Protesting Citizenship: Migrant Activisms

What does it mean to state 'No One is Illegal'? This rallying call is what unifies migrant protests against exclusionary border regimes around the world, bringing migrants, citizens, 'legal' and 'illegal' people onto the streets in ever greater numbers. Indeed, the last decade has witnessed an explosion of immigrant protests, political mobilizations by irregular migrants and pro-migrant activists. This edited collection aims to contribute to the growing body of scholarship on migrant resistance movements and to consider the implications of these struggles for critical understandings of citizenship and borders. It offers a rich series of theoretical and political interventions which together explore the tensions between integrationist and autonomous approaches, and between migrant and activist strategies of invisibility and visibility. By bringing immigrant protests to the heart of debates about citizenship, it also extends discussions about the limits and the possibilities of citizenship as the material and conceptual horizon of critical social analysis, political participation and democracy today.

This book was previously published as a special issue of *Citizenship Studies*.

Imogen Tyler is a Lecturer in Sociology at Lancaster University, UK. She has a long-standing interest in activism, protest and resistance and is the author of the monograph *Revolting Subjects: Social Abjection and Resistance in Neoliberal Britain* (2012).

Katarzyna Marciniak is Professor of Transnational Studies in the English Department at Ohio University, USA. Katarzyna specializes in the discourses of immigration and foreignness, and is one of the initiators of transnational feminist media studies. She is the author of *Alienhood: Citizenship, Exile, and the Logic of Difference* (2006), co-author of *Streets of Crocodiles: Photography, Media, and Postsocialist Landscapes in Poland* (2010), and co-editor of *Transnational Feminism in Film and Media* (2007).

Protesting Citizenship:
Migrant Activisms

Edited by
Imogen Tyler and Katarzyna Marciniak

Routledge
Taylor & Francis Group

LONDON AND NEW YORK

First published 2014
by Routledge
2 Park Square, Milton Park, Abingdon, Oxon, OX14 4RN

and by Routledge
711 Third Avenue, New York, NY 10017

Routledge is an imprint of the Taylor & Francis Group, an informa business

© 2014 Taylor & Francis

British Library Cataloguing in Publication Data
A catalogue record for this book is available from the British Library

ISBN 13: 978-0-415-72864-5

Typeset in Times New Roman
by Taylor & Francis Books

Publisher's Note
The publisher accepts responsibility for any inconsistencies that may have arisen during the conversion of this book from journal articles to book chapters, namely the possible inclusion of journal terminology.

Disclaimer
Every effort has been made to contact copyright holders for their permission to reprint material in this book. The publishers would be grateful to hear from any copyright holder who is not here acknowledged and will undertake to rectify any errors or omissions in future editions of this book.

Contents

Citation Information

The chapters in this book were originally published in *Citizenship Studies*, volume 17, issue 2 (April 2013). When citing this material, please use the original page numbering for each article, as follows:

Chapter 1
Immigrant protest: an introduction
Imogen Tyler and Katarzyna Marciniak
Citizenship Studies, volume 17, issue 2 (April 2013) pp. 143–156

Chapter 2
Impossible protest: noborders in Calais
Joe Rigby and Raphael Schlembach
Citizenship Studies, volume 17, issue 2 (April 2013) pp. 157–172

Chapter 3
No Border: photo essay
Julie Rebouillat
Citizenship Studies, volume 17, issue 2 (April 2013) pp. 173–177

Chapter 4
After citizenship: autonomy of migration, organisational ontology and mobile commons
Dimitris Papadopoulos and Vassilis S. Tsianos
Citizenship Studies, volume 17, issue 2 (April 2013) pp. 178–196

Chapter 5
Immigrant protests in Toronto: diaspora and Sri Lanka's civil war
Ishan Ashutosh
Citizenship Studies, volume 17, issue 2 (April 2013) pp. 197–210

Chapter 6
Naked protest: the maternal politics of citizenship and revolt
Imogen Tyler
Citizenship Studies, volume 17, issue 2 (April 2013) pp. 211–226

Chapter 7

Medical aid as protest: acts of citizenship for unauthorized im/migrants and refugees
Heide Castañeda
Citizenship Studies, volume 17, issue 2 (April 2013) pp. 227–240

Chapter 8

Gagging orders: asylum seekers and paradoxes of freedom and protest in liberal society
Deirdre Conlon and Nick Gill
Citizenship Studies, volume 17, issue 2 (April 2013) pp. 241–259

Chapter 9

Legal/illegal: protesting citizenship in Fortress America
Katarzyna Marciniak
Citizenship Studies, volume 17, issue 2 (April 2013) pp. 260–277

Chapter 10

'I am an American': protesting advertised 'Americanness'
Cynthia Weber
Citizenship Studies, volume 17, issue 2 (April 2013) pp. 278–292

Please direct any queries you may have about the citations to
clsuk.permissions@cengage.com

Notes on Contributors

Ishan Ashutosh, Department of Social Sciences, Northumbria University, Newcastle upon Tyne, UK.

Heide Castañeda, Department of Anthropology, University of South Florida, Tampa, Florida, USA.

Deirdre Conlon, Department of Sociology and Urban Studies, Saint Peter's University, Jersey City, USA.

Nick Gill, Department of Geography, College of Life and Environmental Sciences, University of Exeter, Exeter, UK.

Katarzyna Marciniak, Department of English, University of Ohio, Athens, Ohio, USA.

Dimitris Papadopoulos, School of Management, University of Leicester, Leicester, UK.

Julie Rebouillat, Freelance Photographer, Contre-Faits, Marseille, France.

Joe Rigby, Department of Sociology, Lancaster University, Lancaster, UK.

Raphael Schlembach, School of Education and Social Science, University of Central Lancashire, Preston, UK.

Vassilis S. Tsianos, Department of Sociology, University of Hamburg, Hamburg, Germany.

Imogen Tyler, Department of Sociology, Lancaster University, Lancaster, UK.

Cynthia Weber, Department of International Relations, University of Sussex, Brighton, UK.

Immigrant protest: an introduction

Imogen Tyler[a] and Katarzyna Marciniak[b]

[a]Department of Sociology, Lancaster University, Lancaster LA1 4YW, UK; [b]Department of English, University of Ohio, Athens, OH 45701, USA

The last decade has witnessed an explosion of 'immigrant protests', political mobilizations by irregular migrants and pro-migrant activists. This special issue on 'immigrant protest' has emerged in response to this rise in the visibility of immigrant protests, and its central aim is to contribute to the growing body of scholarship on migrant resistance movements and to consider the implications of these struggles for critical understandings of citizenship. This introduction maps out some of the central issues and themes emerging from the contributions to this issue, exploring the tensions between integrationist and autonomous approaches and theories of migrant activism and resistance and between migrant and activist strategies of invisibility and visibility. By bringing immigrant protests to the heart of debates about citizenship, we hope to further extend discussions about the limits and the possibilities of citizenship as the material and conceptual horizon of critical social analysis and political participation and practice today.

The last decade has witnessed an explosion of 'immigrant protests', political mobilizations by irregular migrants[1] and pro-migrant activists. Indicative examples include the rise of the Sans-Papiers movement in France (see McNevin 2006), the spectacular protests of millions of undocumented Latin American workers in the USA in Spring 2006, under the banner 'A Day Without Immigrants' (see this issue Marciniak, De Genova and Borcila 2011), events which in turn inspired the 'A Day Without Us' marches and strikes in Italy, Greece, Spain, and France in 2011. Refugee activism has become a significant political force in its own right, with coalitions of citizens and noncitizens engaging in various forms of advocacy and resistance around the enforced destitution, dispersal, detention, and deportation of refugee populations (see this issue Conlon and Gill).[2] The upsurge in immigrant protest is a consequence of the intensification of border security measures across the globe in recent decades, the abjectifying effects of which have been well documented by scholars and activists. In the face of the incremental militarization of national and regional borders and the emergence of a 'lucrative political economy of border policing and immigrant detention' (De Genova and Borcila 2011) immigrant protests constitute critical counter-political voices, highlighting and protesting deteriorating conditions for irregular migrants and refugees 'on the ground', exposing the violence engendered by border controls, and challenging the abstract and fetishized political rhetoric of 'illegal immigration'.

New media, such as the Internet, 3G mobile video phones, weblogs, social media, and instant messaging, have inordinately strengthened migrant politics. These technologies are employed to co-ordinate the swarming of bodies on the streets, to capture and upload videos of protests and police violence, and to generate publicity for struggles. The advent of these digital communication systems means that protests staged in one physical place are now transmitted across borders so that even smaller scale protests, such as riots, fires, and hunger strikes by immigration detainees, and individual anti-deportation campaigns have the potential to resonate internationally (Cottle 2011, p. 4). International coalitions such as *the European NoBorders Network* (see this issue Rigby and Schelmach and Rebouillat) and the *No One is Illegal* movement have emerged as important horizontal umbrella networks for protesters to connect and coordinate across borders, transforming online spaces into supranational 'common spaces' (see this issue Papadopoulos and Tsianos).

This special issue on 'Immigrant Protest' has emerged in response to this rise in the visibility of immigrant protests. Its aim is to contribute to the growing body of scholarship on migrant resistance movements and to consider the implications of these struggles for critical understandings of citizenship. The eight articles and one photographic essay, which make up this issue, draw on rich case studies of immigrant protest, ranging from the 2006 uprising by undocumented workers in the USA, a NoBorders camp in Calais, naked protests in immigration detention centers in the UK, art activism at the borders of Europe and the USA, medical activism in Germany, protest marches by Tamil migrants in Toronto, and the everyday strategies of resistance employed by undocumented workers in Europe, who burn passports and forge documents to cross borders. The majority of case studies examined in this issue are drawn from protest and resistance movements at Europe and North America borderzones. As such, this issue makes no claim to represent the full global spectrum and diversity of immigrant protests. Despite this partial perspective, this issue offers an insight into what immigrant protests might tell us about the changing meaning and dynamics of citizenship under neoliberal globalism. As Nicholas De Genova notes, the securitization of migration 'is inextricable from a concomitant securitization of citizenship itself' (De Genova 2007, p. 440). It is our contention that migrant protests against this securitization of citizenship expose the contradictions and inclusionary/exclusionary dynamics of contemporary modalities of citizenship in instructive ways.

Neoliberal citizenship

In 'Why Citizenship Studies?', an introductory essay to the special issue that marked the tenth anniversary issue of this journal in 2007, Peter Nyers notes that:

> one criticism in particular that the journal has sought to address is that citizenship is a concept that is derived from a specifically European lineage and so represents a kind of conceptual imperialism that effaces other ways of being political... for all the innovations in how we conceive of citizenship, the concept remains deeply embedded with practices that divide humanity according to race, ethnicity, gender and geography. (Nyers 2007, p. 2)

One of the aims of this current issue is to revisit this criticism through the lens of the migrant and migrant-allied protests against prevailing regimes and forms of citizenship. To do this, however, it is important to note that citizenship has been dramatically refashioned over the last decade. One of the primary characteristics of the redesign of citizenship in the twenty-first century is the intensification of citizenship as a technology of governance (see Weber 2010, Tyler 2010). As Tyler argues, citizenship has become 'a vast and proliferating bureaucracy from which flow categories of people marginalized by, excluded or disqualified from citizenship and the rights which flow from this status' (Tyler 2010, p. 71). Citizenship has become 'the premier instrumentality' for the subjection 'of those whom states "contain" within their juridical and spatial confines' (De Genova 2007, p. 440). Erik Swyngedouw uses the term 'governance innovation' to describe the ways in which the expansion of purportedly democratic forms, such as citizenship, operates as mechanisms of neoliberal ideologies, as freedoms are retracted from individuals and communities and wealth and power concentrated in the hands of social and political elites and global corporations (Swyngedouw 2005, p. 1992, Tyler 2010). A 'reality gap' has opened up between normative political rhetorics of 'deepening democracy' through citizenship (including the exporting of 'liberal democracy' through the 'war on terror'), and the abjection of 'illegal' populations from the rights and protections of citizenship through the enforcement of often brutal and inhumane immigration controls. This 'liberal paradox' is further complicated by the incongruity between the opening up of international borders to flows of capital and the simultaneous 'damming' of states and regions to 'undesirable' migrants from the Global South: a migratory pull which is paradoxically fueled by market demands for cheap unregulated migrant labor in the Global North (see Hollifield 2004, de Hass 2007).

The securitization of migration takes different national and regional forms but includes the reduction in legal channels for migration, the proliferation of legislation to limit, hierarchize and scale citizenship, the criminalization of 'undesirable' migrants, the emergence of a global business in immigrant prisons, and the normalization of detention and deportation as instruments of governance. The concern of many activists is that the incremental criminalization of migrancy has led to the deepening exploitability of irregular and undocumented migrant populations. As de Genova argues, irregular migrants are 'increasingly terrorized by the state's immigration law enforcement tactics' but are 'all the more enthusiastically desired by employers precisely because they are extraordinarily vulnerable' (De Genova and Borcila 2011). De Genova describes the precarity experienced by irregular migrant populations as 'deportability': 'the fact that the great majority of so-called "illegal" migrants are not deported but instead remain, as labor, under excruciatingly vulnerable socio-political conditions indefinitely' (De Genova and Borcila 2011). Similarly, Sandro Mezzadra suggests that 'European policies on migration, despite their rhetoric, do not aim to hermetically seal European borders. Their objective and their effect is the establishment of a system of dams and eventually *the production of an active process of inclusion of migrant labor by means of its criminalization* (it. clandestinizzazione)' (Mezzadra 2004, our emphasis).

In her examination of this 'active process of inclusion' in the context of the Australian state, Anne McNevin argues that the militarization of state and regional borders (most visibly evident in the mushrooming of for-profit immigrant prisons) operates as 'performances of political closure designed to assuage those made vulnerable by [a] neoliberal economic trajectory' (McNevin 2007a, p. 611). As McNevin's analysis suggests, tough border controls function performatively to placate and appease those citizens whose own dreams of 'the good life' have become increasingly precarious in the face of the erosion of social democracy and welfare provision (see Plant 2011; Berlant 2011). In this context, xenophobia has a specific economic and political function, constituting irregular migrants as scapegoats for deepening inequalities within the borders of neoliberal states (see this issue Marciniak, Tyler 2013).

The neoliberal refashioning of citizenship we are describing has impacted not only on migrants but also on citizens themselves. For example, during the last decade the British government, like many other European governments, has instituted a program of reforms aimed at 'deepening citizenship' through legislation, compulsory citizenship education and the introduction of categories of 'active' and 'earned' citizenship

(Goldsmith 2008; UK Border Agency 2008; Tyler 2010). This 'active citizenship agenda' aims to transform migrant and indigenous populations into productive citizens through policy innovations such as nationalistic education programs, 'forced volunteering', and a 'National Citizenship Service.[3] These governmental programs of social citizenship, which emphasize widening participation, social cohesion, social responsibility, and belonging, pave the way for the introduction of laws, policies, and environmental redesigns which often target disenfranchised young people, but radically curtail the freedoms of all citizens and made them subject to hitherto unimaginable levels of surveillance and policing (see Tyler 2013). Of course, as Giorgio Agamben claims, citizenship has always been 'two-faced', 'the bearer both of subjection to sovereign power and of individual liberties' (Agamben 1998, p. 125). However, the transformation of liberal rights-based notions of citizenship into citizenship as an 'active and productive' mode of neoliberal governance has led some to ask whether the idea of 'modern citizenship' is now defunct (Tyler 2010, p. 71). Indeed, Yoav Peled has argued that within 'liberal democracies', the toxic combination of neoliberal economics and the erosion of civil and political rights have created 'a post-citizenship society' (Peled 2007).

The immigrant protests that have erupted across the globe in the last decade are a response to the 'exclusions, inequalities, hierarchies, securitizations' which have been affected by this refashioning of citizenship (Nyers 2007, p. 2). Yet, inevitably, one of the main strategies of migrants and pro-migrant activists is to demand the rights of citizenship, however problematic or precarious this citizenship may have become. Driven by immediate humanitarian considerations, many migrant advocacy movements focus on challenging existing legal and political frameworks in order to gain migrants' rights and access to legal aid, welfare, and education. The integrationist politics which underpins migrant rights movements are epitomized by the London-based 'Strangers into Citizens' campaign founded in 2006 (and now an international movement) which calls for the naturalization of long-term irregular migrants through appeals to a 'local' notion of citizenship (as living and belonging to place for a period of time). In the USA, the proposed DREAM Act is a program which would offer 'a conditional path to citizenship' for specific categories of 'alien minors' if they graduate from high school and then either serve in the US military for 2 years or complete a college degree. The merits of these kinds of campaigns for naturalization and their positive impact on the lives of migrants and their children should not be minimized. As well as assisting migrants materially, these campaigns, in very concrete ways, challenge the exclusions of citizenship. However, humanitarian or state-based movements campaigning for the inclusion of migrants within existing legal systems of citizenship also risk colluding with the regimes of illegalization which abjectify migrants and their children in the first place. In other words, although these forms of legal and political advocacy are necessary, important, and can be effective, they inevitably reproduce the inclusive/exclusive logic of citizenship, which has been 'designed to fail specific groups and populations' (Tyler 2010).

This brings us to the heart of the paradox which the contributors to the issue variously engage with: immigrant protests are 'acts' against the exclusionary technologies of citizenship, which aim to make visible the violence of citizenship *as regimes of control*. However, in order to effect material changes, protestors are compelled to make their demands in the idiom of the regime of citizenship they are contesting. As McNevin puts it:

> the claims of irregular migrants both challenge and reinscribe existing political identities. On one hand, their assertion of entitlement as rights-bearing subjects despite irregular status contests the exclusivity of citizenship as a measure of political inclusion. Yet their call for

legalization simultaneously reinforces the authority of citizenship as the foremost measure of belonging (McNevin 2007b, p. 670).

One of the enduring lessons of the Sans-Papiers is that they engage in claims for citizenship while also critically questioning citizenship as a system of governance and control. The Sans-Papiers movement began as a struggle by undocumented workers in France for papers and regularization, but it became a movement that more radically questioned the neocolonial function of citizenship itself. As Ababacar Diop, a spokesperson for the Sans-Papiers of St Bernard in Paris notes, 'The struggle of the Sans-Papiers has to go beyond obtaining our papers and must address the underlying questions [. . .] What is the purpose of migration policies? Should frontiers be open? (Diop 1997). Further, as Monika Krause suggests, the Sans-Papiers:

> define themselves not by having fled as 'refugees', not by having come in as 'immigrants', not even by moving as 'migrants' but by the mere fact that they are in

> France without the required documents for residence and work. [. . .] Their status is purely imposed by the state. They ask not for recognition of their status, but

for the

> end of their identity. (Krause 2008, p. 342)

The Sans-Papier movement has inspired important forms of migrant activism, notably the European NoBoders movement, which calls for an end to all border controls, and a body of theoretical work, the 'autonomy of migration' scholarship, which examines 'migratory movements and conflicts in terms that prioritize the subjective practices, the desires, the expectations, and the behaviors of migrants themselves' (Mezzadra 2011, p. 121).

After citizenship

Joe Rigby and Raph Schlembach's article in this issue, 'Impossible Protest: NoBorders in Calais', makes an important contribution to 'autonomy of migration' scholarship. They offer an account of their participation in a NoBorders camp in Calais in June 2009 as a route into thinking about the ways in which political solidarity between migrants and citizens can be mobilized against the politics of 'illegality' instituted by citizenship. The migrants in Calais have made often perilous journeys from a diverse number of places. Whether escaping unbearable lives in refugee camps on the Pakistan and Afghanistan border, economic and political turmoil in post-war Iraq or conflict and/or abject economic conditions in Northern and East Africa, they congregate in this port town on the Northern border of France in the hope of making the sea crossing to Britain. (The UK is widely perceived as a Mecca for migrants, offering better employment prospects for undocumented workers, and better welfare systems than most of mainland Europe.) Within official discourses, the migrants in Calais are produced as an 'illegal presence', and/or as a 'humanitarian problem'. In an attempt to expel migrants from the area, a Red-Cross center providing welfare was closed, brutal policing has been employed to make migrants' daily lives as unlivable as possible, and more recently, the 'Global Calais project' has been initiated (funded by the IOM and the French and British governments) to offer financial incentives to migrants to return home. Rigby and Schlembach detail how, by camping alongside the undocumented migrants, NoBorders activists constitute themselves as another kind of 'illegal' migrant presence at the border. This strategy aims both to make visible the abject conditions for migrants in Calais and the historical and legal contingency of the asphyxiating politics of citizenship which contain them there. Through these methods, Rigby and Schlembach argue that NoBorders activism does manage, if momentarily, to disarticulate the borders between citizens and noncitizens in ways which open up spaces for collective resistance.

Mezzandra argues that one of the problems with the ways in which migrant struggles have been conventionally conceptualized is that they proceed from the perspective of the state, assuming, for instance, 'that migrants want to become citizens' (Mezzadra 2011, p. 121). In their article, 'After Citizenship: Autonomy of Migration, Organisational Ontology and Mobile Commons', Dimitris Papadopoulos and Vassilis Tsianos explore the underside of ever-evolving regimes for the control of migrants from the perspective of migrant autonomy. They argue that the governmental fixation *and* theoretical fixation on 'security', 'mobility control', and 'deportability' fail to take account of the ordinary experiences of people on the move. Drawing on empirical research with irregular migrant workers in Europe, they examine the ways in which migrants share knowledge and engage in forms of mutual support and care in ways which create social spaces below the radar of existing political structures. Papadopoulos and Tsianos theorize this migrant sociality, as a 'mundane ontology of transmigration'. They employ their rich description of the ways of which migrants craft worlds on the move to argue for a rejection of citizenship and the abject security regimes it institutes in favor of what they term 'the mobile commons'.

As we have argued, migrants and activists who engage in integrationist forms of migrant politics are involved in important forms of critical resistance to the exclusions of citizenship, but risk remaining captured within the existing legal frameworks and prevailing regimes of sovereignty which they contest. In contrast, the autonomy of migration approach developed by Papadopoulos and Tsianos focuses on migrancy as a creative and productive form of movement which 'escapes' and always 'exceeds' legal and conceptual frameworks of citizenship. Their aim is 'to cultivate an imaginary and a practical sensibility to what lies after citizenship'. Their starting point is migrants on move – transmigrants – and they argue that the multiplicity of the lives and movements of migrants forces a break with citizenship as a central category in migration policy as well as academic research. Hence, the focus in their article on the ways in which undocumented migrants engage strategies of invisibility and clandestinisty (such as burning their papers, obtaining multiple passports and burning off finger-prints) to avoid capture. Resistance, in their account, precisely means refusing the traps of representation, including the representative politics of citizenship, and embracing modes of being and forms of live that enable mobility. In this account, becoming imperceptible is the most precise and effective tool migrants employ to oppose the individualizing, quantifying, and representational pressures of the settled, constituted geopolitical power.

The apparent incommensurability of integrationist and autonomous approaches to migrancy raise a series of political and theoretical tensions about migrant strategies of in/visibility. We will return to the question of in/visibility shortly. For the moment, we want to note that, by developing neo-Marxist theories of capital and labor, the emergent field of autonomy of migration scholarship usefully mobilizes the category of 'worker' to defetishize the figure of the 'immigrant' or 'illegal'. This focus on 'work' enables a reconceptualization of migrancy as strategies of escape from economic abjection, and migrant resistance as the vital political solidarities and friendships of precarious workers on the move. However, as Papadopoulos and Tsianos concede, reducing migrant mobility to questions of labor and capital is highly problematic. One problem with this argument is that for many migrants, particularly those who are elderly, those who are sick or have disabilities, or those with dependent children, 'movement', 'work', and indeed 'escape' are not their primary goals or available possibilities. Many migrants need to be able to access the medical, welfare support, and education offered by states. Rather, as

Papadopoulos and Tsianos suggest, the most important dimension of the mobile commons they describe is *care*: 'mutual cooperation, friendships, favors that you never return, affective support, trust, care for other people's relatives and children, transnational relations of care, the gift economy between mobile people'. Indeed, the conditions for a livable life for many if not the majority of human beings is the ability to 'lay down roots', create a home, and belong to a physical place and community. As Nick Gill has argued, many migrants desire not mobility, but *stillness*. As he writes: 'the pursuit of stillness among asylum seekers is both a human and political response to their situations – stillness becomes a metric in the struggle between abject migrants and the state' (Gill 2009, p. 6). The avant-garde emphasis within the autonomy of migration scholarship on mobility as a politics of resistance as movement and escape risks diminishing an important focus in migrant scholarship both on forced movement, forms of capture encapsulated by policies of dispersal, and on the forced curtailment of movement, epitomized by immigration detention.

Detention camps for migrants have mushroomed across the globe. In the European Union alone, there are now more than 200 formal detention camps, housing more than 30,000 asylum seekers and migrants awaiting deportation (Dikeç 2009, p. 184). The proliferation of 'border management tools' such as offshore asylum processing, detention centers, and transit camps needs to be considered as part of a global system of 'migrant camp proliferation', which includes refugee camps in Africa and the Middle East. One consequence of the capture of migrants in camps is that they often spend interminable amounts of time in limbo, a state that has been described as 'permanent temporariness'. As Abu Khalil al-Laham, a leading community figure in the Dheisheh Refugee Camp which was established in Palestine in 1949, notes:

> temporariness kills creativity, it kills and prevents initiative … political and social awareness, our general cultural awareness was inhabited by a culture of temporariness that prevented societal development … you cannot plan tomorrow if you live in a state of transit. (Abourahme and Hilal 2009)

The struggles of refugees in 'permanent camps' such as Dheisheh, as well as the protests of those detained in Europe and North America, are reminder that any account of the resistant temporalities of migrancy as escape needs to be balanced with the continued critical, political, and theoretical exegesis of migrant experiences of 'capture', 'temporariness', and the desire to be 'still', to make a home, to make a life, and to belong to a place.

Acts against citizenship

Engin Isin has argued influentially that citizenship can be reclaimed as a site of political potential if understood in terms of acts. By 'acts' he means the practices through which subjects transform themselves into citizens (Isin 2008, p. 18), the activities through which individual subjects and groups 'constitute themselves as […] those to whom the right to have rights is due' (Isin and Nielsen 2008, p. 2). Isin's thesis breaks from formal definitions of citizenship and indeed from a focus on citizens *per se*, to those 'performances, enactments and events' (Walters 2008, p. 192) which produce *relations of citizenship* in any given moment. This redefinition of citizenship has proved fruitful for thinking about the ways in which populations who are disenfranchised by the states in which they reside, and are 'outside of politics' in any normative sense, are able to act in ways that allow them to (temporarily) constitute themselves as political subjects under sometimes extreme conditions of subjugation. The radical potential of immigrant protests precisely resides in the ways in which migrants organize and act despite their lack of access to the rights and protections of citizenship. Indeed, given the increasingly controlling and excluding function of many statist forms of citizenship, migrant activists and scholars have increasingly adopted a language of local, transnational and 'global citizenship' (Hardt and Negri 2000, Cabrera 2008).

Ishan Ashutosh draws on Isin's post-sovereignty citizenship thesis in his examination of a series of protests by Tamil migrants in Toronto, Chennai, London, and Oslo, in the spring of 2009. These protests were a consequence of the escalation of a 25-year civil war between the Sri Lankan government and the Liberation Tigers of Tamil, with protestors calling for a ceasefire and restating their claim for a Tamil state. Through a close analysis of the Toronto protests and the Canadian political and media responses to the protests, Ashutosh explores how these protests operate both within and without the bounds of a single state in ways which unfold critical questions of how we conceive of diasporic protests in relationship to citizenship. Ashutosh concludes that it is productive to think these protests as 'acts of transnational citizenship' which generate Tamil citizenship through the invocation of a symbolic Tamil state (Elem). Ashutosh's contribution reveals both the material and symbolic limits of state-bound notions of citizenship for diasporic communities of forced migrants who always already inhabit and practice multiple forms of citizen identities. Further, it illustrates both the constraints and possibilities of mobilizing a 'citizenship beyond the state' as a material and economic form of resistance against a brutal and violent regime. However, although Ashutosh states a claim for theorizing citizenship beyond the state, his account shows how these protests nevertheless rely on the creation of national identities, if in the form of the collectively imagined (and contested) state of Elem. Further, Ashutosh's account details how negative Canadian political and media responses to the Tamil protests remained firmly bounded with statist notions of belonging. Although 'trans-national citizenship' is proposed as a solution to the multiple contested categories of state-based citizenship in operation, the question remains whether 'citizenship' is the only, or the most useful, way to conceive of the counter-political movements of migrants.

Imogen Tyler's contribution, 'Naked Protest: the Maternal Politics of Citizenship and Revolt', explores this question through a focus on motherhood as a site of collective resistance in migrant and indigenous struggles against the state. This article begins with an account of a 'naked protest' by a group of mothers, refused asylum seekers, and 'illegal immigrants' at Yarl's Wood immigration removal center in England. The protests of the Yarl's Wood mothers might be conceived in Isin's terms as an 'act of citizenship', in that the mother's are demanding their, and their British born children's, 'right to have rights'. However, these women are explicitly *protesting against* the specific regime of citizenship in operation, which has led to the detention and imminent deportation of themselves and their children. In this regard, the naked protest in Yarl's Wood might be more properly understood as an *act against citizenship*. Unfolding the longer history of naked protest, Tyler turns to the extraordinary activism of 'indigenous mothers who employ 'naked protest' to highlight their expropriation from their land by global petroleum companies in the Niger Delta. By tracing connections between the naked protests of mothers in these two seemingly disparate geo-political locations what becomes evident is that 'citizenship is no guarantee of anything' (De Genova 2011). Nyers asks, 'Is there a form of bio-agency capable of resubjectification in a way that does not reproduce the paradoxes of sovereign power?' (Nyers 2004, p. 212). Responding to this question, Tyler argues that 'the mothers in Yarl's Wood and the Niger Delta mothers together enact a political solidarity beyond the bonds of citizenship or statist politics, a solidarity which is grounded in [...] '*umunne* ...

the spirit of shared motherhood' (see Amadiume 1987, p. 56). She suggests that through their invocation of 'natality' these protestors introduce a vital 'tension about value and most particularly the value of life itself' (Khanna 2009, p. 195): a tension which has the capacity to trouble sovereignty *and* the theoretical descriptions of sovereignty which dominate in debates about citizenship and rights. In particular, the rich transnational seam of 'maternal politics' enacted through these protests challenges the 'catastrophic functionalism' and Eurocentrism of Agamben-inspired accounts of bare life, and offers an alternative lens through which to perceive the ethical and political claims made by noncitizens and disenfranchised people (Papadopoulos *et al.* 2008, p. 198). In many respects, Tyler's argument comes close to Papadopoulos and Tsianos' account of the politics of care between migrants in what they term 'the mobile commons', but through a focus on maternal care she offers a distinctly feminist perspective to debates about the limits of citizenship as the horizon for thinking critically about differential modes of capture, displacement, and resistance.

Heide Castañeda contribution to this issue documents the resistance practices of medical activists as a protest against (German) citizenship. Her analysis focuses on the 'Medical Aid for Refugees', a humanitarian organization which offers medical assistance to refugees and undocumented migrants in several German cities. Drawing on ethnographic research with the Berlin branch of this organization, Castañeda illustrates how the statist definitions of migrant 'deservedness' play out within the organization, with refugees and survivors of torture perceived differently to undocumented workers seeking assistance. Further, she details how this organization has been increasingly co-opted by the state, which, far from opposing the 'illegal' medical aid offered by this organization, uses it as an alibi for the exclusionary policies which bar migrants from state-funded medical services. In this respect, the provision of medical aid to migrants works to reinforce rather than challenge statist notions of citizenship which produce irregular migrants as a 'national abject'. While acknowledging these paradoxes, Castañeda suggests that the distinctive ethics associated with providing medical care both troubles and ultimately exceeds citizenship as the primary social relation between people in a given place.

In contrast to the attempts by Ashutosh, Castañeda and Tyler conceptualize migrant protests as acts which trouble statist notions of citizenship as the organizing principle and horizon of politics, while Deirdre Conlon and Nick Gill explore the 'soft' technologies of citizenship deployed to govern migrants in detention and accommodation facilities in the UK and Ireland. Drawing on rich empirical data, Conlon and Gill examine the constraints upon resistance within these borderzones by analyzing the materials, orientation booklets, citizenship classes, and legal self-representation manuals which detained migrants are subject to. They argue that these pedagogical technologies of state-based regimes of citizenship compel detainees to transform themselves into ideal detainees in order that they might escape detention. In the context of detention, 'freedom' is, they claim, a paradoxical concept in as much as freedom is allied with the ability of migrants to successfully engage in practices of self-transformation and adaption to the liberal norms of host nations. Their comparative analysis highlights the ways in which border policing acts upon the bodies of migrants in subtle ways to produce 'desirable' kinds of migrant subjectivity. Conlon and Gill's contribution is important because it insists that critical and theoretical engagement with 'immigrant protest' needs to attend to technologies of self-governance which operate to 'gag' captive migrants. In their account, citizenship emerges as a psycho-social site of struggle which is not external to, but constitutes migrant subjectivity itself.

In/visibility

The majority of contributions to this special issue are concerned with the ways in which migrants and their activist allies engage in political strategies of visibility in order to generate 'outrage' and 'make public' their specific concerns and grievances. As Papadopoulos and Tsianos insist, a series of risks and tensions unfold from political strategies of visibility and representation. In very material ways, becoming visible and demanding rights expose irregular migrants to the full force of state border controls. Hence, for many migrants, making themselves visible through protest is an activity engaged in only as a last resort. As Tyler documents in her account of the naked protest undertaken by mothers in Yarl's wood, some of those who took part in the protest were disciplined and penalized by having their deportations 'fast-tracked'. The punishing effects of visibility lead Papadopoulos and Tsianos to argue that 'visibility, in the context of illegal migration, belongs to the inventory of the technologies for policing migrational flows' (Papadopoulos and Tsianos 2008, p. 229). However, the practices of migrant activists such as the Sans-Papiers reveal that 'becoming perceptible' is also a strategy of resistance. Making migrant experiences visible and audible is often the overarching aim of immigrant protests. As Madjiguène Cissé, a spokeswoman for the Sans-Papiers movement notes, 'In France up until now our fate as immigrants was: either take part in the Republic's process of integration, or be deported like cattle. ... We have made ourselves visible to say that we are here, to say that we are not in hiding but we're just human beings. We are here and we have been here a long time' (Cissé 1997). As Nyers suggests, citizenship struggles are not simply about legal status but are struggles 'for recognition as someone with an audible and corporeal presence that can be described as 'political' (Nyers 2007, p. 3). It is of critical importance that we examine the ways in which irregular migrants and their allies negotiate the contradictions, losses and gains of in/visibility in their interactions with sovereign power.

As noncitizens, irregular migrants have few available routes to self-representation available to them and often have no autonomous public voice. It is not the case, however, that undocumented and irregular migrants are invisible in the public domain; on the contrary, 'immigrants' and the topic of 'immigration' are 'hypervisible' (see Tyler 2006). As Katarzyna Marciniak's contribution to this issue details, the figure of the immigrant is invoked continuously in overdetermined, stereotyped, and stigmatized forms within mainstream media and political rhetoric. It is precisely the hypervisibility of 'the immigrant' and particularly the production of the 'illegal immigrant' as a national abject, which screens the realities of migrant lives from view, and silences migrant voices. This is why one of the central strategies employed by humanitarian organizations is to generate positive forms of migrant representation that can counter xenophobic depictions of immigrants as national abjects. If public discourses depict immigrants as a dehumanized, undifferentiated foreign mass, hoard, influx, etc., the representational strategies adopted by many humanitarian organizations on behalf of migrants are to provoke publics to recognize 'the human face' of specific migrants. Indeed, a favorite device of humanitarian publications is the use of photographic close-ups of migrant faces and first-person accounts of their experiences. These affective technologies of the 'close-up' aim to move the reader in ways that will enable citizens to identify with migrants as 'human beings' (see Tyler 2006, Marciniak and Turowski 2010). In other words, these strategies attempt to humanize refugees and irregular migrants as *subjects who matter*, 'like us'. These kinds of publicity strategies, whether they are appeals made by agents or agencies on behalf of migrants, or whether, they are made by migrants themselves, can be extremely effective.

However, they also exceptionalize the deservingness of specific categories of migrants, such as refugees or children.

Through her photographic practice, art activist Julie Rebouillat focuses attention on the creative strategies which Noborders activists deploy to enable what is 'hidden in plain sight' (the abjection and dehumanization of migrants) to become visible. Rebouillat's method involves being alongside migrants and activists in order to document form of solidarity which might resist the objectification of individual figures. Cindy Weber's multimedia project, 'I am an American': Video Portraits of Unsafe US Citizens', engages with the American Advertising Council's post-9/11 'I am an American' advertizing campaign. In her contribution, she offers a reflective account of her own critical media practice, and the history and political intentions of this work 'as a 'protest' that challenges the normativities that circumscribe who gets to count as a 'citizen'. In a similar vein, Marciniak's account of the traveling poster exhibit, *No Human Being is Illegal! – Posters of the Myths and Realities of the Immigrant Experience* (which was first premiered in Los Angeles 1988, then again in 2007) foregrounds the gains to be made from the creation of alternative frames of visibility for migrant lives:

> [the exhibition] historicizes migration ... and shows complexities of immigration experiences without romanticizing, victimizing, or demonizing migrants. Through a multivocal tonality–anger, empathy, playfulness, poignancy, sarcasm, irony–the exhibition counters the prescribed visuality of illegality by exposing the U.S. citizenship itself as 'illegal'–rooted in the colonization of indigenous people and in neocolonizing practices of exploitation.

Bringing theories of affectivity to bear on the understandings of both immigrant and anti-immigrant protest in the USA, Marciniak argues that the generation of emotional responses through the production of different kinds of political aesthetics is central to the struggles taking place in migrant politics. For example, thorough close analysis, she demonstrates how anti-immigration groups in the USA employ online performance of 'rage' which operates as virtual acts of bordering, which have material effects on immigrant's lives. To counter this anti-immigrant rage, the work of art activists is, she suggests, critical in exposing the ways in which US citizenship is constituted by illegality, whether in terms of the colonization of indigenous people or in its current neocolonizing practices of exploitation. The underlying assumption of the forms of 'art activism' presented in this issue is that the work of creating alternative forms of visibility, or disrupting prevailing norms of representation, clears the ground for the political agency of migrant populations, denaturalizing xenophobic ideologies. It is the capacity for counter-representational practices to generate 'uncertainty about 'common-sense' understandings of belonging that we want to insist upon here. As Simon Faulkner notes, 'uncertainty is a first step in a potential process of declassification that is central to the challenging and reorganization of the political given' (Faulkner 2009). As these three art-orientated contributions to this issue suggest, the works of artists, writers, and filmmakers not only document immigrant protest but are a form of protest in their own right.

Conclusion

Immigrant protests take many forms and involve actors who are very differently positioned in the relation to the state, be they undocumented workers, refugees, detainees, concerned citizens, humanitarian organizations, or NGO's. Multiple factors shape the specificity of immigrant protests, and the political and conceptual language that demands for equality, justice, or rights is made in. Citizenship is a site of struggle within these protests: it is both the goal which many immigrant protesters are striving to achieve and the regime of exclusion which they are protesting against. A consideration of migrant protests and allied movements through the lens of citizenship has foregrounded the role of citizenship policies in generating injustice, exclusion, and immobility (social and geopolitical), and has exposed the limits of state-based notions of citizenship as a category for sustained social and political resistance. One of the central questions explored within this issue is whether the explosion in demands of migrants might be interpreted as part of a counter-political shift from state-based notions of citizenship to 'insurgent' acts of 'transnational citizenship', or 'global citizenship' (Hardt and Negri 2000, Balibar 2006), or whether immigrant protests are important because they enable forms of politics that exceed or refuse to be a politics of citizenship at all (De Genova 2010, p. 105, see this issue Papadopoulos and Tsianos and Tyler). Given that the abjectification of migrants is increasingly an effect of the neoliberalization of citizenship, the question remains to what extent citizenship can or should be mobilized as a productive conceptual framework, or activist vocabulary, for the emancipatory projects of migrants and their allies. The incommensurability of integrationist and autonomous approaches to migrancy and citizenship is an important site of critical and theoretical struggle within citizenship studies and migrancy research today. The tensions that arise from these debates are not, we want to argue, problems to be resolved but are rather are indicative of the daily struggles of irregular migrants on the ground as they encounter the structures of sovereignty which abjectify them. Whether we attempt to think citizenship 'beyond the state' or reject citizenship as the constitutive ground of the political by highlighting alternative forms of political solidarity, and cultivating alternative vocabularies, what is clear is that citizenship is historically contingent and subject to disruption, rupture, and transformation when its contingency is exposed. In bringing immigrant protests to the heart of debates about citizenship, we hope then not to have foregrounded the antagonisms which immigrant protests make explicit, namely the punitive realities of border and immigration controls, in ways which further extend debates about the limits and the possibilities of citizenship as a category of control and resistance.

Notes

1. We are drawing on McNevin's definition of irregular migrants here: 'The term "irregular migrant" refers to non-citizens who have crossed state borders or remain in state territory without the explicit sanction of the host state. It includes recent arrivals as well as longer term residents who lack officially recognised residence and citizenship status [. . .] "Irregular migrant" and "irregular migration" remain awkward terms, not least because they are thoroughly implicated in the state-centric account of citizenship and political belonging. However, since forms of citizenship and political belonging beyond state-centric ones are conceptually underdeveloped, we do not yet have the vocabulary to articulate the ambiguous status of many irregular migrants and residents'. (2007b, p. 655, fn 1.)

2. This introduction has been informed by an empirical research project with asylum advocacy organizations in the UK and the USA. This research was undertaken by Nick Gill, Deirdre Conlon, Ceri Oeppen, and Imogen Tyler in 2011, and was funded by the Economic and Social Research Council, UK (RES-000-22-3928). Please see www.asylum-network.com for more details about this project. This special issue was also made possible by funding for research leave through a Leverhulme Research Fellowship held by Imogen Tyler 2010–2011, and she gratefully acknowledges this support.

3. For details of the UK 'National Citizen Service', see http://webarchive.nationalarchives.gov.uk/+/www.direct.gov.uk/en/YoungPeople/Workandcareers/Workexperienceandvolunteering/NationalCitizenService/index.htm

References

Abourahme, N. and Hilal, S., 2009. Intervention: (self)urbanization and the contours of political space in Dheisheh refugee camp [online], Available from: http://www.jerusalemquarterly.org/ViewArticle.aspx?id=303 [Accessed 17 January 2012].

Agamben, G., 1998. *Homo sacer: sovereign power and bare life*. Translated by D. Heller-Roazen. Stanford, CA: Stanford University Press.

Amadiume, I., 1987. *Male daughters, female husbands: gender and sex in an African society*. London: Zed Books.

Balibar, E., 2006. Strangers as enemies: further reflections on the aporias of transnational citizenship [online], Available from: http://www.globalautonomy.ca/global1/servlet/Xml2pdf?fn=RA_Balibar_Strangers [Accessed 12 January 2012].

Berlant, L., 2011. *Cruel optimism*. Durham: Duke University Press.

Cabrera, L., 2008. *The practice of global citizenship*. New York: Cambridge University Press.

Cissè, M., 1997. The sans-papiers: a woman draws the first lessons [online], Available from: http://www.bok.net/pajol/madjiguene2.en.html [Accessed 15 January 2012].

Cottle, S., 2011. *Transnational protests and the media*. New York: Peter Lang.

de Haas, H., 2007. The myth of invasion: irregular migration from West Africa to the Maghreb and the European Union. *International migration institute* [online]. Available from: http://www.imi.ox.ac.uk/pdfs/Irregular%20migration%20from%20West%20Africa%20-%20Hein%20de%20Haas.pdf [Accessed 4 January 2012].

De Genova, N., 2007. The production of culprits: from deportability to detainability in the aftermath of 'Homeland Security'. *Citizenship studies*, 11 (5), 421–448.

De Genova, N., 2010. The queer politics of migration: reflections on 'illegality' and incorrigibility. *Studies in social justice*, 4 (2), 101–126.

De Genova, N. and Borcila, R., 2011. An image of our future: on the making of migrant 'illegality'. *AREA Chicago* [online], Available from: http://www.areachicago.org/p/issues/immigrations/image-our-future/ [Accessed 3 January 2012].

Dikeç, M., 2009. The 'where' of asylum. *Environment and planning D: society and space*, 27 (2), 183–189.

Diop, A., 1997. The struggle of the 'sans-papiers': realities and perspectives, trans. I. Nappier [online], Available from: http://www.bok.net/pajol/sanspap/sptextes/ababacar2.en.html [Accessed 7 January 2012].

Faulkner, S., 2009. Walking the green line running the border [online], Available from: http://simonsteachingblog.wordpress.com/2009/12/27/traveling-the-green-line-and-the-aesthetics-of-uncertainty/ [Accessed 9 January 2012].

Gill, N., 2009. Longing for stillness: the forced movement of asylum seekers. *M/C journal* [online], 12 (1).

Goldsmith, L., 2008. Citizenship: our common bond [online], Available from: http://image.guardian.co.uk/sys-files/Politics/documents/2008/03/11/citizenship-report-full.pdf [Accessed 19 January 2012].

Hardt, M. and Negri, A., 2000. *Empire*. Cambridge, MA: Harvard University Press.

Hollifield, J., 2004. The emerging migration state. *International migration review*, 38 (3), 885–912.

Isin, E.F., 2008. Theorizing acts of citizenship. *In*: E.F. Isin and G.M. Nielsen, eds. *Acts of citizenship*. London: Zed Books, 15–43.

Isin, E.F. and Nielsen, G.M., 2008. Introduction: acts of citizenship. *In*: E.F. Isin and G.M. Nielsen, eds. *Acts of citizenship*. London: Zed Books, 1–12.

Khanna, R., 2009. Disposability. *Differences: a journal of feminist cultural studies*, 20 (1), 181–198.

Krause, M., 2008. Undocumented migrants: an Arendtian perspective. *European journal of political theory*, 7 (3), 331–348.

Marciniak, K. and Turowski, K., 2010. *Streets of crocodiles: photography, media, and postsocialist landscapes in Poland*. Bristol: Intellect.

McNevin, A., 2006. Political belonging in a neoliberal era: the struggle of the sans-papiers. *Citizenship studies*, 10 (2), 135–151.

McNevin, A., 2007a. The liberal paradox and the politics of asylum in Australia. *Australian journal of political science*, 42 (4), 611–630.

McNevin, A., 2007b. Irregular migrants, neoliberal geographies and spatial frontiers of 'the political'. *Review of international studies*, 33 (4), 655–674.

Mezzadra, S., 2004. Citizenship in motion [online], Available from: http://www.makeworlds.org/node/83 [Accessed 8 January 2012].

Mezzadra, S., 2011. The gaze of autonomy: capitalism, migration, and social struggles. *In*: V. Squire and trans. R. Nunes, eds. *The contested politics of mobility: borderzones and irregularity.* Routledge: New York, 121–142.

Nyers, P., 2004. Introduction: what's left of citizenship? *Citizenship studies*, 8 (3), 203–215.

Nyers, P., 2007. Introduction: why citizenship studies? *Citizenship studies*, 11 (1), 1–4.

Papadopoulos, D. and Tsianos, V., 2008. The autonomy of migration: the animals of undocumented mobility. *In*: A. Hickey-Moody and P. Malins, eds. *Deleuzian encounters: studies in contemporary social issues.* New York: Palgrave, 223–235.

Papadopoulos, D., Stephenson, N. and Tsianos, V., 2008. *Escape routes: control and subversion in the 21st century.* London: Pluto Press.

Peled, Y., 2007. Towards a post-citizenship society? A report from the front. *Citizenship studies*, 11 (1), 95–104.

Plant, R., 2011. *The neoliberal state.* Oxford: Oxford University Press.

Swyngedouw, E., 2005. Governance innovation and the citizen: the Janus face of governance-beyond-the-state. *Urban studies*, 42 (11), 1991–2006.

Tyler, I., 2006. 'Welcome to Britain': the cultural politics of asylum. *European journal of cultural studies*, 9 (2), 185–202.

Tyler, I., 2010. 'Designed to fail: a biopolitics of British citizenship. *Citizenship studies*, 14 (1), 61–74.

Tyler, I., 2013. *Revolting subjects: social abjection and revolt in neoliberal Britain.* London: Zed.

UK Border Agency, 2008. The path for citizenship: next steps in reforming the immigration system [online]. *Border and Immigration Agency Communications Directorate.* London: Available from: http://www.ukba.homeoffice.gov.uk/sitecontent/documents/aboutus/consultations/closedconsultations/pathtocitizenship/pathtocitizenship?view$\frac{1}{4}$Binary [Accessed 6 January 2010] British Home Office.

Walters, W., 2008. Acts of demonstration: mapping the territory of (non-)citizenship. *In*: E.F. Isin and G.M. Nielsen, eds. *Acts of citizenship.* London: Zed Books, 182–206.

Weber, C., 2010. Introduction: design and citizenship. *Citizenship studies*, 14 (1), 1–16.

Impossible protest: noborders in Calais

Joe Rigby[a] and Raphael Schlembach[b]

[a]Department of Sociology, Lancaster University, Lancaster, UK; [b]School of Education and Social Science, University of Central Lancashire, Preston, UK

Since the closure of the Red Cross refugee reception centre in Sangatte, undocumented migrants in Calais hoping to cross the border to Britain have been forced to take refuge in a number of squatted migrant camps, locally known by all as 'the jungles.' Unauthorised shanty-like residences built by the migrants themselves, living conditions in the camps are very poor. In June 2009, European 'noborder' activists set up a week-long protest camp in the area with the intention of confronting the authorities over their treatment of undocumented migrants. In this article, we analyse the June 2009 noborder camp as an instance of 'immigrant protest.' Drawing on ethnographic materials and Jacques Rancière's work on politics and aesthetics, we construct a typology of forms of border control through which to analyse the different ways in which the politics of the noborder camp were staged, performed and policed. Developing a critique of policing practices which threatened to make immigrant protest 'impossible', we highlight moments of protest which, through the affirmation of an 'axiomatic' equality, disrupted and disarticulated the borders between citizens and non-citizens, the political and non-political.

The Afghans that come to the camp do not come for food and blankets, although it is very nice, this is not what we come for. Every time I come to meetings we discuss blankets, but we are not hungry, we do not come for blankets, open the borders. (Afghan Migrant, noborder camp, Calais, June 2009)

How are we to understand this demand, made by a young Afghan migrant, immobilized, because undocumented, in the non-place of the Franco-British border? Is it a claim, an 'act' of citizenship, constitutive of a subject to whom the right to have rights (the right to freedom of movement) is due? (Isin and Nielsen 2008, p. 2). The question could indeed be considered a 'scholastic' one (Bourdieu 1990), divorced from the practical urgency of the situation, were it not for the fact that the statement was itself aimed at questioning, quite directly, the content of the demand 'open the borders'. It was made as an intervention in a meeting held as part of a 'noborders' 'protest camp' which took place in the French port of Calais between 23 and 29 June 2009. The camp, conceived by British, French and Belgian noborder activists and organized and run in cooperation with undocumented migrants and aid organizations in Calais, was intended as a way of confronting the border authorities over their treatment of undocumented migrants trying to reach Britain.

In what follows, we analyse the events and discourses surrounding the June 2009 noborder camp as an instance of 'immigrant protest'. Such a site is, we argue, particularly productive for thinking about the relationship between immigrant protest and contemporary citizenship. It acutely condenses what Imogen Tyler and Katarzyna Marciniak describe in the introduction to this issue as the increasingly visible gap between the democratic promise of citizenship and its mobilization as a mechanism for controlling the movements of people. We show how on the border in Calais, and in the Calais noborder camp, citizenship was less a catalyst for political mobilization than a device for the policing of political subjectivity: part of a sovereign policing apparatus that, through various practices of *im*mobilization, threatened to make acts of protest, or at least 'immigrant protest', impossible. 'Citizenship' was a way of defining and policing the borders of who and what could count as political. Protest in the noborder camp thus necessarily entailed a 'refusal of citizenship as the organizing frame of political subjectivity' (see Tyler, 'Naked Protest' this issue).

There is, perhaps, nothing particularly surprising about this: immigrants cannot protest because they are not citizens. Their lack of political capacity is what defines their situation. Immigrant protest is *per definition* impossible. Yet it happens, or threatened to happen, hence everywhere in Calais the presence of the police. We demonstrate how immigrant protest involved confronting this imputed impossibility through the assertion of an 'axiomatic' equality against sovereign and inegalitarian divisions. We conceptualize such moments of protest as moments of subjective disidentification which, through staging scenes of what Jacques Rancière calls 'dissensus' (2010), call into question the limits of politics and the 'impossibility' of protest.

The intervention reproduced in our epigraph, for instance, was made as a direct challenge to the content of the noborders movement: did the movement, as a political movement, include the physical movement against borders, or not? If so, then why did its meetings revolve around questions of 'food and blankets' and not the border itself? The intervention dramatized the apparent disjuncture between the (citizen) protest and the (non-citizen) movement against borders. In doing so, it called for the verification of the political equality of the movement and the protest against borders.

In order to analyse the different ways in which the politics of the noborder camp were staged, contested and policed, we draw on Jacques Rancière's work on politics and aesthetics to construct a typology of forms of 'border policing' or 'border control'. We think that Rancière offers some significant theoretical resources for rethinking citizenship (for alternative accounts see Nyers 2003, 2008, Panagia 2009). In particular, his maxim that every political community is also an aesthetic community, a particular 'distribution of the sensible' which governs a particular way of doing politics and grants a certain legibility and intelligibility (or not) to political action, alerts us to a key dimension of the political. Politics is not simply concerned with a certain kind of activity, less it be confused with the act of governing or the exercise of power, but crucially with the account given of this or that activity as political or not. This is the 'aesthetic' dimension at the core of the political and a key site of any political struggle.

Using Rancière's work, we demonstrate how citizenship provided one such political aesthetic, one idiom through which the divisions of sovereign politics exerted an effect on the politics of the noborder camp. Drawing on Rancière's (1999, p. 21–42) analytic of 'politics and police', we also show how 'humanitarianism' and 'activism' presented alternative but related prisms through which the border was both contested and regulated. The purpose of constructing this typology is not only to highlight the different forms of political domination, but to show the avenues of protest and political subjectivization that inhere as blind spots *within* these modalities of border control.

We begin with an introduction to the struggle between border authorities and undocumented migrants in Calais, before moving on to an analysis of the policing of a public demonstration held as part of the noborder camp on 27 June 2009. We develop the meeting between protestors and police on 27 June into a paradigm for the conflict over the borders of the political, between the sovereign act of bounding the political and egalitarian acts of protest which tend to undermine every border and every division. Rancière's work is useful to us in this context since instead of assuming or importing a set of positive distinctions – between citizenship and non-citizenship, the political and non-political, the possible and the impossible – it is sensitive to the fact that on the border, and in the protest against it, these become the very objects of dispute. In answer to the question posed by our epigraph, we will argue that 'noborders' is not a claim or an 'act' of citizenship, but an attempt to develop a politics of equality autonomously from the categories of citizenship, sovereignty and the state.

Bienvenue à Calais

Located on the north French coast, Calais overlooks a narrow and heavily trafficked straight of sea to the British port of Dover. Despite being a fully fledged member of the European Union, Britain remains only a partial signatory of the Schengen Agreement – the treaty which in theory requires member states to abolish internal border controls with one another (Europa 2010). In part because of Britain's geographical and political relationship to the rest of Europe, but also in part because of the 'Europeanization' of immigration and asylum law (see Tsianos and Karakayali 2010), the presence of undocumented migrants hoping to reach the UK has become something of a recurrent problem for the Calais authorities. The imaginary of the clandestine migrant, both in Calais and in the rest of Europe, has also become a vehicle for the more general articulation of a complex of anxieties over border security and cooperation, migration and welfare provision, and asylum and citizenship in contemporary Europe (Walters 2008, p. 182).

Calais first staged the play of these specifically European anxieties in 2001–2002. The problem of undocumented migrants residing at the Red Cross refugee reception centre or 'refugee camp' in the nearby village of Sangatte became the subject of European-wide attention. The migrants, it was argued, were using the centre as a base from which to attempt clandestine border-crossings to the UK (Freedman 2004, p. 64–69). Following the termination of the Red Cross' Sangatte operation in 2002, undocumented migrants living in Calais have been forced to take refuge in a number of squatted migrant camps, locally known by all as 'the jungles'. Conceited from discarded materials and disused structures, nestled amongst sand-dunes, scattered across waste lands, or lodged in abandoned industrial zones in and around Calais, living conditions in these 'jungle' camps are very poor. Built by migrants themselves and intended as temporary residences, the intensification of Franco-British border control in the port made the camps into more permanent habitations, with a stay of 6 months or more not being uncommon. A United Nations spokesperson who visited the area in 2009 is reported to have said that he had never visited a refugee camp anywhere in the world with as 'impossibly insanitary conditions' as some of the Calais jungles (cited in Kirby 2009).

The very framing of Calais' 'migrant problem', insofar as it relates to the problem of *non*-European nationals trying, illegitimately, to reach Britain, outlines the contours of a specifically European racism (Balibar 2004, p. 44). Thousands of foreigners or 'migrants', in the sense of non-French nationals, pass through Calais everyday. Yet for some of these 'migrants' – tourists, businesspeople, *European* labourers – their 'migranthood', as far as the border is concerned, is erased (Andersson 2008).

Visiting Calais and straying a little from the neatly kept gardens and parks of the *centre-ville*, what Etienne Balibar (2004) invoked as the spectre of a European apartheid accompanying the development of a nascent European citizenship is given a very worldly apparition: spatial segregation, administrative detention, expulsions, enforced material deprivation, the rule of force for some and the rule of law for others. Among the many stories of police brutality we were told, we heard accounts of how police chased migrants by baton from public parks, corralled them into police vans only to abandon them miles out of town, destroyed their settlements, stole or pissed on their belongings, and contaminated their water supplies with CS gas.

Sandro Mezzadra has suggested that the emergence of such spaces as the Calais jungles within the European space gives the European Union a decidedly 'postcolonial constitution'. They mark a situation in which 'the "metaborder" between metropolis and colonies no longer organizes any stable world cartography' with the consequence that colonialism, and its organizing binary of 'citizen and subject', re-emerges as a stratifying factor 'within the territory of the former metropolises themselves' (Mezzadra 2006, p. 35). In Calais, the borders of the new Europe meet the struggles of migration, and the fissure at the heart of European citizenship is given a particularly callous expression. In Calais, Europe divides into two.

In keeping with this divisive geography, 'camp' has become a recurrent designation in cultural responses to border struggles in Calais: the Red Cross 'refugee camp' at Sangatte, the shanty-like 'jungle-camps' around the port, and the noborders 'protest camp' in June 2009. There are of course significant differences between a camp run by an international agency, a self-organized itinerant camp or slum, and a temporary protest camp organized by activists. Yet such commonplaces perhaps express a truth about some important features of the space of the border.

Giorgio Agamben has proposed the concept of 'camp' as the key to understanding the operation of modern sovereignty (see Agamben 1998, 2005, Diken and Laustsen 2005). Drawing on the politically opposed analyses of biopolitics and sovereignty in the respective works of Michel Foucault and Carl Schmitt, Agamben shows how sovereignty must be understood as a bordering practice, tracing a threshold between inside and outside; or in our context, citizen and non-citizen, documented and undocumented. Border crossings introduce a crisis at the very heart of the space of the border, creating 'a zone of indistinction between outside and inside, exception and rule' (Agamben 1998, p. 170). 'Camp' designates a permanent spatial arrangement for dealing with this crisis, a space in which the tracing of the threshold between inside and outside, citizenship and non-citizenship, is continually being drawn.

Crucially, the tracing of this threshold produces 'a limit-figure of life, a threshold in which life is both inside and outside the juridical order, and this threshold', as Agamben writes, 'is the place of sovereignty' (Agamben 1998, p. 27). Life in the jungle-camps does approach this 'limit-figure', what Agamben calls 'bare' or 'naked life'. The camps are in a sense outside Calais since for those living there the 'normal' civil protections and rights of redress do not apply. And yet precisely because of this, life in the camps is much more closely subject to the scrutiny of the law and the rule of the police.

Agamben's work is important for it complicates the oversimplified notion that the problem of the camps can be solved through a simple granting of citizenship rights. Borderlands and camps do not simply separate citizens and non-citizens. They produce the political existence of the citizen and the bare life of non-citizenship *together*, through their very separation. Hence, confronting the camps necessarily involves a critique of the politics of citizenship, resting as it does on the constitutive scission between bare life and political existence.

Agamben's analyses have been criticized for being pessimistic and totalizing (see Agamben 2004), and for excluding the question of political economy from a consideration of the camps (Mezzadra and Neilson 2003). And it is important not to overemphasise the extent to which the camps are effective in immobilizing migratory movements (Bojadžijev *et al.* 2004, Papadopoulos *et al.* 2008, p. 162–221). The Calais jungles were, after all, not just spaces of immobilization, but largely self-organized sites where migrants planned their next move. Nevertheless, we think that Agamben's concept of the camp is useful for showing how sovereignty provides a powerful motor of depoliticization – 'naturalizing' the right of some to control the movement of others, and that the camp is, like the border, a zone of indistinction, a space of conflict where the distinction between bare life and political existence, citizenship and non-citizenship, is resisted and imposed.

The noborder protest camp reflected this. A similarly liminal space, it accentuated and blurred the boundaries between citizens and non-citizens in different ways. During the week that the camp was held around 1000 noborder activists, undocumented migrants and local youths created and shared a self-managed space located near the centre of the port and some of the migrant 'jungle' camps. Some meetings and political discussions were held in four or five languages, and exchanges, encounters and confrontations occurred which temporarily disrupted the habituses, rhythms and everyday lives of the activist, the citizen and the undocumented. At its most principled level, the camp called for the immediate abolition of controls on the movement of people, and for the intensification of the movement against systems of control dividing people into citizens and non-citizens.

Protestors and police

As part of the planned activities for the noborder camp, a public demonstration was scheduled to take place on 27 June. Some months ahead of the demonstration, the county mayor of the Pas-de-Calais region, Pierre de Bousquet, asserted that whilst the demonstration would be allowed to take place, it would be forbidden for 'the migrants' to take part. They were being forced into demonstrating, he argued, and warned that the *Compagnies Républicaines de Sécurité*, police specializing in public order, would be there to keep his word.

More than simply opposing his police force to the bodies of the protestors, the mayor framed the protest itself within what, following Rancière, we will call a police conception of politics – reflected in, but nevertheless irreducible to, the activities of the actual police. As Rancière puts it: 'The police is, essentially, the law, generally implicit, that defines a party's share or the lack of it' (Rancière 1999, p. 29). When the mayor declares that the migrants have no place on a public demonstration, he speaks with the voice, even promises the force, of the police.

On the day of the demonstration, it was clear that the mayor intended to make good on his promise as roughly 2000 police officers met around 1500 demonstrators. The police operation, which mobilized riot-equipped officers, water-canons, a helicopter, armoured vehicles, police horses and dogs, had the very visible effect of preventing many of 'the migrants' from joining the demonstration. One Iraqi recalled how the police had blocked the roads leading from the site of the noborder camp to the beginning of the demonstration on the port-front. After a short stand-off between a group of protestors and police, officers decided to let the group pass on condition that passports or other identification documents were shown. When our interviewee shrugged his shoulders at the police officer asking him for his passport, the officer replied: 'No passport – then go back to jungle'.

The Iraqi's story was a common one. On the day of the demonstration, the police effectively established border-controls at strategic points around the town centre and the planned route of the demonstration; wherever possible demanding that passports and identity documents should be shown. The words 'no passport – then back to the jungle' became something of a refrain amongst those we asked to reflect on the day of the demonstration.

An Afghan teenager we spoke to described how he had walked with a group of about 400–500 protestors from the noborder camp and had almost reached the agreed starting point of the demonstration, a few kilometres walk from the noborder camp and many of the migrant camps. At one point, the bloc passed an asbestos riddled building squatted by African migrants. Some of the demonstrators went to hand out leaflets and make contact with a group of onlookers. The riot police quickly established lines to separate and prevent contact between the demonstrators and the onlookers. At this point, a plain clothed police officer stopped our interviewee and asked to see his passport. After failing to produce one, the officer nodded tellingly to him: 'if you want my advice, I'd leave the demonstration' – and with that, taking heed, he left the demonstration. He explained all this to us later the same day, adding: 'many people are very afraid of coming on the demonstration. They are afraid that the police will take a serious action on the spot. They are afraid of being deported'.

The policing of protest on 27 June involved restricting protest to those with the proper documentation, and to those with a *recognized and identifiable* citizenship status. The police and the mayor sought to delimit and define the proper place where, and the persons amongst which, politics and protest could take place. Policing literally involved maintaining the border and a certain distance between citizens and non-citizens, 'not so much the disciplining of bodies as a rule governing their appearing, a configuration of occupations and the properties of spaces where these occupations are distributed' (Rancière 1999, p. 29). At stake in the confrontation between protestors and police was the very appearance of subjects in public space:

> Police interventions in public spaces consist primarily not in interpellating demonstrators, but in breaking up demonstrations ... It consists, before all else, in recalling the obviousness of what there is, or rather of what there is not, and its slogan is: "Move along! There is nothing to see here!" The police is that which says that here, on this street, there's nothing to see and so nothing to do but move along. It asserts that the space for circulating is nothing but the space of circulation. (Rancière 2010, p. 37)

The police defended the very perimeters of the possible and the impossible, a certain 'distribution of the sensible' determining 'the place and the stakes of politics as a form of experience' (Rancière 2004, p. 13). The politics of the noborder camp did not begin in some pre-established domain of the political, but in the struggle over whether or not migration could be a site of politics at all. It began with the struggle against the police assertion that 'the space of circulation is nothing but the space of circulation'. This brings us to the 'aesthetic' dimension at the core of political. An originary confrontation revolving around 'what can be seen and what can be said about it, around who has the ability to see and the talent to speak, around the properties of spaces and the possibilities of time' (Rancière 2004, p. 13). We further discuss this policing of the political, this partitioning of the possible and the impossible in the politics of the noborder camp through our typology of border policing below.

Border policing I: sovereignty

Through the physical control of the space of the border, the police force in Calais brings sovereignty concretely into play. The dividing practice of the police, separating citizens from non-citizens, legitimate protestors and border-crossers from the illegitimate, reflects a more global characteristic of the politics of undocumented migration. As Angela Mitropoulos and Brett Neilson note, there is a tendency even *within* political struggles surrounding undocumented migration such as the noborder movement for such movements to fracture on a biopolitical or racialized axis: 'between movement understood in a political register (as political actors and/or forces more or less representable) and movement undertaken in a kinetic sense (as a passage between points on the globe, or from one point to an unknown or unreachable destination)' (Mitropoulos and Neilson 2006).

'Border policing', in this context, relates not just to the fact that those without papers were prevented from demonstrating, but to a more general aesthetic division in the account given of what constitutes a political movement. The separation of 'movement as politics' from 'movement as motion' consistently presents the acts of undocumented migrants, their *movements* as 'bereft of political decision and action', thereby suturing politics to sovereignty and territoriality (Mitropoulos and Neilson 2006).

In the popular language used to describe the border struggle in Calais, a whole aesthetics of sovereignty tends to divide and fracture sociopolitical space. Symptomatic in this respect is the popular designation of the squatted migrant camps as 'jungles'. Insofar as some of the camps were situated in small wooded areas, the camps really did resemble 'jungle' or 'forest' dwellings. Still other camps were set amongst sand dunes or in disused buildings, but more or less all of them were referred to as 'jungles'.

This description of the migrant camps as 'jungles' rehearses an older opposition between city and forest which, for centuries, has played an important role in the development of modern sovereignty. The most infamous deployment of this imagery in political theory is of course the Hobbesian narrative of 'the state of nature' as the violent and unruly state of human coexistence before the establishment of sovereign political rule. Political life, for Hobbes, is only possible on condition that a sovereign power exists which is capable of effectively ruling on conflicts of interest and matters of security, or else politics becomes impossible and life reverts to being 'nasty, brutish and short'.

In a classical sovereign gesture opposing the state of nature to the rule of law the French Immigration Minister, Eric Besson, speaking of his intention to destroy the Calais migrant camps in April 2009 remarked: 'the law of the jungle will not rule either here in Calais or anywhere else in France'. 'The jungle will not exist anymore' (BBC News 2009). The problem with this temporalized and temporalizing picture, however, is that the existence of the Calais jungles is not a consequence of the absence of rule. They are the consequence of a series of undeniably political decisions on the part of British and French governments, including the decision to withhold even the most basic forms of assistance to undocumented migrants in Calais:

> The state of nature is, in truth, a state of exception, in which the city appears for an instant... *tanquam dissoluta* [as if it were dissolved]. The foundation [of the city] is thus not an event achieved once and for all but is continually operative in the civil state in the form of the sovereign decision. What is more, the latter refers immediately to the life (and not the free will) of the citizens... Yet this life is not simply natural reproductive life, the *zoe* of the Greeks, nor *bios*, a qualified form of life. It is, rather, the bare [naked] life of *homo sacer* and the *wargus*, a zone of indistinction and continuous transition between man and beast, nature and culture. (Agamben 1998, p. 109)

Sovereign authority founds itself on the identification of a non-political element, bare or naked life, within the political realm. When this bare or naked life becomes the subject of political regulation and decision, politics becomes *biopolitics*: 'literally the decision concerning the unpolitical' (Agamben 1998, p. 173). The police officer's refrain, 'no passport – back to the jungle', outlaws or abandons the undocumented migrants from the city, the site of politics, to a condition of bare or naked life in the state of nature – excluded from politics but nevertheless subject to power.

To an extent, the jungle-camps are experienced as a machine of naked life, stigmatizing their inhabitants, 'immobilizing' individuals in their identity as excluded others (Bauman 1991, p. 68). One of our interviewees noted the social production of the stigma they carried: 'some people say that Afghan people are not clean, but we live in the jungle, how can we be clean, in the jungle it is not possible to be clean'.

Yet the aesthetics of sovereignty did not go unchallenged, and the line separating bare life and political existence is not one that can easily be drawn with any finality. Besson's sovereign gesture is founded on a 'mythological' power sustaining the fantasy that he can, and does, keep the spheres of 'city' and 'jungle' apart. The need for the actual police, their show of force and weapons, signals the contingency of this boundary, not its immutability (Rancière 1999, p. 28, Agamben 2000, p. 104–105). One of our interviewees protested against the desocializing and dehumanizing nature of his subjection: 'We don't want to live forever in the jungle, are we not human, why they treat us like this, are we not humans, are we not all brothers?' Sovereignty denies this commonality, it is, as Esposito notes, 'the not being in common of individuals, the political form of their desocialization' (2008, p. 61). Our interviewee's challenge was thus to the perceptual frame of sovereignty, to the sense of what was common between us from that defined by sovereignty and the police. His specific challenge to us as interviewers was to openly admit that, positively, he was not an equal – that he did not 'count' as a brother, whilst at the same time verifying that he was human, an equal, and a brother.

Far from directly claiming citizenship rights or affirming a different identity and way of life from that forced on him by the police, his protest proceeded *via negativa*. It consisted not in the affirmation of one kind of political community against the one that excluded him, but in demonstrating the 'impossible' community of the world where his humanity and fraternity was valid and the world where it was not. He invoked 'humanity' and 'fraternity' not as regulative ideals against which the reality of the world came up hopelessly short, but put them to use as part of the 'configuration of the given', as inscriptions which give equality a form of visibility (Rancière 2010, p. 68).

Significantly then, and herein lies the specific force of his challenge to sovereignty and the police, he did not claim to speak only for himself, or on behalf of some excluded others, but in place of *anyone*. His protest constructed, against the partial and conditional 'universalism' of the police order, a singular case of universality *by means of an assumption of equality*. What sovereignty cannot tolerate is the universal claim of equality across, or *in spite of* the citizen/non-citizen divide: the coming of a 'whatever' subject, rejecting all properties of identity and representable conditions of belonging (Agamben 1993, p. 87). 'Properly' speaking, of course, we are not all brothers. Fraternity here has the structure of an aesthetic 'as if', implying a certain substitutability or equivalence, *as if* we are all brothers (Rancière 2009, p. 278–280).

Equality *as* substitutability is axiomatic to his protest; hence, instead of *identifying* with the substantive content of his suffering, protest entailed a disidentification with his position, or lack of position, in the social order. A disidentification which simultaneously called for a disidentification on the part of the whole community from the community as such: 'are we not human, are we not *all* brothers'. 'The opening up of a subject space where anyone can be counted since it is the space where those of no account are counted, where a connection is made between having a part and having no part' (Rancière 1999, p. 36). His protest made manifest this dissensus between having a part and having no part. It staged the 'dissensual' or 'impossible' presence of 'two worlds in one' (Rancière 2010, p. 36–37). We are *all* human, we are *all* brothers, or we are not.

Border policing II: humanitarianism

In March 2008 Calais elected a new town mayor, Natacha Bouchart. Upon being elected, Bouchart responded to fears that a 'Sangatte mark II' was to be established to deal with the problem of undocumented migrants living in the jungles. Between 1999 and 2002 when the Red Cross ran its Sangatte operation, it is estimated that in excess of 75,000 migrants passed through the centre (Walters 2008, p. 182). There would be 'no new Sangatte' asserted Bouchart. Taking a soft line on the problem of undocumented migrants in Calais, such as providing them with food and shelter, she argued, would only encourage attempts at clandestine border crossings from the port (Sparks 2008).

The creation of a new Sangatte-style refugee camp has been consistently presented as a 'humanitarian' alternative to the contemporary border regime in Calais. In the absence of such an arrangement, destitute migrants rely on the goodwill and charity of individuals and organizations, such as *Association SALAM* and *La Belle Etoile* for food on a daily basis. For their opposition to the hard-line policing strategy, such individuals and groups have been threatened with criminal charges through what has come to be known as the *délit de solidarité*, or 'crime of solidarity'. Article L622-1 of the French Penal code makes it illegal to assist, directly or indirectly, the arrival, movement or residence of persons irregularly present on the French territory. The offence is punishable by a €30,000 fine or up to 5 years in prison. Whilst the law is primarily used to convict people engaged in people trafficking, it is also the background against which the activities of individuals and organizations assisting those living in the jungles have been disciplined and curtailed.

The organizing networks for the noborder camp recognized that they were entering a field already framed by the work of civil society and humanitarian organizations. The *délit de solidarité* had, to a certain extent, 'politicized' the issue of basic material assistance to undocumented migrants in Calais. Nevertheless, noborder activists were keen to challenge what, in 'humanitarianism', they saw as a limited framework of understanding. Some activists were even highly critical of the aid organizations' work (albeit recognising that differences existed between the various ones). During a meeting held in the noborder camp, one stressed the role that humanitarianism played in maintaining the domination of the state, reproducing it on a voluntary level. 'The state relies on you', was his charge to the representatives of aid organizations.

There was a definite attempt by some in the noborder camp to move beyond a simple opposition between humanitarianism and politics. To this end, food and shelter and washing facilities were available for anyone who came to the camp and a medical treatment centre was established on site, run by first-aid trained activists. There was of course no question of being able to provide anything like the level of care, permanent habitation and subsistence required. But all these activities became a central part of the struggle to achieve a sense of collective security and self-organization in the camp and materialize a different kind of political space in Calais.

Despite this, the immediate situation of the migrants living in Calais was so bad that, even in the space for political discussions made possible by the camp, humanitarian sentiments often overrode more explicitly political discussions. This caused audible frustration within the camp, best expressed by the individual whose statement provides the opening epigraph to this article: 'The Afghans that come to the camp do not come for food and blankets, although it is very nice, this is not what we come for. Every time I come to meetings we discuss blankets, but we are not hungry, we do not come for blankets, open the borders!' The overall consequence of this humanitarianism was that the politics of the noborder camp risked remaining confined to a consensus set by the space of the border, and hence sovereignty, itself.

Symptomatic in this respect was the prevalent valorization of humanitarian 'realism', typically contrasted with the 'idealism' of the 'noborder' position, even when the suffering caused by the border, and not just some contingent feature of it, was manifestly what was at stake. Such 'realism' is part of a 'police logic of order, which asserts, in all circumstances, that it is the only thing possible to do' (Rancière 1999, p. 132). Protest on 'humanitarian realist' grounds reduces protest to a contest over 'the possible' which can only ever mean, at a fundamental level, a conservative acceptance of the existing framework for grasping problems and their solutions. Protest is not 'the art of the possible', but rather 'the art of the *impossible* – it changes the very parameters of what is considered 'possible' in the existing constellation' (Žižek 1999, p. 199).

In fact the Calais migrants have no shortage of 'impossible' stories concerning their journeys and escapes. When viewed from the perspective of those trying to cross the border, humanitarian 'realism' is in fact thoroughly 'idealist', subordinating the material struggle against the border to the problem of rights and their recognition. Here idealism is, as always, an apparatus for purging or disavowing material antagonisms. One group of migrants we spoke to highlighted the continuity between war in Afghanistan and their struggle against the border authorities in Calais. 'If we categorize the whole journey [from Afghanistan to Calais], this here [Calais] is more difficult than the whole journey'. Asked how the situation they faced in Calais compared to the situation they faced in Afghanistan, one replied bluntly, 'no, no, Calais *is* Afghanistan'.

This 'impossible' claim of a single world of Calais and Afghanistan is precisely what the border is there to deny. It is significant, in this respect, that the majority of would-be border crossers held up in Calais originate from countries that have had or continue to have some colonial and/or imperial relationship to Britain – their desired destination. In 2009, the majority of undocumented migrants in the Calais jungles were from Afghanistan and Iraq. Other significant groups included migrants from Iran, the Congo, Sudan, Ethiopia and Eritrea. Their movements constitute a *reversal* of the flow of imperial expansion, refusals of the 'naturalness' of their subordinated positions in these 'other' worlds (Mitropoulos 2007a, p. 129–130).

Within the noborders movement, the concept of 'the autonomy of migration' has been developed as a way of orientating noborder politics around an insistence on the constituent and political element of migratory movements. As Bojadžijev *et al.* (2010) point out, developing their account of the autonomy of migration thesis, 'the border regime does not transform of its own accord, but rather obtains its dynamic from the forms of migratory movements'. This is not to attribute an isolated 'agency' to migrants, but simply to appreciate that although migration is 'entangled within relations of power and domination ... this does not mean that migrants are forever condemned to reproducing these relations in the same way'. Migration and mobility are both a source of exploitation *and* 'the symptom of flight from relations of exploitation and oppression' (Bojadžijev *et al.* 2010). The wager of 'the autonomy of migration' is, then, that the border, like the factory, is both a site of suffering and a vector of antagonism.

At stake in the struggle over the border in Calais, but also in the mediation of this struggle in public discourse, in the practice of professional sociology, journalism and so on, is the control of the borders of the political itself:

> In presenting the act of migration as something outside the field of politics [as economic, familial, criminal, humanitarian, environmental] the very definition of what a [political] movement and politics is remains tied to the organization of democratic representation in a

very precise sense, and so, *in turn*, the terrain in which migration occurs appears as that which must be controlled, regulated, and mediated. (Mitropoulos 2007a, p. 131)

In terms of 'protest', the autonomy of migration thesis helps to conceptualize the border as a site of struggle. When compared to other analytical frameworks, 'autonomy' reintroduces dissensus into the border struggle in Calais. It is a determined act of de-classification and disidentification, an exodus from the existing and proliferating categories of migration. The autonomy of migration proposes an analytic through which to make migration not simply visible, but visible as an activity: the act of an equal will and intellect. 'Equality is not given, nor is it claimed; it is practiced, it is *verified*' (Rancière 1991, p. 137). And it can only be verified if there is something common on both sides of the border. The autonomy of migration '*opens the possibility* for analytically and practically connecting various struggles within the context of migration' for creating a framework for 'a broader movement in the concerns of migrants', 'beyond basic pity and general human rights' (Bojadžijev *et al.* 2010 our emphasis).

'We must never look only to the tip of the iceberg', urges Moulier-Boutang, 'the institutionalized forms, or the word of the people ... supposing that, as soon as they aren't saying anything, they aren't acting ... the silences, the refusals, and the flight [are] something active' (2001, p. 227). To restrict our discussion of protest to those moments when injustice was 'obviously' challenged would be, we argue to redraw the perceptible divisions of the police order which sees in undocumented migration only the symptom or malaise of some other economic, military, humanitarian or criminal dysfunction.

Border policing III: activism

In contrast to the relatively invisible and/or apolitical construal of migrant subjectivity in Calais, the activities of citizen-activists were highly visible. Almost *any* act by a 'protester' was seen as politically motivated, and thereby subject to the limitations set by the local authorities and police. Arrests were made for the most mundane of activities, attempts to leaflet shoppers in the town centre were prevented, and flyers, activist newspapers and even toilet rolls were confiscated. Police barred a planned football match that the press had been invited to and which was to take place on a pitch not far from the noborder camp with mixed teams of migrants, activists and local youths. A trip to the local supermarket, which would have otherwise only taken a few minutes, could take in excess of an hour as activists underwent passport controls anytime they strayed far from the site of the noborder camp. These policing tactics, however, far from making protest 'impossible' for the activists, in effect made it very difficult for activists to act in a way which was not considered 'protest'. Indeed, it was hardly possible to walk around the town without being recognized as 'one of the noborder', and challenged by Calais residents on political motivation, violence and anarchism.

The local press ran sensationalist stories dramatizing an impending violent clash between noborder 'militants' and police. On 27 June, the day of the public demonstration, half the town centre was shut down. The front page of the daily paper *Nord Littoral* carried an image of noborder activists dressed in black, donning hoods and face scarves: 'Day of truth for the no-borders', 'D-Day has arrived' ran the headlines. The popular mediation of the noborder camp tended to emphasise the relationship between the noborder activists and the police, effectively restricting what was considered intelligible as political action to the actions of the noborder 'activists'. Whilst the mainstream accounts of the noborder camp did not go unchallenged in the form of alternative media, still other 'actions' did little to unsettle the validity of this image of activism.

In any case, the spectacular opposition between noborder activists and the police, dramatized by both sides, in fact masks a more fundamental identity between them. Invariably in this picture what gets presented as 'activism' essentially remains defined by the state. Recall the mayor's declaration that the protest of 27 June would indeed be able to take place, only that 'the migrants' were to have no part in it. In the event, the protest was strictly limited to a previously agreed and heavily guarded route, away from the town centre and ferry-port. Policing the separation between migrants and activists involved not only denying undocumented migrants the capacity of protest, but also framing protest and 'activism' in a particularly statist way.

Wherever 'activism' remains defined by the state, even if this means opposition to it, it fails to put itself 'at a distance to the state', denying 'at bottom any active autonomy, any real independence, any affirmative political virtuality, to what rises up in the enraged rebel of good faith. "Down with repression!" leads no further than a *placed* reactive' (Badiou 2009, p. 32). That is, 'activism' had both a place and an identity in the context of the border struggles which tended to limit the contours of protest to a reaction to the regulations, discourses, categories and practices of the state.

One British activist, for instance, super-glued his hands to the doors of the Town Hall in Calais, his bare back carrying a bold penned message: 'showers for the migrants!' The assumption behind this kind of action is that the 'exclusion' of undocumented migrants from systems of political representation calls for an 'activism' which will 'represent the unrepresented'. But this notion of 'representing the unrepresented', whilst introducing issues which were certainly not on the mainstream political agenda, in fact reinforces the very same divisions it seeks to oppose. The 'excluded' ('the migrants!') become 'included' through this call for recognition, a call which in marking a political deficiency or lack only ends up reaffirming, rather than challenging, the necessity of a sovereign power capable of recognizing it (Mitropoulos 2007a, p. 131).

In this sense then, 'activism' is much less a synonym for political action than a definition of it, a 'distribution of the sensible' circumscribing 'what actions and dispositions might be deemed properly political and therefore, by contrast, those which are not'. Moreover, what gets deemed as 'protest' in this conception of politics is 'for the most part, the kinds of [actions] that make representational claims possible… One does not speak, or act, for oneself, but for others' (Mitropoulos 2007b). This matching of interests to be represented with positions and identities in fact *forecloses* protest. Since everybody, 'including the excluded', is already accounted for, the mechanisms of appearance whereby the 'impossible' community of citizens and non-citizens could be demonstrated or staged are in advance effaced (Rancière 1999, p. 116). The 'excluded' are 'included' through the very discourse of exclusion, thereby closing 'spaces of dissensus by plugging intervals and patching up any possible gaps between appearance and reality, law and fact' (Rancière 2010, p. 71).

'Activism' is the other side of what remains after the separation of movement as motion from movement as politics. Whilst there was much talk and criticism in the camp about the appropriate vocabulary with which to refer to 'the migrants', there was less practical interrogation about the limitations which 'activist' identity placed on the approach to border protest. But in separating the protest from the movement against borders, the border became a more global instrument of political domination, and not just one affecting 'the migrants'.

The separation of movement as politics from movement as motion divides 'word' from 'action'. Protest is permitted, possible, solicited even, so long as it is not connected to any concrete threat of change. In this context, protest literally becomes a matter of 'spectacle', in Guy Debord's sense. The spectacle as 'the culmination of humanity's internal separation' (Debord 1967, p. 20) exiling art from life, images from action. At first glance, the society of the spectacle seems to radically affirm and valorize 'appearances', making politics and protest into a question of appearances. Yet, it is actually the precise opposite. 'Appearance' stands not simply for an image, but for the *arrival* of something which marks a difference or initiates a change, a *reconfiguration* of 'the space where parties, parts, or the lack of parts have been defined', which *undoes* 'the perceptible divisions of the police order' (Rancière 1999, p. 30, 95–105, see also Žižek 1999, p. 191–198).

'Post-politics' is another word for this 'disappearance of appearance', this severing of the link between words and action (Diken and Laustsen 2005, p. 170). In post-politics anything can be political, so long as it is disconnected from a sense of movement understood as the possibility of real change. It is thus the very antithesis of dissensus. In post-politics, the spectacle of a border protest without consequence coincides with the biopolitics of border struggles pushed to the limits of bare life:

> To the media devices which control and handle the public word thus corresponds the technological devices which register and identify naked life: between these two extremes of a word without body and a body without word the space of what we formerly called politics is increasingly more reduced and exiguous. (Agamben cited in Diken and Laustsen 2005, p. 65)

There were, however, and continue to be, practical attempts to overcome this division between the protest and the movement against borders. Following the noborder camp in 2009, a new organization in Calais has been established, 'Calais Migrant Solidarity'. Instead of simply campaigning on behalf of the Calais migrants, the group take their directions from the border struggles of the migrants themselves, offering practical support, monitoring police activity, documenting and where possible preventing arrests and the destruction of migrant settlements. There are of course limitations to this kind of 'resistance', but in disarticulating the implicit border (and hierarchy) between 'protest' and 'movement', Calais Migrant Solidarity perhaps presents a challenge to post-politics. A new politics? A new politics beyond citizenship?

Conclusion

'At stake in every politics of border control is the control of the borders of the political' (Mitropoulos 2007a, p. 131). Or, put differently, an essential part of any political dispute concerns the very 'politicity' of the dispute itself (Rancière 2010, p. 35). In this paper, we have analysed the play of this conflict as it played out in the context of the Calais noborder camp. Each of the *dispositifs* of border control which we have analysed, from 'citizenship' and 'sovereignty' through to 'humanitarianism' and 'activism', define a particular 'distribution of the sensible', a particular aesthetics of politics, a certain mapping of 'the visible, the intelligible and also of the possible' (Rancière 2006) that we found to be particularly effective in the way the politics of the noborder camp was staged, regulated and contested.

In making a terminological distinction between 'protest' and 'police', we hope to have shown that the internal dynamism which animates our diagrams of border control is not reducible to a power struggle over what can and cannot count as political. 'Protest' and 'police' work according to two totally contradictory logics. 'Police' works according to inegalitarian logic which always sets out to police the borders of the political through defining not only the space and subjects of politics, but also the space of non-politics. From the perspective of the police, the *dispositifs* define strategies for controlling the borders of the political: relations of visibility between power, knowledge and the subject, particular definitions of politics and the subjects that are proper to it.

'Protest', by contrast, proceeds through an egalitarian logic which explodes every border of the political, '*displacing* the borders of what is acknowledged as "the" political' (Rancière 2010, p. 149 our emphasis). It is a displacement which occurs from within a given regime of the perceptible but, since equality is not a 'property' of the arrangement, by a logic which does not 'belong' to it. Strictly speaking then, from this perspective, equality is indeed 'impossible', but this does not mean that it cannot exert an effect.

We have shown some of the ways in which the logic of equality disrupted the activities and distributions of the police and how certain inscriptions of equality are put to use within the different modalities of border control, even if their effectiveness tends to be subordinated to the distributions of places, properties and roles (Rancière 2010, p. 207). Policing does not so much as 'deny' equality, it 'wrongs' equality, and protest occurs wherever the verification of equality is obliged to turn into the disputation of this wrong (Rancière 1992, p. 59).

Our conclusions resonate with a question posed by Imogen Tyler; that is, if citizenship is deployed (if not 'designed') 'for purposes of disenfranchisement and political dispossession, in what sense can it be said to retain any radical promise for social justice?' (Tyler 2010, p. 72). Historically, citizenship has been built on exceptions: the exception of colonial subjects, of women, of the non-propertied classes, the young, the mad, and so on. This is, we would argue, a consequence of conceptualizing citizenship in terms of a property which individuals can, and therefore cannot, possess. The demand of 'citizenship for all' does not escape this quandary (Hindess 2004).

The novelty and hence the promise of 'noborder' politics lies not in its demand of 'freedom of movement for all', not as an 'act' or claim of citizenship, but in its capacity to disrupt the tentative ways in which the borders of the political are policed and produced. That the critique of one form of border control has a tendency to call another figure of the police into existence, as we move from sovereignty, to humanitarianism, to activism, shows, we believe, not only the importance of thinking through the complexities of the relationship between politics and movement (Mitropoulos and Neilson 2006), but also the importance of thinking through equality, not as a property or end, but as a political axiom – not least for a movement which privileges the struggle against borders in the fight for emancipation.

Acknowledgements

The ethnographic material for this paper was collected by the authors during their participation in the Calais noborder camp, June 2009, and through their involvement in the UK noborders movement more generally. The authors thank Imogen Tyler and Katarzyna Marciniak for their support in preparing this article for publication, Bülent Diken and John Urry for their comments on earlier drafts, and the two anonymous reviewers from *Citizenship Studies* for their generous comments and criticisms. They also thank all those who made the 2009 Calais noborder camp possible, and in particular our interviewees.

References

Agamben, G., 1993. *The coming community*. Minneapolis, MN: University of Minnesota Press.
Agamben, G., 1998. *Homo sacer: sovereign power and bare life*. Stanford, CA: Stanford University Press.
Agamben, G., 2000. *Means without end: notes on politics*. Minneapolis, MN: University of Minnesota Press.
Agamben, G., 2004. 'I am sure you are more pessimistic than I am . . .' An Interview with Giorgio Agamben, Vacarme. *Rethinking marxism*, 16 (2), 115–124.
Agamben, G., 2005. *State of exception*. Chicago, IL: University of Chicago Press.

Andersson, R., 2008. *A criminal confusion*, [online]. ASA Globalog, Immigration. Available from: http://blog.theasa.org/?cat=49 [Accessed 30 August 10].

Badiou, A., 2009. *Theory of the subject*. London: Continuum.

Balibar, E., 2004. *We, the people of Europe? reflections on transnational citizenship*. Princeton, NJ: Princeton University Press.

Bauman, Z., 1991. *Modernity and ambivalence*. Cambridge, MA: Polity.

BBC News, 2009. *France 'to shut down Calais camp'*, [online]. Available from: http://news.bbc.co.uk/1/hi/8014940.stm [Accessed 30 August 10].

Bojadžijev, M., Karakayalı, S. and Trott, B., 2010. Recuperating the sideshows of capitalism: the autonomy of migration today. *e-flux*, 17, 1–9.

Bojadžijev, M., Karakayalı, S. and Tsianos, V., 2004. Le mystère de l'arrivée. des camps et des spectres. *Multitudes*, 19, 41–52.

Bourdieu, P., 1990. The scholastic point of view. *Cultural anthropology*, 5 (4), 380–391.

Debord, G., 1967. *The society of the spectacle*. London: Rebel Press.

Diken, B. and Laustsen, C.B., 2005. *The culture of exception: sociology facing the camp*. Abingdon: Routledge.

Esposito, R., 2008. *Bios: biopolitics and philosophy*. Minneapolis, MN: University of Minnesota Press.

Europa, 2010. *The Schengen area and cooperation*, [online]. Europa: Summaries of EU legislation. Available from: http://europa.eu/legislation_summaries/justice_freedom_security/free_movement_of_persons_asylum_immigration/l33020_en.htm [Accessed 10 December 2010].

Freedman, J., 2004. *Immigration and insecurity in France*. Aldershot: Ashgate Publishing.

Hindess, B., 2004. Citizenship for all. *Citizenship studies*, 8 (3), 305–315.

Isin, E.F. and Nielsen, G.M., 2008. Introduction. *In*: E.F. Isin and G.M. Nielsen, eds. *Acts of citizenship*. New York: Zed Books, 1–12.

Kirby, E.J., 2009. *Hope dims in Calais 'jungle'*, [online]. From Our Own Correspondent, BBC Radio 4. Available from: http://news.bbc.co.uk/1/hi/programmes/from_our_own_correspondent/8262800.stm [Accessed 30 August 2010].

Mezzadra, S., 2006. Citizen and subject: a postcolonial constitution for the European union. *Situations*, 1 (2), 31–42.

Mezzadra, S. and Neilson, B., 2003. Available from: http://www.borderlands.net.au/vol2no1_2003/mezzadra_neilson.html [Accessed 27 February 12] Né qui, né altrove – migration, detention, desertion: a dialogue [online]. *Borderlands*, 2 (1).

Mitropoulos, A., 2007a. Autonomy, recognition, movement. *In*: S. Shukaitis, D. Graeber and E. Biddle, eds. *Constituent imagination: militant investigations collective theorization*. Oakland, CA: AK Press, 127–136.

Mitropoulos, A., 2007b. Activism bound. On the borders of politics: activism, democracy, labour. *Department of gender and cultural studies seminar series*, 1 June 2007, University of Sydney [online]. Available from: http://s0metim3s.com/2007/06/30/on-the-borders-of-the-political/ [Accessed 27 February 12].

Mitropoulos, A. and Neilson, B., 2006. Available from: http://www.vacarme.org/article484.html [Accessed 27 February 12] Exceptional times, Non-governmental spacings, and impolitical movements [online]. *Vacarme*.

Moulier-Boutang, Y., 2001. The art of flight: an interview with Yann Moulier-Boutang, Stany Grelet. *Rethinking marxism: a journal of economics, culture and society*, 13 (3), 227–235.

Nyers, P., 2003. Abject cosmopolitanism: the politics of protection in the anti-deportation movement. *Third world quarterly*, 24 (6), 1069–1093.

Nyers, P., 2008. No one is illegal between city and nation. *In*: E.F. Isin and G.M. Nielsen, eds. *Acts of citizenship*. New York, NY: Zed Books, 160–181.

Panagia, D., 2009. The improper event: on Jacques Rancière's mannerism - thinking citizenship series. *Citizenship studies*, 13 (3), 297–308.

Papadopoulos, D., Stephenson, N. and Tsianos, V., 2008. *Escape routes: control and subversion in the 21st century*. London: Pluto Press.

Rancière, J., 1991. *The ignorant schoolmaster: five lessons in intellectual emancipation*. Stanford, CA: Stanford University Press.

Rancière, J., 1992. Politics, identification, and subjectivization. *October*, 61, 58–64.

Rancière, J., 1999. *Disagreement: politics and philosophy*. Minneapolis, MN: University of Minnesota Press.

Rancière, J., 2004. *The politics of aesthetics: the distribution of the sensible*. London: Continuum.

Rancière, J., 2006. *Our police order: what can be said, seen, and done. Interview with Truls Lie and Jacques Ranciere*, [online]. Eurozine. Available from: http://www.eurozine.com/articles/2006-08-11-lieranciere-en.html [Accessed 30 August 2010].

Rancière, J., 2009. Should democracy come? ethics and politics in Derrida. *In*: P. Cheah and S. Guerlac, eds. *Derrida and the time of the politcal*. Durham: Duke University Press.

Rancière, J., 2010. *Dissesnsus: on politics and aesthetics*. London: Continuum.

Sparks, I., 2008. *There will be no second Sangatte refugee camp, says new mayor of Calais*, [online]. The Daily Mail. Available from: http://www.dailymail.co.uk/news/article-540568/There-second-Sangatte-refugee-camp-says-new-mayor-Calais.html [Accessed 30 August 10].

Tsianos, V. and Karakayali, S., 2010. Transnational migration and the emergence of the European border regime: an ethnographic analysis. *European journal of social theory*, 13 (3), 373–387.

Tyler, I., 2010. Designed to fail: a biopolitics of British citizenship. *Citizenship studies*, 14 (1), 61–74.

Walters, W., 2008. Acts of demonstration: mapping the territory of (non-) citizenship. *In*: E.F. Isin and G.M. Nielsen, eds. *Acts of citizenship*. London: Zed Books, 182–206.

Žižek, S., 1999. *The ticklish subject: the absent centre of political ontology*. London: Verso.

No Border: photo essay

Julie Rebouillat

Contre-Faits, Marseille, France

Editor's note

Julie Rebouillat is a freelance photographer who collaborates with the art-activist organisation *Contre-Faits*. She has been interested in the issue of borders and migration since 2008. She is currently working on a series of photographs looking at the daily lives of irregular migrants in the border regions of Europe (Calais, Igoumenitsa). She has also conducted projects investigating the struggle of NoBorder activists and the camps which have been organised at strategic points in 'Fortress Europe' to demand the opening of borders to all (Calais, Brussels).

Her approach is based on immersion; she values taking the time to make contact with people in order to provide an intimate representation of their daily lives, as opposed to the often sensationalised and distancing images of the mass media. In Calais, for example, she spent 1 month living in a squat with African migrants. At the NoBorder camps, her photographs were also taken from an inside perspective, in order to share the NoBorder activists' point of view on the camp and actions.

The following images are taken from two projects carried out at the NoBorder camps at Calais (June 2009) and Brussels (October 2010).

Imogen Tyler

For more details about Julie's work, see http://www.contre-faits.org

After citizenship: autonomy of migration, organisational ontology and mobile commons

Dimitris Papadopoulos[a] and Vassilis S. Tsianos[b]

[a]School of Management, University of Leicester, Leicester LE1 7RH, UK; [b]Department of Sociology, University of Hamburg, Allende-Platz 1, 20146 Hamburg, Germany

This paper explores the relevance of the autonomy of migration approach for understanding the role of citizenship in the sovereign control of mobility. There is an insurgent configuration of ordinary experiences of mobility emerging against this regime of control. At its core is the sharing of knowledge and infrastructures of connectivity, affective cooperation, mutual support and care among people on the move. The sovereign regime of mobility control is displaced on the level on which it attempts to take hold: the everyday movements of migrants. The frenetic fixation with security is challenged by the creation of common worlds of existence; the obsession with governance is replaced by inhabiting social spaces below the radar of existing political structures. This paper attempts to contribute to a reconstruction of this mundane ontology of transmigration, an ontology which we will describe as the mobile commons of migration.

For Sarah, Sidik and Indres who are on the road right now

1. Sapik in Europe

Do I use Facebook to stay in contact with my family? – No, all you need is a mobile phone. At home, up there, they don't have anything except mobiles. Sometimes you just beep them so that they can see from your area code, where you are and that you've done a step further. In Facebook I have recovered some friends that I have lost for years – now they live in Paris. Last year, after the Pagani camp I wanted to continue to Germany together with a friend. We traveled through Macedonia and Serbia until Hungary, where we split. We prepared everything, we had every part of the route as a copy from Google Earth with us, printed in Internet cafes. And we used GPS on our mobiles. My friend took a train to Germany, but he fell asleep and had to drop out in Vienna where they caught him. I was arrested in Hungary and brought to a camp for six weeks. They threatened me to remain detained for years if I wouldn't want leave the country voluntarily. So I decided to return to Greece. In Serbia the police stole all of my money and my mobile phone and together with many others I was brought to a cell. Such a thing I didn't ever experience in Greece. When I finally arrived in Macedonia the police asked me if I was on my way to Serbia or to Greece. They showed me the path and even gave me some coins to make a phone call. I already spoke on the phone with a friend who through Evros came to Athens where he now lives. He tells me that actually it is very cheap in Evros, only $400. And this is certainly linked to the fingerprint questions. If you try to make it through the islands it is much more difficult without being fingerprinted. That's why it is more expensive. In Evros you can pass without much money and without fingerprints. (Interview with Sapik, Lesvos, Greece, 7 September 2010)

The shared knowledge, affective cooperation, mutual support and care between migrants when they are on the road or when they arrive somewhere is the main topic of this paper. Here, we attempt to contribute to a reconstruction of this flat mundane ontology of the moving people, an ontology which we will describe as the *mobile commons* of migration. Sapik reminds us what it means to cross the borders into Europe. Once one is in Europe an even more brutally patrolled border stands in the way: European citizenship. Our focus on the mobile commons does not attempt to question citizenship and its possible importance in certain situations but rather to open, as Peter Linebaugh says, a chink in the wall and explore the possibilities that lie behind the horizon of contempoary European discourses and practices of citizenship. For many, citizenship appears as a wall indeed. There is no doubt that citizenship is hard fought between those who try to restrict it and those who invest in the efficacy of citizenship as a potential guarantor of rights, justice and liberation. Such critical investments can be found in the idea of citizenship beyond sovereignty and the state which will be discussed later or in ideas of local citizenship, citizen labs, transnational citizenship, global citizenship, or acts of citizenship. But whatever the definition of citizenship is, it operates as a wall when it represents the ultimate horizon of political practice and social analysis – this is the argument that this paper will try to develop. In order to respond to the increasing securitisation and abjection through citizenship, one could see as a possible solution the invention of another qualifying adjective to the concept of citizenship. But this is not the aim of this paper. Rather the methodological principle guiding this work is to see through the chink in the wall, to cultivate an imaginary and a practical sensibility to what lies after citizenship. And what we see through this chink is the mundane organisational practices of mobile people. Our starting point will be migrants on the ground, on the road – transmigrants. It is the multiplicity of these lives and movements of people that forces a break not with citizenship as such but with it as a central category in migration policy as well as academic research.

2. Labour and migration

Despite the fierce labour struggles and social struggles that were played out in the past decades on a global scale, the ghost of *the* working class as the avant-garde of social change is disappearing. The spectre of the working class undergoes a transmutation which threatens equally political institutions and the fragile identities of the populations in the Global North: the spectre of the migrant worker. For almost 40 years now, the response was to exclude mobility from the constitution of polity. Mobility was also seen as external to labour, and class was thought independent of movement. But migration not only brings the current political system into turmoil, it also destabilises and recomposes what class is. The question of the past decades was how to suppress and silence migrants. Now this question is rendered obsolete by the very fact that people did not stop moving, creating new lives elsewhere, mixing with the native working classes and capital did not stop capitalising on them. We are facing a new situation, one which is dominated by a different question: not how to immobilise migrants but how to institutionalise mobility. The concern today is how to codify mobility, how to make it productive and sustainable, and how to combine it with a new political order and the decline of sovereignty.

This is a moment when the cards of labour, mobility and sovereignty are mixed and redistributed again. We used to think of mobility as a movement through space. And this is of course true: migration is applied geopolitics on the ground. This approach focussed on the idea of territoriality in conceptualising mobility. Consider the spatial strategies of territorialisation in the workhouse which attempted to capture the wandering mob in

Europe of the late Middle Ages (Ignatieff 1978, Federici 2004) or the first foreign worker hostels of the Gastarbeiter era (von Oswald 2002), to name just two examples. The governance of mobile populations now appears as an important site for the exercise of control and the genesis of biopower. The recurring pattern was the attempt to suffocate mobility by terminating it. Mobility–immobility was the driving conflict. In these conditions, immobility is associated primarily with terrioriality, docile labour, becoming native and integration with the local people; mobility is conceived as sabotage, insubordination, escape, untrained work, multiple belongings. Nation state–territory–people is the golden triptych of capitalist sovereignty. But as soon as mobility becomes fused with labour and with the structures of sovereignty which try to contain it, a new perspective on mobility emerges: mobility as a movement in time.

In conditions in which migration becomes one of the main forces in the production and reproduction of capital, the role of control is not to suppress mobility. The role of migration control is to make different time registers of the entry in the productive sphere along the path of mobile populations compatible. In particular, it attempts to render the speed of absorption into the local labour markets compatible with the speed of flows of mobile populations. Migration control is about speed and its regulation. Migration control works as an equaliser between labour markets and migratory movements. For example, camps are less a form of blocking the circulation of mobility; they reinsert irregular migration back into the productive logics of society by making out of irregular mobility, either controllable populations or illegalised people; camps are *speed boxes* of migratory movements.

From forced migration to managed migration during the 1950s and 1960s, mobility was governed productively by territorialising movements and inserting them into the spatial regulation of working bodies (see the work of Castles and Miller 2003, Karakayali 2008). As we move to the temporal regime of mobility control, the main concern is to transform ungovernable streams to governable subjects of mobility that adjust to the needs of local labour markets. Of course we know that the needs of local labour markets are not 'natural' – just pure numbers depicting how much workforce each market can absorb – but they are politically over-determined by issues related to security, nationalism, populist gambling of mainstream political parties, neoliberal policies, etc. This is what the border regime does: it is not there to block migration; it tries to institutionalise it by controlling its speed and magnitude (De Genova and Peutz 2010). The control of mobility is effectively performed through the exercise of sovereignty. Sovereignty is not about sovereign borders. Secure borders do not exist and cannot exist; sovereignty is the futile attempt to regulate the porosity of borders: this can be conceived of as *porocracy* (see chapter 11 in Papadopoulos *et al.* 2008).

Institutionalising the temporal intensities of mobility is what is needed in order to insert migration into labour in conditions in which spatialisation is not enough. Legal or illegal, regular or irregular, managed or unauthorised migration is directly entangled to labour and its local contingencies (see Alberti 2011). So, in order to understand migration we need to rethink the changing forms of exploitation which is at the heart of the current regime of accumulation. The intensification of labour, that is the duration of labour and the intensity of labour are the main two dimensions that define the degree of exploitation (Nichols 1980). Inserting mobility into labour compels us to expand this understanding of appropriation of labour: the intensification of exploitation needs to be complemented by another mode or surplus value extraction which goes beyond the working day and involves the whole existence of the worker. We are not only dealing with an intensification of exploitation but also with its extensification. Exploitation extends across the whole existential conditions of living labour, the lines of fight and exploitation multiply and traverse different domains of life.

This complicates the meaning of labour power which becomes variable capital in the valorisation process. The neoliberal counter-revolution intensified exploitation by expanding the appropriation of labour power beyond the mere capacity to produce. In order to be able to become and remain productive, people mobilise their social and personal investments – social relations, non-work related skills, informal networks, ideas and their capacity to be mobile (Dyer-Witheford 1999, Negri 2005). As work – in order to become productive – becomes incorporated into the non-labour sphere, the exploitation of labour power takes place through the contingencies of the lives of each individual worker; it becomes embodied, that is it becomes an indissoluble characteristic of the whole situated existence of living labour (Moulier Boutang 2012). Intensification and extensification of exploitation have both created a different pattern of surplus value extraction: capitalism becomes embodied, ingrained in every part of the body and in every social activity. One of the key dimensions of the embodiment of capitalist relations is extracting surplus value from the very fact that bodies can become mobile in the most averse circumstances (Alberti 2011). The institutionalisation of mobility is the attempt to include mobility as one of the core ingredients of labour exploitation. This happens by creating different regimes and types of labour in order to reinsert specific segments of the mobile classes into the global labour market. The current increase in research on processes of differential inclusion of migrants in contemporary Global North societies (Bosniak 2006, Anderson 2010) testifies for this fusion of mobility, labour and sovereignty. Differential inclusion means that different modalities of entry into a country and different residence statuses – mainly through immigration controls and legal requirements – create different subjects of labour.

3.   Differential inclusion is citizenship is control

The differential inclusion of mobile populations points always to the way labour, mobility and security are all directly connected with the machinations of sovereignty. The toll to govern this tripartite relationship is citizenship. Of course, the process of differential inclusion is not exclusively related to the modern politics of citizenship. On the contrary, differential inclusion accompanies multiple forms of belonging and multiple forms of the production of difference in different historical periods. The different ways of inclusion of the poor in the European medieval city; the temporary enslavement of white labourers in the British colonies; the freed black slave owners in the American South; the thin line between free and unfree as well as between waged and unpaid labour which varies historically, socially and culturally and produces different forms of social stratification; the different racisms that were mobilised to fragment black peoples and include them in different positions in polity – all this are just few examples showing the contingent historical configuration of differential inclusion (see for instance Lowe 1996, Brass and Linden 1997, Lucassen and Lucassen 1997, Steinfeld 2001, Glenn 2004). Thus, when we talk of differential inclusion this is not to highlight its historical novelty or historical uniqueness, rather we want to argue that the specificity of today's differential inclusion functions through citizenship: the term citizenship is used in this paper as a specific form of governance that regulates the relation between *r*ights and *r*epresentation. This double-R axiom is the foundation of modern polity. Rights are considered as crucial for governing migration (who is subject to rights and who is not is a crucial way to create different segments of citizens). But representation has increasingly played a role in defining who is entitled to have rights and what kind of rights one is entitled to have. Cultural identity and collective affects of belonging emerge among mobile or marginalised populations which create a social subject that then can become a subject of rights. Only through representation are rights possible. Citizenship is the form of governing this unstable and dangerous balance of the double-R axiom. Too much representation of a certain group (e.g. Sans Papiers) without rights can create a potential explosive social situation because this particular group is socially active without having any legal, social or political rights. Too restricted a representation of a social group makes exclusion and structural racism apparent (as the 2005 Banlieus uprising in France showed).

Imagine a scale where we have on the one pole full rights and on the other complete illegalisation and invisibility. It is somewhere between these two extreme poles that a cut is placed. This cut is citizenship. Where the cut is placed is a political question (e.g. in the current conditions affected by the crisis and the broader conservative backlash the cut moves towards illegalisation and invisibility). Citizenship is this toll of sovereign governance that regulates the balance between rights and representation and renders certain populations as legitimate bearers of rights while other populations are marked as inexistent. In her work on British citizenship, Tyler (2010) shows persuasively how selective and by design exclusionary the practice of citizenship is (for a description of similar practices in the postcolonial context of Cyprus see the important work of Trimikliniotis 2009). Tyler analyses the 1981 Nationality Act – which is still the cornerstone of current politics of citizenship and immigration in Britain – and shows that it was designed to exclude the peoples of the ex-colonies by protecting only the right to British citizenship by those who had a lineage to someone born on the British island.

> The passage of this Act through parliament was thus a significant event in the history of British race relations, a moment when, through citizenship, racism was implicitly incorporated within the judicial body of the state becoming an active component part of its operational system of 'legal justice'. (Tyler 2010)

We can think of the 1981 Nationality Act as a cut (that is a particular configuration of citizenship) in this scale which has on the one pole full rights and on the other complete illegalisation in conditions of Thatcher's 1980s Britain. Once the cut is positioned, certain groups have different tools for changing the place of the cut, most importantly demonstrations, uprisings, social mobilisations and protests (and sometimes academic social research can contribute to this also). Tyler (2010) describes how the Brixton riots of 1981 and the broader civil unrest of that period can be read as a response to the exclusionary design and function of the 1981 Nationality Act. More generally, we can say that it is through all these struggles that sovereignty is pushed towards the pole of full rights. And there are always long periods of backlash when there is a growing anti-immigrant sentiment and the cut is pushed back towards the pole of illegalisation.

4. The impossible citizenship

There is a paradox in this function of citizenship as the regulatory mechanism of inclusion and exclusion: the more a society moves towards citizenship, the more it creates the conditions for its disappearance as a form of governance. If you include everyone and if you assign rights to everyone, citizenship becomes obsolete. 'Citizenship for all' is an impossible term. Citizenship is 'designed to fail' (Tyler 2010), and it is always 'incomplete' (Gunsteren 1998). Or else, imagine a society which assigns citizenship to everyone. In this fictional society, citizenship is not connected to rights or any other legal status, it is a mere social ritual. Citizenship would be granted automatically to every denizen and to the extent that, as in any society, rituals for social cohesion are important, everyone who wants to demonstrate a strong identification with this society can buy in almost every convenience shop a Home Office Citizenship Medal® for £8.99. You can wear it every day or just forget it in a drawer or lose it. This fictional society would be very different, of course, than the societies we know. But probably the most important difference is that this society would not have borders. To think this the other way round: citizenship is coexistent with borders. Citizenship is coexistent with the exercise of sovereign control, as Bridget Anderson, Nandita Sharma and Cynthia Wright show in their research (e.g. Anderson *et al.* 2009). The more we talk about security, the more we talk about citizenship. This is the predicament of citizenship. It feeds from the power of sovereignty to erect and maintain borders – borders that it cannot ultimately fully control. Citizenship cannot be thought outside of sovereignty and control.

O'Connell Davidson's (2010) work on trafficking exemplifies this function of citizenship from another perspective, namely how in the name of protecting human rights and liberal citizenship sovereign control promotes a tougher take on the freedom of mobility and leads to the introduction of restrictive migration measures as pro-human rights policies. In this sense, we can think of citizenship as a form of governance that performs exclusion not inclusion. Whatever qualifying attribute we add to citizenship – accidental, activist, irregular, imperfect, biological, sexual, reversible, unrecognized (Gunsteren 1998, Bell and Binnie 2004, Sassen 2004, Nyers 2009) – it cannot avoid an optic which looks at peoples' movements from the perspective of control. The vision that citizenship is inherently liberal can be historically revealed as a fiction. There is no global unified citizenship and this because citizenship exists only as one of the tools that are deployed to build up national sovereignty. It is, thus, limited to the territorial space of the nation state and stops where the borders of a country stop – while the rest of a country's activities (such capital movements, trade, circulation of elite populations, war, etc.) can extend beyond its borders. The limits of citizenship are the limits of sovereignty. But liberal citizenship is not only problematic because it excludes by design everyone who is outside its borders, but also because there is a long history of actively 'denationalising' dangerous or unwelcomed citizens and of creating categories of citizenship which can be viewed as accidental (Nyers 2006) or reversible (Tsianos and Pieper 2011). And these limits are even more obvious if we look at citizenship from a global perspective: different national citizenships are bound to the strict hierarchy of the global world system, in which certain countries and their citizenships are far more valued and powerful than others (Balibar and Wallerstein 1991).

Liberal citizenship is a fiction and could not be materialised in the post-WWII period. Elsewhere, we used the term post-liberal conditions to discuss how these ambivalences of citizenship push liberal democracies to their limits (Papadopoulos *et al.* 2008, see also Buckel *et al.* 2010). The example of the denationalisation of one of the most prominent Dutch politicians, the Somali-Dutch Hirsi Ali exemplifies this form of post-liberal politics. Hirsi Ali, a paradigmatic liberal citizen well known for her critical stance towards Islam in Holland, was stripped of her Dutch citizenship (and her seat in the Dutch parliament) when it became public that some narrative elements of her asylum case were fictional. What from a legalist perspective appears as a correct procedure, demonstrates the paradox and ultimately the impossibility of liberal citizenship. Hirsi Ali lost her citizenship although she was fully embodying and practising its core values. In post-liberal conditions, citizenship has to be always protected from expanding too much and including somebody who 'should not' be in. Citizenship in post-liberalism decouples lived embodied existence and the singular subject of rights of a certain nation by making citizenship *principally* reversible (Tsianos and Pieper 2011). Not even her lived and active belonging to the Dutch community could deter the exclusionary logic of citizenship.

Thus, understanding and theorising migration in terms of differential inclusion and citizenship is a necessary and important step in analysing the current configuration of sovereign control. But at the same time, when we perceive migration through the lens of citizenship, we always contribute to the creation of its others, of its outside. This is because citizenship as a non-exclusionary category, citizenship for all, is a contradiction in terms. Citizenship is an important tool for creating possibilities for certain groups to be included, but it can never respond to the question which migration poses to capitalist sovereignty: what about all those who are mobile and cannot be included, that is the *majority* of the mobile populations?

5. Autonomy of migration revisited

In order to be able to answer this question we need to shift our perspective from the order of sovereign control to the primacy of migrants' mobility, that is to read capitalism through migration and to understand sovereignty through mobility, rather than the other way round.

This represents probably the most important insight of the autonomous approach to migration: the attempt to see migration not simply as a response to political and economic necessities, but as a constituent force in the formation of polity and social life (Rodriguez 1996, Karakayali and Tsianos 2005, Papadopoulos *et al.* 2008, Mezzadra 2010). Yann Moulier Boutang (1998) has offered an impressive account of this movement historically. The autonomy of migration approach foregrounds that migration is not primarily a movement that is defined and acts by making claims to institutional power. It rather means that the very movement *itself* becomes a political movement and a social movement. The autonomy of migration thesis highlights the social and subjective aspects of mobility before control. It rejects understanding migration as a mere response to economic and social malaise (e.g. Jessop and Sum 2006). Instead migration is autonomous, meaning that it has the capacity to develop its own logics, its own motivation, its own trajectories that control comes later to respond to, not the other way round (Transit Migration Forschungsgruppe 2006). This does not of course mean that mobility operates independently of control. Very often, it is subjected to it and succumbs to a violent state or to private interventions that attempt to tame it; probably the politics of detention and deportation is the best example of such violence which shows how migrant mobility can be halted and brutally controlled (see Tyler's contribution to this issue and Schuster 2003).

There is no space for romanticisation of nomadism and migration in the autonomy of migration approach. Migration grapples with the harsh, often deadly, realities of control. However, the point is migration is not just responding to them. Rather it creates new realities that allow migrants to exercise their own mobility against or beyond existing control. In this sense, the autonomy of migration thesis is about training our senses to see movement before capital (but not independent from it) and mobility before control (but not as disconnected from it). One of the most common critiques of the autonomy of migration approach (Düvell 2006, Sharma 2008) is that it substitutes all these different migrant subjectivities and the diverse concrete spatialities of movements into a new big narration of migration. The term migration supposedly homogenises and effectively erases the diverse lived experiences of migrants *vis-à-vis* the state. We agree, of course, that migration encompasses a broad spectrum of practices of mobility: humanitarian, forced, war, environmental, cultural, economic, circular, seasonal and internal migration – all these are radically different types of migrant mobility. All these migrations are, however, not neutral definitions of migrational movements. Much of our empirical research – among of course a myriad of similar studies in the field of transnationalism – shows when, where and how a young transmigrant, to use just an example here, can be attributed the category of an unaccompanied refugee minor or could be considered as somebody who circulates between the country of origin and the country of destination or as an economic migrant is less self-evident than it appears in the first instance (O'Connell Davidson 2011). Furthermore, the underlying drive behind these migratory movements is also usually obscure. One can, for example, understand migration as the exercising of agency from below in the diffuse conditions of globalisation (Appadurai 1996); or as a metaphor for a fluid modernity that is driven by an ever increasing penetration of the neoliberal doctrine (Bauman 2007); or even as an approach inspired by complexity theory in which all different forms of mobility – from tourism to transnational terrorism – exist equally next to each other (Urry 2003).

But subsuming all these different types, cases and approaches to migration under the concept of migration does not mean flattening out their differences; rather, it attempts to articulate their commonalities which stem from all these different *struggles for movement* that confront the regimes of mobility control. The supposedly abstract and homogenising category of migration does not attempt to unify all the existing multiplicity of movements under one single logic, but to signify that all these singularities contribute to an affective and generic gesture of freedom that evade the concrete violence and control of moving people. Migration in the autonomy of migration approach refers to a kind of politics that neither entails uniformity nor abstraction; rather, it relies on struggles for movement that escape and subsequently delegitimise and derail sovereign control. So, the first meaning of migration in the autonomy of migration approach is an empirical one: the real struggles, practices, tactics that escape control. This approach to migration is important because it is an answer to the heterogenising practices of state regulation of mobility: sovereignty breaks the connectivity between multiple migratory subjects in order to make them visible and render them governable subjects of mobility. And it does this through operationalising the category of the citizen in order to create different classes of citizens. The heterogenising effects of power should not be confused here with the multiplicity of mobile subjectivities and struggles. These are effaced at the expense of making clearly defined heterogeneous objects of governance. The second meaning of migration in the autonomy of migration approach appears here: migration nurtures the belief in the possibility to be free to move. It is true that this second meaning of migration in the autonomy of migration approach is figurative. It is a figure that embodies virtuality as secure, free and warm as it can get in the harsh conditions of sovereign control which gives strength to people to move when they are on the road. Migration, in this second sense is more related to an affective imaginary, and it exists as potentia and virtuality that becomes actualised and materialised through the diverse movements of people.

6.   'I work only for papers' – the illegalisation of migration

This double dimension of autonomy of migration can be best exemplified in an emblematic type of migration: illegalised border crossing. It is from this perspective that we need to analyse mobility that fails out of citizenship and is excluded from it. When migrants are considered as irregular citizens, they are commonly conceived either as criminals or as being forced to move, not as active creators of the realities they find themselves in or of the realities they create when they move (for a typical example see Jordan and Düvell 2002). This constructs them as irregular or unauthorised subjects. It is not primarily the legal context that creates the category of the illegal migrant, but it is the political and theoretical view that does not allow for forms of agency that is not driven by external necessities; the legal context only follows to consolidate this perspective and standardise them into manageable categories.

However, in conditions where illegal migration has become one of the main, or probably the main, migration route to the societies of the Global North (on this see the detailed work of Karakayali 2008), irregularity can always be perceived in a double perspective: either from the perspective of citizenship – which attempts to disclose how irregularity is produced and maintained through control and through the responding acts of migrants – or from the perspective of mobile migrants that use clandestinity in order to facilitate their everyday movements. The difference here is very small but of importance for understanding the autonomy of migration approach: contesting irregularity is *not* a political act in itself. Irregularity is a practice of governance that *illegalises* migrants in order to control them through the current arrangement of borders, securitisation and public safety. Irregularity makes sense only as *illegalisation* of migrants through the machinic order of sovereignty and the governance of citizenship not as an indented (or even unintended) political act of migrants.

Research on irregularity and citizenship is a necessary and important analytical tool, but focussing solely on this seems to be superseded not only by the practices of migration itself but also by the current processes of migration control. From the perspective of the current digitalised, porocratic configuration of control, mobility is not the enemy. Mobility is considered a necessary, in fact, social and economically indispensable element of current European societies: it only needs to be institutionalised through discourses of citizenship in order to sustain the new flexible configuration of labour that relies on extensified exploitation – as discussed earlier in Section 2. This creates of course a political problem for every approach to migration through citizenship. The more one tries to support rights and representation through citizenship, the more one contributes to the restriction of movement. This is a dilemma that is well known to activist organisations that engage with migration and border radical politics (see Rigby and Schlembach in this issue). The dilemma is that migrants do not usually get involved in political mobilisations about migration *as such*. Migrants tend to become invisible, to disappear, to disidentify themselves (Broeders and Engbersen 2007, and the various examples in Chapter 11 and 12 in Papadopoulos *et al.* 2008). And when migrants mobilise politically, they only do it in a strategic way because they encounter a *particular* and *direct* form of discrimination in a concrete situation.

Many of the transmigrants we talked to in the camps of Pagani and Igoumenitsa (Greece) in the past 3 years used the phrase 'I work only for papers'. Initially we struggled to understand this phrase: On the one hand, we know that a lot of them work in the worst possible conditions, without being documented and only for money. On the other hand, 'papers' – that is the necessary documents which one needs in order to make it to the target destination – is not something which 'you work for', rather we think of 'papers' as something which one is legally entitled to (or not). But these transmigrants challenged two of the widespread assumptions of what a migrant is: firstly, the assumption that migrants are labourers where their subjectivity is defined by their capacity to offer their labour power in 'foreign' labour markets. Secondly, the very distinction between legality and illegality by questioning the dualism between those who are legal subjects of citizenship (if they have 'papers') and those who are illegal subjects outside of citizenship (if they do not have 'papers'). These transmigrants turn both of these assumptions on their heads: Not only is work secondary for their subjectivity, but they see that the *actual* work they do is the *work* for acquiring 'papers' – something which Vasta (2011) describes as 'irregular formality' to articulate the fluidity between irregular and regular statuses from the migrant point of view. This is a double blasphemy against the logic of labour as well as the logic of citizenship. In fact, these transmigrants do not even intend to play the game of political participation in our institutions and practices or engage in acts of citizenship through mobilising their subjectivity as citizens or as workers. Or we could even say that they would engage in any act of political participation if this would help them to get the necessary 'papers'.

7. The politics of migration

The forms of political action that migrants engage cannot be confused with a mobilisation that resembles the action of a collective historical or political subject. The very conditions of current migration defy the possibility of constructing a viable intentional and permanent subjectivity. It also defies the whole subject-form, whether this is related to the liberal governmental subject or the radical subject of social change. To the extent that one cannot build liberal democracies with migration, to the same extent one cannot do Leninist politics with it. It is impossible to adapt migration to our own political targets be it right, left, liberal or radical left. And if this happens, it will only be for a short period of time, until the new migration wave arrives, until new relations of care between mobile migrants are built on the ground, until new transnational mobile communities emerge that undermine any permanence of classical representational politics.

The spectre of migration will never become a new working class. It will always remain a spectre, which comes in the night through the backdoor of your nation on a smuggled vessel, by using false papers, by crossing hundreds of miles of snowed mountains, by changing one's own identity, by destroying the skin of one's own fingertips with acid and a knife to avoid identification, by overstaying a visa, an au pair contract, or the regular tourist period of stay. The spectre of migration will always remain a spectre, one that is much more present though than any of the political ghosts summoned in the history of political thought and political struggle in order to fulfil the desire for securitisation or revolution alike. The spectre of migration will always be with us, among us, more real than anything else: cleaning your home, cleaning your office, cleaning your roads, cleaning your buses, taking care of your kids, fixing your computer, fixing your car, providing sex, providing care, providing babysitting, ironing your shirts, answering your phone calls, doing your gardening, building your house, collecting your strawberries, living in the flat next door. Migrants do not hold the place of a historical or a political subject as such, rather they tend to become imperceptible to history (see chapter 6 and 12 in Papadopoulos *et al.* 2008). But the more they do this, the more they change history by undermining the sovereign pillars of contemporary societies. The more the paranoid enterprise of a securitising sovereignty and the toxic discourse of public safety intensifies, the more it becomes inoperative to sustain capitalist production and capitalist polity.

The approach we are presenting here breaks with the dominant integrationist canon of migration studies which maintains the fundamental assumption that migrants' practices become political only if they become integrated into an existing polity – be it in the country of origin or in the country of destination or in one of the countries through which transmigrants pass. The cohesion of this polity is taken for granted and migrants' political practices *are* political only if they address and operate in it (for an extended critique of integrationism see Glick-Schiller and Çaglar 2008, Hess *et al.* 2009). So, what kind of politics do migrants do if we reject integrationism? What are the politics of migration when they cross borders? What kinds of politics are performed when people become mobile despite the restrictions of migration controls? What kind of politics characterise all these migrant practices which neither attempt to integrate people into an existing polity nor to systematically resist this polity?

Following Rancière (1998), we rather see migrants political practices not as acts of resistance but as attempts to create a new situation that allows those who have no part – to enter and change the conditions of social existence altogether. How else can we understand the silent and mundane transformations that happen when migrants who clandestinely defy the borders that block their future expose the limits of liberal citizenship without ever intending it? These are politics which transform the political without ever addressing it in its own terms and practices. Migrants' politics develop their own codes, their own practices, their own logics which are almost imperceptible from the perspective of existing political action: firstly, because we are not trained to perceive them as 'proper' politics and, secondly, because they create an excess that *cannot* be addressed *in* the existing system of political representation. But these politics are so powerful that they change the very conditions of a certain situation and the very conditions of existence of the participating actors (Tsianos *et al.* 2012).

Migrants' politics are in this sense *non-politics* (that is non-representable in the dominant existing polity). With Asef Bayat we could call them 'social non-movements'. In his work on recent social and political change in the Muslim Middle East, Bayat (2010) describes the invisible everyday activities that prepared all these radical transformations – non-movements because for years they were sustained and nurtured silently through the everyday and seemingly non-political experiences and actions of people. It is these non-movements that when they were confronted with the brutality of the state, they crafted a non-identitarian collectivity of insurrection. In a similar vein, Zibechi (2011) describes the struggles of the urban poor and the indigenous movements in South America as anti-representational politics. Their aim is to appropriate and self-organise social territory in cities or rural areas in the midst of a strict and immovable order of political and social power. These struggles create, in the words of Zibechi, post-capitalist 'societies in movement'.

The mundane gestures of sociality that nurture people when they are in the move or arrive and try to settle in a new place, these 'societies in movement' are imperceptible from the perspective of an existing polity. The more the migrants become imperceptible, the more they become like everyone. Becoming everyone is the death of citizenship. The moment when you buy your Home Office Citizenship Medal® for the price of £8.99 in every corner of the British island will be the moment in which freedom of movement will be a reality. But becoming everyone is not an event to come. It is not salvation awaiting, it is the universal strategy of mobility when it moves through places and continents and even when it becomes clandestine and passes through the biopolitical controls of sovereignty. It is a magical moment of transformation in the objectivity of the present. Becoming everyone is a move based on respect and care of the worlds we are creating when we leave behind marked and secure social positions and selves; becoming everyone is a necessary strategy of everyday survival for migrants on the road and for migrants facing racism when they try to settle in a place.

Crossing Calais can be seen as an 'act of citizenship' (Isin and Nielsen 2008) only to the extent that the very moment of hiding in a lorry is an illegalised activity. From the perspective of migrants, this is an act of immediate *justice* for sustaining their everyday life. Let us put it in a different way, to the extent that migration undermines the securitisation of sovereignty by its very existence, to the same extent it undermines the liberal as well as radical left political projects and announces – together with many other social movements of course – a different form of politics. This sounds perhaps disappointing, but there are reasons to celebrate also. It forces both, capitalism as well as its opponents to change their strategies and to take seriously the principle guiding migrants' mobility: *'freedom of movement* for myself, my children, my friends, my relatives, my fellow travellers and the people who deserve it'. Migration is forcing us to repudiate the implicit avant-gardism of earlier versions of the autonomy of migration approach (Mezzadra 2001, Bojadzijev *et al.* 2004, Papadopoulos and Tsianos 2007). An avant-gardism which by attempting to improve citizenship and change governance tries to realign migrants with the working classes ('Migrants and precarious workers together!') and to resurrect a new social protagonism of migration. Of course, there is a growing proximity between migrant labour and precarious labour since migrant labour becomes increasingly precarised (especially after the 2008 economic crisis) and precarious labour becomes increasingly mobile. However, if there is a potential for transversal politics between the worlds of migration and precarity, this is not in a form of solidarity or in the creation of a new hybrid political subject. Rather, we believe that where migrants and precarious workers meet is in sharing the same urban spaces and that both of them, from their very different positions and with very different aims, participate in the metropolitan uprisings of European cities.

8. 'Making connections' and the gift economy of migration

On 27 August 2009 together with an Amnesty International Representative, we organised a meeting with a group of young transmigrants in one of central cafe snack bars of Mytilini (Greece). Mytilini was at this time a heavily used route for crossing from Turkey into Greece. As a result, the detention camps were overcrowded. Responding to this situation, there was a no borders mobilisation organised on the island in August 2009, which resulted in the closure of this camp (Alberti 2010, Lafazani 2011).[1] Many of the detainees escaped the camp without being registered and their fingerprints being taken in EURODAC, a centralised Euro-wide database of fingerprints of asylum applicants and illegalised immigrants. Many of the migrants we met that afternoon were women in their twenties coming from different cities in the Horn of Africa. They told us that some of them have previously worked as domestic carers and workers in Saudi Arabia and Dubai. The working conditions there were very bad, so they decided to migrate again, this time to Canada because relatives and friends told them that they had better experiences as domestic workers. They used different routes to arrive in Turkey and then eventually crossed the EU border to Greece on a boat. They were intercepted by Frontex patrols, the European border security agency, and had to destroy their boat so that they will be transported as shipwrecked asylum seekers to a camp Greece. They preferred this because they were confident that they would be able to meet other people on the move in the camp and check possibilities to continue their journey, rather than simply be arrested and returned immediately back to Turkey (for an extensive discussion of this context see the ethnographic research of Ibrahim 2010). They were interned in the Pagani camp. The Amnesty International Representative explained that they were released after 38 days with no formal procedure for claiming asylum, but on the condition they leave the country voluntarily and return to their countries of origin (Panagiotidis and Tsianos 2006).

What was the most striking aspect of this encounter was that none of our discussants looked or behaved in a way that would fit the image of the typical illegalised victim circulating in media and mainstream politics. They protested against detention and complained how they were treated by the border police, but one could not see the picture of misery, exploitation and oppression that they had suffered while they were interned in horrendous conditions in the Pagani camp. Rather they looked tired, calm, decided and optimist. When we were parting ways, we asked them how they were going to spend the rest of the day. They replied that they did not know, but the next thing they were going to do was to go to cybercafe to check emails and their Facebook accounts: 'Making connections. Making our route' they said before leaving. (Later we got to know through a contact of a friend that some of them are not as planned in Canada but working in Norway.)

In the same way that 'migrants as agents' do not do the politics we expect them to do, 'migrants as victims' do not behave as victims should. Rather than being the isolated, individualised victim, these young women appeared to negotiate the difficult and dangerous lives they live through the continuous recourse to the idea of some sort of 'social connections' that will help them to move on and continue their journey. In a strange way, you had the feeling that when they were talking they were referring to a 'we', without ever describing it, a 'we' which has the potential to recode or even to interrupt the logic of the border control and detention. Virtual spaces such as chatrooms, facebook, emails as well as the spaces of the camps and of migrant neighbourhoods are the spaces that help one stay mobile, collect information about routes, possibilities for survival and learn tactics of existence (Panagiotidis and Tsianos 2006, Kuster 2011). This is a knowledge and affective reservoir that offers vital resources and energies to migrants on the road or when they arrive in a new place. This 'mobile commons' needs to be continuously updated and extended; and it is the innumerable uncoordinated but cooperative actions of mobile people that contribute to its making.

People on the move create a world of knowledge, of information, of tricks for survival, of mutual care, of social relations, of services exchange, of solidarity and sociability that can be shared, used and where people contribute to sustain and expand it. This is the world that facilates Sapik's movements as described in the interview excerpt at the beginning of this paper. However, it is not just that Sapik uses all these invisible resources to remain mobile, but that by actually using them and by remaining mobile he contributes to expand and circulate this knowledge for coming migrants. This contribution is neither related to the good intentions of those who participate nor to a presumably 'natural' solidarity 'reflex' between migrants. Migration, as we described it in this paper, is by definition a process which relies on a multitude of other persons and things. This extreme dependability can only be managed through reciprocity, and reciprocity between migrants means the multiplication of access to mobility for others. Multiplying access is the gift economy of migration. This is the world of the mobile commons. This is a second world, *World 2*, and beyond the world most of us experience as subjects of rights, as citizens, and as political activists (Papadopoulos 2006). World 2 – the world of transmigrants whether they are on the road, in a new country, or in a new neighbourhood, whether they are settled, clandestine, have refugee status, or are documented workers – is the world that exists as a common world in the making.

9. Organising the mobile commons

The mobile commons is neither private nor public, neither state owned nor part of civil society; rather it exists to the extent that people share it and generate it as they are mobile and when they arrive somewhere. But beyond its use and actualisation, it is equally important to partake in the creation of the mobile commons, in the making of a common non-proprietary and non-enclosed world of mobility (as discussed by Anderson *et al.* 2009). The making of the commons is the continuation of life through 'commoning' (Linebaugh 2008) the immediate sociality and materiality of existence (Papadopoulos 2012). This is a flight into a world where the primary condition of existence is the immersion into the worlds you inhabit and share with other people, animals, plants and the soil as you move. The knowledge and practices of mobility circulate beyond the enclosures of public, private and civil society institutions, and they are cooperatively produced in the commons and through the commons (Bollier 2003, Peuter and Dyer-Witheford 2010).

Autonomy of migration is less a discourse about investigating contemporary migration as a social subject against the workings of sovereignty and capital and more an organising practice for supporting and facilitating freedom of movement. Here, we mean a form of organising which goes beyond the traditional question of mobilising migrants against their oppression and for their rights in existing institutions such as trade unions or civil society organisations (Bishop 2011). We rather understand organisation as the practice of producing alternative ontologies, that is alternative everyday forms of existence and alternative *forms of life* (Winner 1986). Migration – as the empirical reality of struggles that evade the control of mobility and as the virtual imaginary of the freedom of movement – is autonomous, that is it can remain autonomous to the extent that it creates such forms of life. We call the organisational ontology of these other forms of life *mobile commons*: the ability to cultivate, generate and regenerate the contents, practices and affects that facilitate the movements of mobile people.

The mobile commons comprise of:

- the invisible *knowledge of mobility* that circulates between the people on the move (knowledge about border crossings, routes, shelters, hubs, escape routes, resting places; knowledge about policing and surveillance, ways to defy control, strategies against biosurveillance, etc.) but also between transmigrants attempting to settle in a place (knowledge about existing communities, social support, educational resources, access to health, ethnic economies, micro-banks, etc.).
- an *infrastucture of connectivity* which is crucial to distributing these knowledges and for facilitating the circular logistics of support to stay mobile: collecting, updating and evaluating knowledge by using a wide range of platforms and media – from the embodied knowledge travelling from mouth to mouth to social networks sites, geolocation technologies and alternative databases and communication streams.
- a multiplicity of *informal economies*. The mobile commons is not outside of existing relations of production, reproduction and even exploitation. It covers all these economic activities and services that cannot not be easily accessed through the public sector or privately: how to find (and let alone pay) a doctor or a lawyer; how to find short-term work or more permanent working arrangements, send and receive money, communicate with friends, family and fellow travellers, make it through the economies of smuggling, get the necessary papers for your move, pay for your rent and find the right person 'to talk to'.
- diverse forms of transnational *communities of justice*: alliances and coalitions between different groups, local governments, political organisation, NGOs, etc.; access to power; the selective organisation of campaigns in collaboration with local groups and other social movements and civil society organisations; the organisation of camps or support actions.

- the last and probably most crucial dimension of the mobile commons is the *politics of care*, care as the general dimension of caring for the other as well as immediate relations of care and support: mutual cooperation, friendships, favours that you never return, affective support, trust, care for other people's relatives and children, transnational relations of care, the gift economy between mobile people, etc. (see an impressive account on this in Bishop 2011, see also Puig De La Bellacasa 2012).

The mobile commons, that is the real world of moving people, is assembled and materialised in these fields of everyday life. The autonomy of migration approach we are arguing for here can be thought as a contribution to facilitate migration movements though multiplying, spreading, and extending any of these properties of the mobile commons. The term autonomy in 'autonomy of migration' refers to a multiplicity of actors who install relations of justice on the ground in the midst of current capitalist power and sovereign control. In fact, the autonomy of migration approach is only possible if it contributes to creating conditions of thick everyday performative and practical justice so that everyday mobility, clandestine or open, becomes possible. This is a form of thick justice which creates new *forms of life* that sustain migrants' ordinary movements. The sustaining of such forms of life is driven by the immediacy of the quest for justice. And from the perspective of migration justice is the making of daily social relations, connections and conditions that evade the control of mobility.

Justice here resembles an affective index that designates how appropriate are the means used to arrive somewhere, the limits of what one can endure throughout this journey, and, most importantly, it indicates what is just and unjust in conditions that are by design outside of formalised law. The justice of the mobile commons is the moral economy of migration. It is similar to what Thompson (1971) called the moral economy of the poor: the immediate feeling and judgement of the crowd about what is just and what is unjust in relation to the everyday conditions of existence, such as the price of food or the prohibition of using the commons. From the perspective of migration, justice cannot be achieved only through the assignment of rights and citizenship or through attempts to organise migrants in unions and parties (although we want to note here that all of these are in certain conditions indispensable, necessary and crucial for migrants) but through changing ordinary existence in a way that allows people to move when they want or need to and to maintain a liveable life when they reside in a certain place. The mobile commons are migrants' resource and path for surviving the pressures of sovereignty and capitalist exploitation. Autonomy of migration has been for too long concerned with the discourse about citizenship rights, differential inclusion and control and so little with the ontology of migration. A materialist autonomist perspective on migration is about betraying the discourse of security and citizenship in defence of everyday sociability of mobile people and the worlds they are creating. The mobile commons is the ontology of transmigration.

10.   Coda

Since we met Sapik in the summer of 2009 in the Pagani camp, we have been regularly taking to him on the phone or in the net. He became a co-researcher and a research adviser. Sapik has a very active Facebook life and his account is linked to a very well-informed and useful blog about mobility and transit issues relevant to his peoples. Sapik is a true commoner in the mobile commons. Suddenly, while writing this paper, it became impossible to contact him. We were very concerned. For many years now, there is a steep increase in fascist and racist attacks in Greece, and Sapik could be one of their targets since he is a well-known and active figure in his community. Thankfully, he contacted us and said that he was doing well. He had left the island and moved to Athens. He said that he was very scared when he experienced the racisct riots in Athens. But he went to Athens because he wanted to understand 'what is happening in this country'. He was not hopeful that the big mobilisations against the government and the imposed austerity measures in May and June 2011 would be successful. His voice was quiet. We asked him when he would go back to the island where, at least in comparison to Athens, things are much more secure for him. He did not reply, and the silence indicated that we did not understand what he was saying. He was in Athens in order to understand the current situation in Greece. He said that he did not know when he would be able to contact us again. And he no longer has a Facebook account. He had to close his account because he was threatened by neo-fascist users. Then he said goodbye and hung up. Very shortly after this phonecall, we received a text message with a new Facebook name and a smily.

11. Coda 2

In the period between submitting the first version of the paper, waiting for the reviews and reworking this paper for the final submission, Sapik decided to leave his clandestine existence in Greece. Although he was satisfied with his life there and had already built a strong community, close links to political activists and a stable way to make his living, he wanted to leave behind the life without papers: 'I want to live like you', he told us. He recently arrived in a city in Northern Europe and claimed asylum. He was strongly supported through his connections in his transnational community and the euro-wide activist networks and his lawyer is confident that he will be granted asylum. Just few days before finishing this paper, we talked to Sapik and he told us that he was preparing his illegal trip back to Greece. We were very surprised, even horrified, when he said that he was firmly decided to leave the country and effectively drop his asylum case despite that his application was progressing very well. 'There is no love here!', he said, 'see you in Greece'.

Acknowledgements

Many of the ideas presented here were developed in conversations with our fellow traveller Hywel Bishop. We are truly grateful to him. Special thanks go to our editor, Imogen Tyler, for her insightful suggestions and encouragement and to Gabriella Alberti, Nicholas De Genova, Dagmar Diesner and Aida Ibrahim for their generous comments on our work. We would like to thank Nelli Kambouri, Brigitta Kuster, Dimitri Parsanoglou and Nico Trimiklinioti for sharing with us their thoughts about our common fieldwork. Some of the empirical and theoretical research presented here was funded by the European Commission FP7 programme *MIG@NET: Transnational Digital Networks, Migration and Gender*.

Note

1. See also the documentation of the *Welcome to Europe* network: http://w2eu.net/nobordertv/pagani-detention-center-2/pagani-detention-center/ [Accessed 1 December 2011].

References

Alberti, G., 2010. Across the borders of Lesvos: the gendering of migrants' detention in the Aegean. *Feminist review*, 94 (1), 138–147.

Alberti, G., 2011. *Transient working lives: migrant women's everyday politics in London's hospitality industry*, School of Social Sciences, Cardiff University. Unpublished PhD dissertation.

Anderson, B., 2010. Migration, immigration controls and the fashioning of precarious workers. *Work, employment & society*, 24 (2), 300–317.

Anderson, B., Sharma, N. and Wright, C., 2009. Editorial: why no borders? *Refuge*, 26, 5–18.

Appadurai, A., 1996. *Modernity at large: cultural dimensions of globalization*. Minneapolis, MN: University of Minnesota Press.

Balibar, E. and Wallerstein, I.M., 1991. *Race, nation, class: ambiguous identities*. London: Verso.

Bauman, Z., 2007. *Liquid times: living in an age of uncertainty*. Cambridge, MA: Polity Press.

Bayat, A., 2010. *Life as politics. How ordinary people change the Middle East*. Amsterdam: Amsterdam University Press.

Bell, D. and Binnie, J., 2004. Authenticating queer apace: citizenship, urbanism and governance. *Urban studies*, 41 (9), 1807–1820.

Bishop, H., 2011. *The worlds that migrants are making: the politics of care and transnational mobility*, Cardiff University, Cardiff. Unpublished PhD dissertation.

Bojadzijev, M., Karakayali, S. and Tsianos, V., 2004. Le mystère de l'arrivée. Des camps et des spectres. *Multitudes*, 19, 41–52.

Bollier, D., 2003. *Silent theft. The private plunder of our common wealth*. London: Routledge.

Bosniak, L., 2006. *The citizen and the alien: dilemmas of contemporary membership*. Princeton, NJ: Princeton University Press.

Brass, T. and Linden, M.V.D., 1997. *Free and unfree labour: the debate continues*. Bern: Peter Lang & International Institute of Social History.

Broeders, D. and Engbersen, G., 2007. The fight against illegal migration. *Identification policies and immigrants' counterstrategies. American behavioral scientist*, 50 (12), 1592–1609.

Buckel, S., Fischer-Lescano, A. and Oberndorfer, L., 2010. Postneoliberale Rechtsordnung? Suchprozesse in der Krise. *Kritische justiz*, 4, 375–383.

Castles, S. and Miller, M.J., 2003. *The age of migration. International population movements in the modern world*. Basingstoke: Palgrave Macmillan.

De Genova, N. and Peutz, N.M., 2010. *The deportation regime: sovereignty, space, and the freedom of movement*. Durham: Duke University Press.

Dyer-Witheford, N., 1999. *Cyber-Marx: cycles and circuits of struggle in high-technology capitalism*. Urbana, IL: University of Illinois Press.

Düvell, F., 2006. *Europäische und internationale migration. Einführung in historische, soziologische und politische Analysen*. Hamburg: Lit.

Federici, S., 2004. *Caliban and the witch*. New York, NY: Autonomedia.

Glenn, E.N., 2004. *Unequal freedom. How race and gender shaped American citizenship and labor*. Cambridge, MA: Harvard University Press.

Glick-Schiller, N. and Çaglar, A., 2008. *Migrant incorporation and city scale: towards a theory of locality in migration studies*. Malmö: Malmö Institute for Studies of Migration, Diversity and Welfare & Department of International Migration and Ethnic Relations, Malmö University.

Gunsteren, H.V., 1998. *A theory of citizenship: organizing plurality in contemporary democracies*. Boulder, CO: Westview Press.

Hess, S., Binder, J. and Moser, J., 2009. *No integration. Kulturwissenschaftliche Beiträge zur Integrationsdebatte in Europa*. Bielefeld: Transcript.

Ibrahim, A., 2010. Eritreische Frauen auf der Flucht. *In*: ConnectionE.V. Pro Asyl, ed. *Eritrea: Desertion, Flucht & Asyl*. Frankfurt: Pro Asyl, 36–48.

Ignatieff, M., 1978. *A just measure of pain: the penitentiary in the industrial revolution, 1750-1850*. New York, NY: Columbia University Press.

Isin, E. and Nielsen, G.M., eds, 2008. *Acts of citizenship*. London: Zed Books.

Jessop, B. and Sum, N.-L., 2006. *Beyond the regulation approach: putting capitalist economies in their place*. Cheltenham: Edward Elgar.

Jordan, B. and Düvell, F., 2002. *Irregular migration: the dilemmas of transnational mobility*. Cheltenham: Edward Elgar.

Karakayali, S., 2008. *Gespenster der Migration: zur Genealogie illegaler Einwanderung in der Bundesrepublik Deutschland*. Bielefeld: Transcript.

Karakayali, S. and Tsianos, V., 2005. Mapping the order of new migration. Undokumentierte Arbeit und die Autonomie der Migration. *Peripherie*, 97/98, 35–64.

Kuster, B., 2011. Camps und Heterotopien der Gegenwart. À props de Rien ne vaut que la vie, mais la vie même ne vaut rien. *In*: M.-H. Gutberlet and S. Helff, eds. *Die Kunst der Migration. Aktuelle Positionen zum europäisch-afrikanischen Diskurs*. Bielefeld: Transcript, 147–157.

Lafazani, O., 2011. The border from the border: Critical perspectives on EU borders migration policies and beyond, In: Paper presented at the conference Border regions in transition XI, 6–9 September 2011, Geneva, Switzerland.

Linebaugh, P., 2008. *The Magna Carta manifesto: liberties and commons for all.* Berkeley, CA: University of California Press.

Lowe, L., 1996. *Immigrant acts: on Asian American cultural politics.* Durham: Duke University Press.

Lucassen, J. and Lucassen, L., 1997. *Migration, migration history, history: old paradigms and new perspectives.* Bern: International Institute of Social History.

Mezzadra, S., 2001. *Diritto di fuga. Migrazioni, cittadinanza, globalizzazione.* Verona: Ombre Corte.

Mezzadra, S., 2010. The gaze of autonomy. Capitalism, migration and social struggles. *In:* V. Squire, ed. *The contested politics of mobility. Borderzones and irregularity.* New York, NY: Routledge, 121–142.

Moulier Boutang, Y., 1998. *De l'esclavage au salariat. Economie historique du salariat bridé.* Paris: Presses Universitaires de France.

Moulier Boutang, Y., 2012. *Cognitive capitalism.* Cambridge, MA: Polity Press.

Negri, A., 2005. *The politics of subversion: a manifesto for the twenty-first century.* Cambridge, MA: Cambridge Polity.

Nichols, T. ed., 1980. *Capital and labour: studies in the capitalist labour process.* London: Fontana.

Nyers, P., 2006. The accidental citizen: acts of sovereignty and (un)making citizenship. *Economy and society*, 35 (1), 22–41.

Nyers, P. ed., 2009. *Securitizations of citizenship.* London: Routledge.

O'Connell Davidson, J., 2010. New slavery, old binaries: human trafficking and the borders of 'freedom'. *Global networks*, 10 (2), 244–261.

O'Connell Davidson, J., 2011. Moving children? child trafficking, child migration, and child rights. *Critical social policy*, 31 (3), 454–477.

Panagiotidis, E. and Tsianos, V., 2006. Denaturalising the camp. *In:* Transit Migration Forschungsgruppe, ed. *Turbulente ränder. neue perspektiven auf migration an den grenzen Europas.* Bielefeld: Transcript, 59–88.

Papadopoulos, D., 2006. World 2. On the significance and impossibility of articulation. *Culture, theory and critique*, 47, 165–179.

Papadopoulos, D., 2012. Worlding justice/commoning matter. *Occasion: interdisciplinary studies in the humanities*, 3 (15 March) [online]. Available from: http://occasion.stanford.edu/node/79.

Papadopoulos, D. and Tsianos, V., 2007. The autonomy of migration: The animals of undocumented mobility. *In:* A. Hickey-Moody and P. Malins, eds. *Deleuzian encounters. Studies in contemporary social issues.* Basingstoke: Palgrave Macmillan, 223–235.

Papadopoulos, D., Stephenson, N. and Tsianos, V., 2008. *Escape routes. control and subversion in the 21st century.* London: Pluto Press.

Peuter, G.D. and Dyer-Witheford, N., 2010. Commons and cooperatives. *Affinities: a journal of radical theory, culture, and action*, 4, 30–56.

Puig De La Bellacasa, M., 2012. 'Nothing comes without its world': thinking with care. *The Sociological Review*, 60(2), 197–216.

Rancière, J., 1998. *Disagreement: politics and philosophy.* Minneapolis, MN: University of Minnesota Press.

Rodriguez, N., 1996. The battle for the border: notes on autonomous migration, transnational communities, and the state. *Social justice*, 23 (3), 21–37.

Sassen, S., 2004. The repositioning of citizenship: emergent subjects and spaces for politics. *In:* P.A. Passavant and J. Dean, eds. *Empire's new clothes: reading Hardt and Negri.* New York, NY: Routledge, 175–198.

Schuster, L., 2003. *The use and abuse of political asylum in Britain and Germany.* London: Frank Cass.

Sharma, N., 2008. Escape artists: migrants and the politics of naming. *Subjectivity*, 29, 467–476.

Steinfeld, R.J., 2001. *Coercion, contract, and free labor in the nineteenth century.* Cambridge, MA: Cambridge University Press.

Thompson, E.P., 1971. The moral economy of the English crowd in the eighteenth century. *Past & Present*, 50, 76–136.

Transit Migration Forschungsgruppe, ed., 2006. *Turbulente ränder. neue perspektiven auf migration an den grenzen europas*. Bielefeld: Transcript.

Trimikliniotis, N., 2009. Nationality and citizenship in Cyprus since 1945: Communal citizenship, gendered nationality and the adventures of a post-colonial subject in a divided country. *In*: R. BauböCk, B. Perchinig and W. Sievers, eds. *Citizenship policies in the new Europe*. 2nd ed. Amsterdam: Amsterdam University Press, 389–418.

Tsianos, V. and Pieper, M., 2011. Postliberale assemblagen. rassismus in zeiten der gleichheit. *In*: S. Friedrich, ed. *Rassismus in der leistungsgesellschaft. analysen und kritische perspektiven zu den rassistischen normalisierungsprozessen der 'sarrazindebatte'*. Münster: Edition Assemblage, 114–133.

Tsianos, V., Papadopoulos, D. and Stephenson, N., 2012. This is class war from above and they are winning it. What is to be done? *Rethinking marxism: a journal of economics, culture & society*, 24 (3), 448–457.

Tyler, I., 2010. Designed to fail: a biopolitics of British citizenship. *Citizenship studies*, 14 (1), 61–74.

Urry, J., 2003. *Global complexity*. Cambridge, MA: Polity.

Vasta, E., 2011. Immigrants and the paper market: borrowing, renting and buying identities. *Ethnic and racial studies*, 34 (2), 187–206.

Von Oswald, A., 2002. Volkswagen, Wolfsburg und die italienischen 'Gastarbeiter'. *Archiv für sozialgeschichte*, 42, 55–79.

Winner, L., 1986. *The whale and the reactor: a search for limits in an age of high technology*. Chicago, IL: University of Chicago Press.

Zibechi, R., 2011. *Territorien des widerstands. eine politische kartografie der urbanen peripherien lateinamerikas*. Hamburg: Assoziation A.

Immigrant protests in Toronto: diaspora and Sri Lanka's civil war

Dr Ishan Ashutosh

Department of Social Sciences, Northumbria University, Newcastle upon Tyne, NE1 8ST, UK

As Sri Lanka's civil war escalated in the spring of 2009, protests led by the Sri Lankan Tamil diaspora in Toronto appealed for an immediate ceasefire agreement between the Sri Lankan government and the Liberation Tigers of Tamil Eelam (LTTE). Held simultaneously in Chennai, London, and Oslo, the protests called for an end to the hostilities in Sri Lanka as well as recognition of the legitimacy of Tamil Eelam, a separate nation state for Tamils in Sri Lanka. Based on interviews and media coverage in Toronto, this article investigates how these 'immigrant protests' constituted 'transnational acts of citizenship'. I examine the Toronto protests through three acts in the protest that challenged the exclusions of national citizenship by moving from Toronto's streets, statist discourses of Canadian citizenship, and the violence of war in Sri Lanka. Although these transnational acts of citizenship were rendered inaudible in public culture, the article concludes by exploring the possibilities of citizenship and belonging in the Sri Lankan Tamil diaspora following the defeat of the LTTE.

Over a quarter of Sri Lanka's Tamil population now live dispersed across countries of refuge in Western Europe, India, Malaysia, Singapore, Australia, and Canada (International Crisis Group 2010). With a population of 1 million people, the Sri Lankan Tamil diaspora has been characterized as an 'asylum diaspora' produced out of the violence of displacement in Sri Lanka's quarter-century civil war and marginalization in countries of settlement (McDowell 1996). Toronto has been inextricably tied to the conflict in Sri Lanka, particularly after the 1983 anti-Tamil pogroms, an event that became known as 'Black July' in which hundreds of Tamils were killed and with approximately 200,000–300,000 Tamils fleeing Sri Lanka (Samarasinghe 2009). In the months that followed, the Canadian government introduced special immigration provisions that allowed Sri Lankans to apply for asylum as well as priority processing for those who had family residing in Canada (Aruliah 1994). Today, Toronto acts as a central node of the Tamil diaspora, and has the status as the most populous city of Sri Lankan Tamils outside Sri Lanka.[1] In Toronto's eastern suburbs where Tamil businesses and residences are concentrated, memorials to the war in the form of photographs, flags, and murals protest the exclusions of the Sri Lankan state and the exile of diaspora. As violence escalated in Sri Lanka in 2008 and 2009, Toronto's downtown became the exemplary site of immigrant protests that demanded recognition of the oppression of Tamils and the legitimacy of Tamil Eelam, a separate state and homeland for Sri Lankan Tamils. The protests in Toronto lead to crucial questions that ask how transnational practices for national recognition enact citizenship and in the process produce citizens, outsiders, and aliens (Bosniak 2006, Marciniak 2006).

Drawing on interviews, protest literature, and media coverage of the protests in the Canadian press, I extend Isin's (2008) theorization of 'acts of citizenship' to suggest that the Toronto protests represent transnational acts of citizenship. These acts were positioned against the limits of national membership in Sri Lanka and searched for new forms of belonging in the Tamil diaspora. As the articles in this special issue of *Citizenship Studies* collectively argue, immigrant protests are the grounded and concrete acts *for* citizenship, for inclusion, and to be heard by another (Isin 2008, p. 24). Immigrant protests are also acts *against* the limits of political membership and (un-)belonging that underwrite citizenship (Derrida and Beardsworth 1994, see Tyler and Marciniak in this issue). I argue that the demands for recognition in the Toronto protests refused the categorization of citizens and outsiders along binaristic national lines, and as I will show in the following sections, placed citizenship in a transnational context.

Examining the protests as transnational acts of citizenship brings attention to both the limits of national citizenship and the 'long-distance nationalism' of diaspora that aims to transform the isomorphism between nation, state, territory, and citizenship (Anderson 1992, Fuglerud 1999, Schiller and Fouron 2001). Recent conceptions of citizenship in relation to immigration have focused on the extension of political participation to immigrants living outside national territory (Basch *et al.* 1994, Stasiulis 2002, 2008, Isin and Turner 2007), including institutional responses by states to integrate migrant practices that constitute 'transnational citizenship' (Bauböck 1994, 2003). On the other hand, the counter-hegemonic activities of immigrants outlined as 'transnationalism from below' (Mahler 1998, Smith and Guarnizo 1998) have challenged the monopoly of the nation state in determining the contours of citizenship and identity (Isin and Wood 1999). Protestors made claims for Eelam through their status as immigrants, refugees, and an oppressed minority group that has excluded them from Sri Lanka and countries of settlement. Their acts focused on the limits of national citizenship while also creating new forms of diasporic participation that attempted to re-imagine belonging beyond the territories of the nation state. I contend that the lasting activism of the Toronto protests does not lie in their interventions in Sri Lanka's civil war, but in the challenges they pose to the politics of citizenship, when subjects are caught between their ejection from the national community and new practices of belonging in the diaspora.

In the sections below, I discuss three transnational geographies that framed the protests. First, I examine the production of urban spaces of citizenship through the protests, before turning to the scale of the state and its response to the protests. Second, I investigate how the Canadian response to the demands for Eelam reinforced divisions between citizens and outsiders through the language of obligations of citizenship. Finally, I link my analysis of the Tamil protests in Toronto to a wider discussion of citizenship in the global Tamil diaspora and the war in Sri Lanka. I explore the figurative role of Eelam in the Sri Lankan Tamil diaspora and the ways in which Eelam continues to be mobilized in attempts to imagine forms of belonging, claims for recognition, representation, and justice beyond rights guaranteed and limited by nation states. Collectively, these three moments of protest highlight the possibilities, challenges, and the limits of transnational acts of citizenship.

Spaces of citizenship: protesting Sri Lanka's civil war

The tenuous 2002 ceasefire agreement between the government of Sri Lanka and the Liberation Tigers of Tamil Eelam (LTTE) had broken down by 2005. Military operations against the LTTE resumed in the months following the November 2005 presidential victory of Mahinda Rajapaksa who vowed to defeat the organization. After the bombing of an army bus in Colombo, the Sri Lankan government officially withdrew from the ceasefire agreement in January 2008 (Wickramasinghe 2009). Norwegian peace negotiator Jon Hanssen-Bauer lamented: 'a chance has been lost by and for the Sri Lankan people. This is a very negative development for Sri Lanka and civilians are the ones who will suffer' (*Spiegel* 2008). As fighting intensified, the war in Sri Lanka brought protestors onto downtown Toronto's streets as part of larger transnational political practices in the Sri Lankan Tamil diaspora. Protests across the Sri Lankan Tamil diaspora spoke to oppressions against Tamils in Sri Lanka and their exile in countries of refuge. Analyses of immigrant protests as acts of citizenship, therefore, must examine participation and exclusion in both sending and receiving societies, as well as within the wider context of diasporic activity and belonging.

Sri Lanka's military offensive against LTTE strongholds continued in the north of the country in 2009. In January, the army captured the LTTE headquarters of Kilinochchi, confirming for many Tamils in Toronto what they had long suspected – that the government had always sought a military solution to the conflict. The headlines in the conservative Canadian newspaper, *National Post*, insisted that the Sri Lankan civil war was now headed towards a 'decisive showdown' (Bell 2008). Protests for civilians trapped between the remaining LTTE base in Mullaitivu and the Sri Lankan army took the form of human chains in downtown Toronto (*CTV Toronto* 2009a). Earlier, in October 2008, the Tamil Nadu political party Dravida Munnetra Kazhagam (DMK) organized a human chain in Chennai, India (Murari 2008). By mid-March 2009, human chains encompassed Toronto's downtown core with at least 45,000 people taking part in the protest (*CTV Toronto* 2009b), highlighting the power of Sri Lankan Tamils in Toronto through coordinated protests across urban locales in countries of exile. A few weeks later over 3000 people protested around Parliament in London's Westminster, closing the bridge and the tube station (*Press Trust of India* 2009). Meanwhile, in Sydney, 1000 protestors demanded that Australian Prime Minister Kevin Rudd appeal to the government of Sri Lanka for an immediate ceasefire (*Sydney Morning Herald* 2009). In conjunction with the protest in Sydney, 15,000 protestors in Toronto and 5 hunger strikers in Ottawa hoped that their protests would lead to the Canadian government demanding that the Sri Lankan government halt their military campaign.

On the weekend of 9–10 May 2009, a series of protests were held throughout Toronto. The protests followed news that the number of civilians killed in Sri Lanka had climbed to at least 9000, with 16,700 wounded with the shelling of a 14-square-kilometre 'no-fire zone' (Tran 2009). Shortly thereafter, UN spokesperson Gordon Weiss stated that in Sri Lanka the fear of a 'bloodbath has become reality' (Nessman 2009). The march on 9 May 2009 made its way through downtown Toronto and ended in front of Toronto's City Hall, the streets otherwise deserted in a severe thunderstorm. Along the way, a group of young boys were uncharacteristically jubilant in the otherwise sombre procession and led the chant, 'stop the genocide'. Other protestors, alongside their families, tightly gripped umbrellas with the map of Tamil Eelam emblazoned on red and yellow cloth. Together, they called for a ceasefire in the Sri Lankan civil war. Protestors also sought to reverse what Cheran (1999, p. 4) described as the international indifference to the war that has killed over 70,000 people (*BBC News* 2010), a 'forgotten' war, a war that was 'too far – both metaphorically and literally – from strategic concerns of the West'.

As the protesters circled south toward Toronto City Hall, the clouds dissipated. Suddenly, the protests were joined by bemused passers-by, one group of tourists frantically snapping photographs, mistaking the protest for an Independence Day Parade.

A Steelworkers Union group joined in the protest, their banner obscured by a large poster of a fanged, devil-horned Mahinda Rajapaksa standing over destroyed villages and refugee camps with blood dripping from his mouth. Teenagers weaved in and out of the march, distributing pamphlets to the few onlookers. One protestor handed out an information pamphlet prepared by the Tamil Canadian Graduate Students Association that posed the question 'aren't we human enough to be cared?' The pamphlet, also distributed at protests in Washington, D.C. and Ottawa, described Tamils as Sri Lanka's 'forgotten people' and presented a history of Tamil exclusions from the post-colonial state (Anon, *Pray for Us*). Another pamphlet detailed a new mission proposed by the Canadian Tamil Congress (CTC), 'No to Sri Lanka', that demanded a 'boycott [of] Sri Lanka as a form of consumer activism'. The pamphlet targeted Sri Lanka's export and tourist industry, as well as foreign investment (*No to Sri Lanka* 2009). The global trade of Sri Lankan goods, the pamphlet argued, 'funds expenditure on its army, navy, and air force' which constitutes 20% of 'the country's gross domestic products compared with about 3% in India and Pakistan' (*No to Sri Lanka* 2009). The *No to Sri Lanka* campaign's website lists retailers that import clothing from Sri Lanka, and thereby rescales citizenship to everyday consumptive practices that link neoliberal commodity flows with the Sri Lankan state's militarization. These calls for consumer citizenship (Grewal 2005) connect the transnational circulation of commodities with the violence of the Sri Lankan state. The protests, moreover, attempted to counter the military advertising that, in the name of national security, has become a steady feature of Sri Lankan popular culture (De Mel 2007).

Near City Hall, the protest became increasingly charged, with the chants of 'stop the genocide' becoming 'LTTE freedom fighters!' The protestors further expressed support for the LTTE and its leader Velupillai Prabhakaran with affirmations of 'Prabhakaran! Our Leader!' These slogans reflect an ongoing investment in politics in Sri Lanka as well as connections within the Tamil diaspora. As Fuglerud (1999, p. 155) has provocatively proposed, the LTTE are a marker of the shared spaces between the diaspora and Sri Lanka, for the LTTE are both 'there *and* here, at both ends of the road – whether this road leads to London, Toronto or Oslo'.

A protestor on behalf of the International Communist League handed me a pamphlet that departed from the seemingly unified chorus praising the LTTE. Unlike others who stressed the rapidly deteriorating conditions in Sri Lanka and the urgency of Eelam as the only source for recognition and belonging for Sri Lankan Tamils, for this protestor Eelam was primarily a source of critique reserved for the Canadian and American governments. He argued that the Canadian government could not on the one hand 'ban the LTTE' by declaring them a terrorist organization in 2006, but on the other, remain silent through claims of impartiality and nonintervention in domestic affairs during the Sri Lankan government's latest military offensive. Such opinions were bolstered in his handout, the Trotskyist League of Canada's newspaper, *The Spartacist Canada*, which featured the story titled 'Army Bloodbath in Sri Lanka. Defend the Tamil People!' Although the Trotskyist League upheld the 'self determination for the Tamil people', they were clear to 'give no political support to the LTTE – bourgeois nationalists who, carrying out the logic of nationalism, have staged their own inter-ethnic attacks' (*Workers Vanguard* 2009). Their solidarity with Sri Lankan Tamils was instead a function of the League's internationalism that places Eelam in 'the fight for Marxist workers parties throughout the region that can unite the working people and oppressed in the struggle for workers' revolutions in [Sri] Lanka and throughout South Asia' (*Workers Vanguard* 2009). The Trotskyist League's presence in the protests illustrates the tensions that pervade the transnational politics of the protests. The gathering of different identities – refugees, immigrants, tourists, nationalists, and Marxists – expose the internal struggles taking place over the meaning of Eelam, Tamil nationalism, and political membership across sites. The internationalism of the Trotskyist League and their rejection of nationalism conflict with the particular demands of many protesters that were making a case for Eelam, for the LTTE as an expression of diasporic belonging and as a counter to the persecution of Tamils by the Sri Lankan state.

In these protests across the Tamil diaspora, citizenship was produced through the occupation and visibility in city spaces in which different notions of citizenship, justice, and political participation were contested. Unlike the Medieval European city where the concept of citizenship first emerged (Turner 2005), the protests used the city to illuminate exclusions in Sri Lanka as well as to produce new diasporic forms of inclusion. The protests were concrete manifestations of what Holston and Appadurai (1996, p. 188) detailed as urban citizenship that challenged the monopoly of national categories of belonging:

> with their concentrations of the nonlocal, the strange, the mixed, and the public, cities engage most palpably the tumult of citizenship. Their crowds catalyze processes which decisively expand and erode the rules, meanings, and practices of citizenship. Their streets conflate identities of territory and contract with those of race, religion, class, culture, and gender to produce the reactive ingredients of both progressive and reactionary political movements.

More recently, Sassen (2006, p. 314) argued that citizenship practices in the city produce multi-sited 'nexuses where the formation of new claims materializes and assumes concrete forms'. Protests in and across cities are the spaces where transnational acts of citizenship are staged, connecting Toronto with other urban sites: Jaffna, Colombo, Chennai, Sydney, and London. Their demands for recognition that extended across national borders, however, also produced distinctions between citizens and outsiders. Media coverage of the protests fixed the demands of the protests as beyond the claims of national citizenship and relegated protestors to outsiders who tested the obligations of (Canadian) citizens.

Fortress Toronto: the protests and the production of Canadian citizens

By the time of the protests, representations of Eelam had become largely inseparable from the global reach of the LTTE, with the diaspora acting as the organization's economic and symbolic 'backbone' (Fair 2005, p. 139). In April 2006, Canada declared the LTTE a terrorist organization (*CBC News* 2006), a move in step with discourses of national security following the 11 September 2011 attacks in the USA. Canadian Prime Minister Stephen Harper's decision came one month after the release of the *Human Rights Watch* (2006) report, *Funding the Final War: LTTE intimidation and extortion in the Tamil diaspora*. According to the report, the Sri Lankan Tamil diaspora's financial support for the LTTE, which in the late 1990s ranged between Cdn $1,000,000 and $12,000,000 per year, was achieved through coercion (*Human Rights Watch* 2006, p. 19). The Human Rights Watch report chronicled incidents of vandalism to temples and residences as well as violence committed against Sri Lankan Tamils in Canada and their family in Sri Lanka and elsewhere in the diaspora over their refusal to send donations to the LTTE. During my research in Toronto, Sri Lankan Tamils rarely countered the coercion of the LTTE, though many viewed the report's findings as a distraction to the violence and oppression of Tamils in Sri Lanka, with Human Rights Watch effectively absolving the militarism of the Sri Lankan state in the process. That the LTTE were championed as 'freedom fighters' in the Toronto protests not only complicated facile distinctions between choice and force, but also pointed to the larger dismissal of Eelam by the Canadian government.

With the failure of the ceasefire agreement and the return to war, demands for Eelam in Canada went unheeded over fears of support for the LTTE. Tamil organizations had also sought to place the fight for Eelam as equivalent to the recognition of difference that constitutes Canadian citizenship rights. The legitimacy of Eelam was framed in relation to national rights bestowed on all Canadian citizens. For instance, one year following the government's declaration of the LTTE as a terrorist organization, the CTC argued that Tamil self-determination resonates with the fundamental values of Canadian citizenship. In an Ottawa press conference, CTC spokesman Satheejan Gugananthan (*Canadian Tamil Congress* 2007) responded to the decision taken by the Harper administration:

> We are asking the Government of Canada to show courage and foresight by supporting a Tamil bid for self-determination in what is currently Sri Lanka's north and east... Please send the message that the principles in our Charter of Rights and Freedoms – like equality, like freedom of expression – ought to apply to the entire human race. This includes the Tamils of Sri Lanka.

The Charter of Rights and Freedoms, enshrined in Canada's 1982 Constitution Act, secures the rights of individuals and of minority groups in Canada. By invoking the protections of state citizenship, the CTC tied the exclusions of the Sri Lankan state with the promise of equality and recognition of difference that lies at the center of Canadian citizenship and multiculturalism. With the breakdown of the ceasefire agreement, calls for recognition of Eelam and Tamil self-determination were expressed through Canadian multiculturalism, such as the 2007 hoisting of Eelam flags by students during York University's Multicultural Week. The range of acts, from press releases to the raising of flags, demanded the protections of citizenship while also challenging their exclusions from national membership in Sri Lanka and Canada.

During the 2009 protests in Toronto, the hoisting of Eelam flags was often represented by popular media and the state as acts that demarcated Canadians from (noncitizen) protesters. Declared as the national flag of Eelam by the LTTE in 1990, the flag is composed of two crossed AK-47s centered on a tiger surrounded by a ring of bullets. The tiger represents Dravidian civilization with specific reference to the pre-colonial Chola Dynasty, the empire based in present-day Tamil Nadu that in the eleventh century stretched to Southeast Asia and Sri Lanka. Flown from the diaspora, the Eelam flag conjures the global dispersal of Tamils to sites well beyond South and Southeast Asia. Though Eelam flags have been a consistent feature memorializing the war and Tamil exile in the Toronto's suburbs in which the majority of the city's immigrants live, their presence in the protests in front of City Hall and the Ontario Legislative Building had alas caught the eye of politicians. They were quick to raise the spectre of terrorism, suggesting that the very act of protesting constitutes a threat to national security. Ontario Premier Dalton McGuinty objected to the waving of Eelam flags by stating that it has a detrimental impact on the cause for Eelam and represents the 'wrong way' of protesting (Howlett and Bonoguore 2009). Former Member of Parliament Minister for International Cooperation Bev Oda commented that the Eelam flags 'say[s] to Canadians that... the terrorist organization [the LTTE] is part of the demonstrations that happened' (*CP 24* 2009a, Wingrove *et al.* 2009). These statements not only worked to delegitimize the calls for Eelam, but did so by evacuating the demands of the protests under the threats of terrorism.

The protests in front of Toronto City Hall and the Canadian Parliament Building in Ottawa discussed in the previous section culminated in a demonstration on Toronto's Gardiner Expressway, the primary east-west highway along Toronto's waterfront that connects downtown with the city's suburbs. On Sunday, 10 May over 2000 protestors occupied and closed Toronto's Gardiner Expressway for 6 hours (Van Rijn 2009). Toronto

Police Chief Bill Blair described the 'occupation of the Gardiner' as creating 'a very dangerous situation and they [the protesters] have used children to do it'. Moreover, Blair stated that the protestors on the Gardiner Expressway have 'escalated the situation well beyond merely a democratic process into an unlawful assembly' (Lewington and Makin 2009). Ontario Police Patrol Commissioner Julian Fantino echoed Blair's statement in stating that 'one sector of society' was holding the city 'hostage' (Lewington and Makin 2009). By 'storming' the Gardiner Expressway (*CP 24* 2009b), the protesters were depicted as terrorists, trespassing their rights to the city and imprisoning Canadian citizens.

Two days after protestors closed the Gardiner Expressway, *Globe and Mail* columnist Christie Blatchford (2009) supported the sentiments of the Ontario and Toronto Police in asking 'whose rights are really being trampled?'

> The truth is, no one really knows how many Tamils are in Toronto, or Canada ...

> This is what Torontonians are wrestling with, not rage about traffic snarls, not racism, not a failure to understand the complexities of the civil war in Sri Lanka or its attendant loss of life. We live in a country where we don't even know how many of our fellows are Tamils from Sri Lanka, but are simultaneously asked to accept on faith that they are properly and legally here and to extend to them every privilege conferred by Canadian citizenship – and to suck it up without complaint.

While Blatchford's criticism represents an extreme reaction to the protests, her views, much like the responses by politicians, stress the language of tolerance and civility that are central to discourses of Canadian multiculturalism. As such, the protestors are rhetorically 'cast out' (Razack 2007) from the Canadian political body. The protests were framed as acts against Canadian citizenship and as a failure of the protestors to meet the obligations of membership in the Canadian national community. The transnational acts of protest were extinguished in the consolidation of a national community that barred Sri Lankan Tamils and their sympathizers. Protestors were treated as outsiders that pollute the national body (Malkki 1995), resulting in demarcations between citizens and aliens, Canadian selves and Tamil others. The reactions to the protests run parallel to Ehrkamp's (2006, p. 1677) analysis of assimilation discourses in Germany that 'other' and exclude Turkish migrants while establishing norms for 'native residents'. Despite attempts by Tamil organizations and protesters to locate the politics of Eelam as congruent with the ideals of Canadian citizenship, their acts were anesthetized through discourses of multicultural tolerance. Images and myths of Canada's and Toronto's harmonious diversity became the mechanism through which the Tamil protests were scripted as a challenge to Canadian citizens (Basu 2009) and reinforced dominant discourses of Canadian acceptance and the affirmation of liberal democratic values.

Shortly after the Gardiner Expressway protests, *Toronto Star* columnist Rosie DiManno argued that the protests succeeded in their claims for Eelam:

> The Tamil tactics have been a whopping success as Instructive Geopolitics 101. The constancy of their demonstrations has received front-page coverage for weeks. They have forced us to pay attention to crimes against humanity occurring far away. (DiManno 2009)

Despite the success of the protestors at raising awareness, in many respects the war remained 'far away'. The state used the visibility of the protests to contrast membership and belonging in Canada from transnational and diasporic politics that merge experiences and exclusions across sites.

Alive in diaspora: Eelam in the wake of the LTTE

Moving beyond the reception of the protests in Canada leads to the fundamental paradoxes of national citizenship exposed by Sri Lanka's civil war. The protests posed questions of how human rights, participation, and identity might be reconceptualized and represented through transnational acts of citizenship. Protesting Sri Lanka's civil war in Toronto laid bare the hidden continuities between colonial and post-colonial domination and subject making that act as the basis for national membership and rights (Scott 1999). In *Abiding by Sri Lanka: on peace, place, and postcoloniality*, Ismail (2005) deconstructs Sinhala and Tamil nationalist histories in order to reveal that they both depict their ethnic group identity as undifferentiated wholes antagonistic to each other. Sinhala and Tamil nationalist narratives thereby elide Sri Lanka's religious, ethnic, regional, and linguistic diversity, revealing that democracy 'turns out to be hostile to peace' (Ismail 2005, p. 119). Peace, in the context of the Sri Lankan civil war, is another form of domination predicated on the rule of the majority over the minority (Ismail 2005), in which the ethnic other is a reminder of the fiction of ethnicity and national illusions of ethnic singularity (Derrida 2005, Korf 2006). The protests, then, were acts of citizenship that illuminate the limits of political membership fundamental to representative democracy. Sri Lanka's civil war is not an event simply occurring elsewhere, but its violence is a basic reflection of the constitution of membership and belonging. The war signals the turn from majoritarian to 'predatory identities' in which 'the existence of even the smallest minority within national boundaries is seen as an intolerable deficit in the purity of the national whole' (Appadurai 2006, p. 53).

Ratinam, a refugee who arrived in Toronto from Sri Lanka in the early 1990s, attended a number of protests in April and May 2009 when not covering for a co-worker also busy in the protest at the new downtown condominium where they worked as security guards. Born in Jaffna in 1936, Ratinam encountered the production of national majorities and minorities in colonial and post-colonial Sri Lanka that included the disenfranchisement of Hill Country or Indian Tamils concentrated in Sri Lanka's tea plantations following Sri Lanka's independence in 1948 (Daniel 1996), the 1956 Sinhala Only Act, and two decades later, the militarization of the Sri Lankan state and the transformation of the non-violent struggle for Eelam to the guerrilla tactics of the LTTE. Between the Sri Lankan government and the LTTE, Ratinam explains, 'there is no difference. No justice. But we have no alternative. We have to support [the LTTE]'. His sentiments raise questions regarding how the Toronto protest, the wider struggle for Eelam, and the conditions of the Tamil diaspora reflect the inequalities of post-coloniality that Mbembe (2001, p. 111) has argued, 'produces a situation of disempowerment for both ruled and rulers'. Ratinam remains committed to Eelam, but finds little hope in the LTTE, an organization that Ratinam argues has vacated the urgency of a Tamil homeland in the name of propping up the LTTE's leader, Velupillai Prabhakaran. Though he marched in the protests, Ratinam told me, 'I will never say victory! I will never say *Jai* [long live] Prabhakaran because my heart does not allow me to do that' (personal interview with author, 2008). Ratinam's presence then represents a politics silenced by the militant cries of the protesters and the coverage in the Canadian press. Given the paucity of alternatives to the violence of the Sri Lankan state and the LTTE, Ratinam surrenders by saying that 'it is better to be punished by your own man than someone else'. The LTTE, in other words, while no less exclusionary than the government, has become an uneasy source of identification as the primary representation of Eelam. Ratinam's participation in the protests, therefore, was a recognition of the violence of the Sri Lankan state and the LTTE as much as it was also a search for alternatives.

One week after the Gardiner Expressway protest, the Sri Lankan government announced that they had killed Prabhakaran. Sri Lankan newspapers celebrated, with the *Daily News* running the headline, 'Megalomaniac terrorist Prabhakaran killed' (Wijayapala 2009, *CBC News* 2009), accompanied by an image of his lifeless head, serving as proof of the government's military victory. Following the government's announcement, pro-Eelam websites responded that he was in fact alive. The LTTE's 'International Relations Head' S. Pathmanathan made a statement on Prabhakaran's safety and the ongoing cause for Eelam:

> I wish to inform the Global Tamil community distressed witnessing the final events of the war that our beloved leader Velupillai Pirapaharan is alive and safe. He will continue to lead the quest for dignity and freedom for the Tamil people. The Tamil freedom struggle is a just cause and will not be quashed by the events of the last 24 h. Truth and justice will always prevail. (*TamilNet* 2009b)

Prabhakaran's purported death, confirmed by the LTTE one week later on *TamilNet* (2009e), laid bare the political vacuum created of Tamil nationalism in Sri Lanka and the depleted imaginaries of Eelam propped up by the LTTE. It also proved to be the grounds for new transnational acts of citizenship that attempt to reconcile political membership, nationalism, and state-based rights.

On the heels of the protest and the Sri Lankan government's declared victory over the LTTE, new practices of diasporic citizenship emerged. Pro-Eelam websites, most notably *Tamilnet*, called for the formation of a 'transnational government of Tamil Eelam'. The struggle for Eelam continues despite the defeat of the LTTE, and indeed now emphasizes the role of diaspora and democratic practice. A *TamilNet* editorial described the movement toward transnational governance:

> Transnational governance is not an elite exercise coming from the above and asking the people to vote. Such an exercise, when not orientated in the grass root, is always exposed to the danger of getting hijacked or succumbing to intimidation. But when it is formed with a clear bearing and mandate, through a series of democratic exercises among the diaspora in different parts of the world and if constituently linked from top to bottom, such a structure will be withstanding and cannot be ignored or sabotaged by anyone. (*TamilNet* 2009c)

The language of grassroots activism and democratic practices represents a reconceptualization of Eelam distinct from the alliances between diaspora and the LTTE. In doing so, calls for transnational governance also move notions of belonging and citizenship beyond the borders of state territory. Another statement on the 'Transnational Government for Tamil Eelam' indicated that the transnational government would continue to exist as an independent body in diaspora regardless of the territorial establishment of autonomy of a Tamil homeland in Sri Lanka. Imagining Eelam unshackled from the LTTE and the Sri Lankan state represents an ongoing attempt to transform the relationship between membership, territory, and the imaginative geographies of homeland in which communications technology assist in the production of national belonging (Jeganathan 1998, Whitaker 2004).

With the call for a transnational government, Eelam was placed within the wider context of diasporic groups. The struggle for Eelam was now made according to emergent forms of global citizenship and diasporic belonging that provide new avenues for transnational acts of citizenship:

> Among the very few classical as well as living cultures of humanity, such as the Chinese, Hebrews and Arabs, the Tamils, especially the Eezham Tamils,[2] have become an endangered identity. The world neither protected them nor allowed them to protect themselves... If the present world system is working against them in toto and if the world doesn't have enough appetite to look into their righteous aspirations, then the Tamils... should come out with introducing something innovative and creative to the world system itself. If the oppression to their nationalism is trans-national, the Eezham Tamils have to respond by forming a trans-national government fully responsible to them based on democracy, to negotiate with the world and to look after their own affairs. (*TamilNet* 2009d)

The diaspora's continued call for Eelam represents a transnationalism from below, a movement not cultivated or regulated by states, but fostered through collectivities in a transnational socio-spatial field. Such practices re-imagine notions of home and belonging (Staeheli and Nagel 2006) that move across borders between the diaspora and Sri Lanka. These new practices attempt to produce a political body and forms of citizenship more accountable and rights guaranteeing than the nation state.

Conclusion

> Ensuring that the nation's outpouring of joy at the defeat of terrorism leaves no room for anyone's feelings to be hurt in any manner is the greatest tribute we can pay to our Motherland. – Sri Lankan President Mahinda Rajapaksa in an interview following defeat of the LTTE. (Reddy 2009)
>
> The Tamil Diaspora will not give up. The Sri Lankan regime continues to unleash terror on our people who have been silenced by brute force and unimaginable atrocities. 'Mother India' and International community remain silent. But we, the Tamil Diaspora, will see to that Justice is done. Tamil Eelam will be freed. – Protestor in Toronto who participated in the Gardiner Expressway protest. (*TamilNet* 2009a)

In a recent editorial in *Political Geography,* Jazeel and Ruwanpura (2009) used Rajapaksa's victory speech, an excerpt of which appears above, as an inquiry into the contours of citizenship and belonging in 'post-war' Sri Lanka. Dissent, Jazeel argues, represents Sri Lanka's new minority. Indeed, under the backdrop of military victory and broadcasts of LTTE cadres killed in the final weeks of war, Rajapaksa claimed that defeat of the LTTE is also a defeat for the very concept of national minorities. As Rajapaksa made clear, citizenship in 'post-war' Sri Lanka consists of wholehearted alignment with statist discourses of patriotism as the obligations of membership that silences any form of dissent. Membership is predicated on a loyalty to the state in which the only expression acceptable is an outpouring of joy to the vaunted motherland. Sri Lanka follows the trajectory of post-colonial nationalism that Frantz Fanon cautioned against as nationalism's 'pitfall' in which anti-colonial nationalism gives way to ultra-nationalism, chauvinism, and finally, to racism (Fanon 1963, p. 156). Sri Lankan Tamils defeated in the war lie outside the Sri Lankan nation, with the Sri Lankan Tamil diaspora remaining in exile. Countering Rajapaksa's claims, the Toronto protests represented transnational acts of citizenship that made demands on their 'host' governments to recognize exclusions of the Sri Lankan state and Tamil self-determination. Their acts to be heard in their countries of residence, citizenship, and exile sought to elicit change in the international indifference to the Sri Lankan war. In the calls for Eelam, the protests also demanded inclusion for Tamils in the diaspora.

The second passage above comes from the diaspora, through the words of a protester discussing the significance of their protests in Toronto. Although the 25-year civil war had been regularly marked through solemn ceremonies such as the annual 'Black July' commemorations of the 1983 anti-Tamil pogroms, the 2008 and 2009 protests were significant because they constituted transnational acts of citizenship. Attempts by protestors to be heard, however, were represented as hostile acts of outsiders and not as those of claims-making citizens. Alongside suspicions of terrorism, Canadian political and public responses to the protests, reduced their acts to 'tests of tolerance'. The claims and demands made in the protests could not be contained with prevailing norms and ideals of Canadian citizenship, and the complex transnational politics enacted on the streets were eviscerated in Canadian exigencies for national unity. Buried under dominant representations of the protest, however, lies the lasting importance of the Toronto protests as acts of citizenship. The protests situated citizenship and exclusion in a transnational field that encompassed Canada, Sri Lanka, and the diaspora. As acts of citizenship, the protests point to the limits of national membership and belonging in a transnational field. For Tamils living in Toronto, Oslo, Kuala Lumpur, and Chennai, the protests were a collective diasporic nationalism of over 1 million Sri Lankan Tamils living in exile across the world. The diasporic practices of belonging in the protests sought to extend and universalize the freedom and egalitarianism that underwrite national citizenship to Tamils in Sri Lanka and the diaspora. Through transnational acts of citizenship, the Sri Lankan Tamil diaspora produced new forms of political participation in which the struggle for Eelam remains alive in diaspora.

Notes

1. Estimates of Toronto's Sri Lankan Tamil population have widely varied. In the 2006 Census (Statistics Canada 2006), 29,245 persons in Toronto reported 'Tamil' as their ethnic origin, 80,615 as 'Sri Lankan', and 3360 as 'Sinhalese'. Other estimates, based on interviews with the Tamil community, place the Sri Lankan Tamil population in Canada at over 200,000 and with 90% living in Toronto (Sandercock *et al.* 2004). During the Tamil protests, Toronto's Tamil population became a point of contention in the coverage in *Toronto Star* (English 2009).
2. Eezham is an alternative spelling for Eelam.

References

Anderson, B., 1992. *Long-distance nationalism: world capitalism and the rise of identity politics.* Amsterdam: Center for Asian Studies Amsterdam.

Anon, Pray for us. stop the silent genocide of Tamils in Sri Lanka [online]. Available from: http://www.justice4tamils.com/campaign.aspx [Accessed 28 December 2011].

Appadurai, A., 2006. *Fear of small numbers: an essay on the geography of anger.* Durham: Duke University Press.

Aruliah, A., 1994. Accepted on compassionate grounds: an admission profile of Tamil immigrants in Canada. *Refuge*, 14 (4), 10–14.

Basch, L., Glick-Schiller, N. and Blanc-Szanton, C., 1994. *Nations unbound: transnational projects, postcolonial predicaments, and deterritorialized nation-states.* New York: Gordon and Breach.

Basu, R., 2009. *Spaces of sub/urban/altern cosmopolitanism – creating multilingual geographies of resistance,* Annual association of American geographers Conference. Las Vegas.

Bauböck, R., 1994. *Transnational citizenship.* Edward Elgar: Aldershot and Brookfield.

Bauböck, R., 2003. Towards a political theory of migrant transnationalism. *International migration review*, 37 (3), 700–723.

Bell, S., 2008. *Inside Sri Lanka: an 'island of blood'* [online]. National Post, 19 September. Available from: http://www.nationalpost.com/most_popular/story.html?id=808303 [Accessed 28 December 2011].

Blatchford, C., 2009. *Whose rights are really being trampled?* [online]. Globe and Mail, 12 May. Available from: http://v1.theglobeandmail.com/servlet/story/LAC.20090512.BLATCH12 ART2244/TPStory/TENILLE+BONOGUORE [Accessed 31 August 2010].

Bosniak, L., 2006. *The citizen and the alien: dilemmas of contemporary membership.* Princeton: Princeton University Press.

British Broadcasting Corporation, 2010. *Country profile: Sri Lanka* [online]. Available from: http://news.bbc.co.uk/2/hi/south_asia/country_profiles/1168427.stm [Accessed 28 December 2011].

Canadian Tamil Congress, 2007. Canada's Tamils urge Harper government to recognize Tamil state [online]. 4 April. Available from: www.ctconline.ca/pdf/PR_04_04_07.pdf [Accessed 10 September 2010].

CBC News. 2006. *Canada adds Tamil Tigers to list of terrorist groups* [online]. 10 April. Available from: http://www.cbc.ca/canada/story/2006/04/10/tamils-terror-designation.html [Accessed 28 December 2011].

CBC News. 2009. *Body of Tamil Tiger leader found, Sri Lanka's army says* [online]. 19 May. Available from: http://www.cbc.ca/world/story/2009/05/19/sri-lanka-tamil-tigersvelupillai-body385.html [Accessed 28 December 2011].

Cheran, R., 1999. Sri Lanka: human rights in the context of civil war. *Refuge*, 18 (2), 4–9.

CP 24, 2009a. *Red Tamil flags at protests don't represent terrorist group, demonstrators say* [online]. 11 May. Available from: http://www.cp24.com/servlet/an/local/CTVNews/20090511/090511_tamil_protest/20090511/?hub=CP24Home [Accessed 28 December 2011].

CP 24, 2009b. *Police tolerance of Tamil protests may lessen after highway storming: expert* [online]. 11 May. Available from: http://www.cp24.com/servlet/an/local/CTVNews/20090511/090511_tamilpolice/20090511/?hub=CP24Home [Accessed 28 December 2011].

CTV Toronto, 2009a. *Tamils forms human chain in downtown T.O.* [online]. 30 January. Available from: http://toronto.ctv.ca/servlet/an/local/CTVNews/20090130/tamil_protest_090130/20090130/?hub=TorontoNewHome [Accessed 28 December 2011].

CTV Toronto, 2009b. *Roads close as thousands of Tamils protest in T.O.* [online]. 16 March. Available from: http://toronto.ctv.ca/servlet/an/local/CTVNews/20090316/tamils_090316/20090316?hub=TorontoHome [Accessed 28 December 2011].

Daniel, E.V., 1996. *Charred lullabies: chapters in an anthropography of violence*. Princeton: Princeton University Press.

De Mel, N., 2007. *Militarizing Sri Lanka: popular culture, memory and narrative in the armed conflict*. New Delhi: Sage.

Derrida, J. and Beardsworth, R., 1994. Nietzsche and the machine: interview with Jacques Derrida by Richard Beardsworth. *Journal of nietzsche studies*, 7, 7–66.

Derrida, J., 2005. *Rogues: two essays on reason*. Stanford: Stanford University Press.

DiManno, R., 2009. *Tamils get in staid old city's face* [online]. Toronto Star, 14 May. Available from: http://www.thestar.com/article/634125 [Accessed 28 December 2011].

Ehrkamp, P., 2006. We Turks are no Germans: assimilation discourses and the dialectical construction of identities in Germany. *Environment and planning A*, 38 (9), 1673–1692.

English, K., 2009. *The truth about Tamil Statistics* [online]. Toronto Star, 3 April. Available from: http://www.thestar.com/article/613815 [Accessed 28 December 2011].

Fair, C., 2005. Diaspora involvement in insurgencies: insights from the Khalistan and Tamil Eelam movements. *Nationalism and ethnic politics*, 11 (1), 125–156.

Fanon, F., 1963. *The wretched of the earth*. New York: Grove Press, Inc.

Fuglerud, O., 1999. *Life on the outside: the Tamil diaspora and long-distance nationalism*. London: Pluto Press.

Grewal, I., 2005. *Transnational America*. Durham: Duke University Press.

Holston, J. and Appadurai, A., 1996. Cities and citizenship. *Public culture*, 8 (2), 187–204.

Howlett, K. and Bonoguore, T., 2009. *McGuinty urges protesters not to carry Tamil Tiger flag* [online]. *Globe and Mail*, 12 May. Available from: http://v1.theglobeandmail.com/servlet/story/RTGAM.20090512.wtamilflag0512/BNStory/Front/ [Accessed 28 December 2011].

Human Rights Watch, 2006. *Funding the 'final war:' LTTE intimidation and extortion in the Tamil diaspora*. New York: Human Rights Watch, 18(1).

International Crisis Group, 2010. *The Sri Lankan Tamil diaspora after the LTTE* [online]. Asia. Available from: http://www.crisisgroup.org/en/regions/asia/south-asia/sri-lanka/186-the-sri-lankan-tamil-diaspora-after-the-ltte.aspx [Accessed 28 December 2011].

Isin, E., 2008. Theorizing acts of citizenship. *In*: E. Isin and G. Nielsen, eds. *Acts of citizenship*. London and New York: Zed Books, 15–43.

Isin, E.F. and Turner, B.S., 2007. Investigating citizenship: an agenda for citizenship studies. *Citizenship studies*, 11 (1), 5–17.

Isin, E.F. and Wood, P.K., 1999. *Citizenship and identity*. Thousand Oaks: Sage.

Ismail, Q., 2005. *Abiding by Sri Lanka: on peace, place, and postcoloniality*. Minneapolis: University of Minnesota Press.

Jazeel, T. and Ruwanpura, K.N., 2009. Dissent: Sri Lanka's new minority? *Political geography*, 28 (7), 385–387.

Jeganathan, P., 1998. Eelam.com: place, nation, and imagi-nation in cyberspace. *Public culture*, 10 (3), 515–528.

Korf, B., 2006. Who is the rogue? discourse, power and spatial politics in post-war Sri Lanka. *Political geography*, 25 (3), 279–297.

Lewington, J. and Makin, K., 2009. *Tamil protest surprises Toronto* [online]. *Globe and Mail*, 11 May. Available from: http://v1.theglobeandmail.com/servlet/story/RTGAM.20090510.wtamilprotest0510/BNStory/TENILLE+BONOGUORE/ [Accessed 28 December 2011].

Mahler, S., 1998. Theoretical and empirical contributions toward a research agenda for transnationalism. *In*: M.P. Smith and L.E. Guarnizo, eds. *Transnationalism from below*. New Brunswick: Transaction Publishers, 64–94.

Malkki, L., 1995. Refugees and exile: from 'refugee studies' to the national order of things. *Annual review of anthropology*, 24, 495–523.

Marciniak, K., 2006. *Alienhood: citizenship, exile, and the logic of difference*. Minneapolis: University of Minnesota Press.

Mbembe, A., 2001. *On the postcolony*. Berkeley: University of California Press.

McDowell, C., 1996. *A Tamil asylum diaspora: migration, settlement and politics in Switzerland*. Providence: Berghahn.

Murari, S., 2008. *Indian Tamils in human chain protest over Sri Lanka* [online]. Reuters. Available from: http://www.reuters.com/article/idUSTRE49N3L720081024 [Accessed 28 December 2011].

Nessman, R., 2009. *UN condemns 'bloodbath' in war zone* [online]. *Globe and Mail*, May 11. Available from: http://v1.theglobeandmail.com/servlet/story/RTGAM.20090511.wsrilanka0511/BNStory/National [Accessed 28 December 2011].

No to Sri Lanka, 2009. *No to Sri Lanka: consumers making the right choice against genocide* [online]. Available from: http://www.notosrilanka.com/about-us. [Accessed May 12, 2009].

Press Trust of India, 2009. Tamils protest in London for ceasefire in Lanka. 7 April 2009.

Razack, S., 2007. *Casting out: the eviction of Muslims from western law and politics*. Toronto: University of Toronto Press.

Reddy, B.M., 2009. *Sri Lanka draws up resettlement plan for displaced* [online]. The Hindu, 22 May. Available from: http://www.hindu.com/2009/05/22/stories/2009052258200100.htm [Accessed 30 September 2010].

Samarasinghe, S.W.R. de A., 2009. Sri Lanka: the challenge of postwar peace building, state building, and nation building. *Nationalism and ethnic politics*, 15 (3/4), 436–461.

Sandercock, L., Dickout, L. and Winkler, T., 2004. The quest for an inclusive city: an exploration of Sri Lankan Tamil experience of integration in Toronto and Vancouver. *Research on immigration and integration in the metropolis*, 04–12.

Sassen, S., 2006. *Territory, authority, rights: from medieval to global assemblages*. Princeton: Princeton University Press.

Schiller, N.G. and Fouron, G., 2001. *Georges woke up Laughing: long-distance nationalism and the search for home*. Durham: Duke University Press.

Scott, D., 1999. *Refashioning futures: criticism after postcoloniality*. Princeton: Princeton University Press.

Smith, M.P. and Guarnizo, L., eds, 1998. *Transnationalism from below*. New Brunswick: Transaction Publishers.

Spiegel, 2008. *Civilians are the ones who will suffer* [online]. Spiegel, 1 January 2008. Available from: http://www.spiegel.de/international/world/0,1518,529920,00.html [Accessed 28 December 2011].

Staeheli, L. and Nagel, C., 2006. Topographies of home and citizenship: Arab-American activists in the United States. *Environment and planning A*, 38 (9), 1599–1614.

Stasiulis, D., 2002. Introduction: reconfiguring Canadian citizenship. *Citizenship studies*, 6 (4), 365–375.

Stasiulis, D., 2008. The migration-citizenship nexus. *In*: E.G. Isin, ed. *Recasting the social in citizenship*. Toronto: University of Toronto Press, 134–161.

Statistics Canada, 2006. *Census of Population, Statistics Canada catalogue no. 97-562-XCB2006006 (Toronto, Code535)* [online]. Available from: http://www12.statcan.gc.ca/census-recensement/2006/dp-pd/tbt/Rp-eng.cfm?TABID=1&LANG=E&APATH=3&DETAIL=0&DIM=0&FL=A&FREE=0&GC=01&GK=1&GRP=1&PID=92333&PRID=0&PTYPE=88971,97154&S=0&SHOWALL=0&SUB=0&Temporal=2006&THEME=80&VID=0&VNAMEE=&VNAMEF= [Accessed 28 December 2011].

Sydney Morning Herald, 2009. *Tamil protestors converge on PM's lodge* [online]. Available from: http://news.smh.com.au/breaking-news-national/tamil-protesters-converge-on-pms-lodge-20090414-a539.html [Accessed 28 December 2011].

Tamilnet, 2009a. *Tamil diaspora agitates as civilian death toll rises* [online]. 11 May. Available from: http://www.tamilnet.com/art.html?catid=13&artid=29331 [Accessed 28 December 2011].

TamilNet, 2009b. *War crime in the massacre of LTTE officials* [online]. 19 May. Available from: http://www.tamilnet.com/art.html?catid=13&artid=29409 [Accessed 28 December 2011].

TamilNet, 2009c. *A roadmap to liberation* [online]. 11 August. Available from: http://www.tamilnet.com/art.html?catid=99&artid=29987 [Accessed 28 December 2011].

TamilNet, 2009d. *Setting the hands of the clock right* [online]. 1 June. Available from: http://www.tamilnet.com/art.html?catid=99&artid=29504 [Accessed 28 December 2011].

TamilNet, 2009e. *Claims and scepticism sans evidence* [online]. 25 May. Available from: http://www.tamilnet.com/art.html?catid=13&artid=29446 [Accessed 28 December 2011].

Tran, M., 2009. Sri Lanka army shelled no-fire zone says UN agency [online]. *Guardian*, 1 May. Available from: http://www.guardian.co.uk/world/2009/may/01/srilanka-nofire-satellite-pictures-un [Accessed 28 December 2011].

Turner, B., 2005. Citizenship. *In*: T. Bennett, L. Grossberg and M. Morris, eds. *New keywords: a revised vocabulary of culture and society*. Malden and Oxford: Blackwell, 29–32.

Van Rijn, N., 2009. *Gardiner chaos averted* [online]. Toronto Star, 11 May. Available from: http://www.thestar.com/news/gta/article/632257 [Accessed 28 December 2011].

Whitaker, M., 2004. Tamilnet.com: some reflections on popular anthropology, nationalism, and the internet. *Anthropological quarterly*, 77 (3), 469–498.

Wickramasinghe, N., 2009. Sri Lanka in 2008: waging war for peace. *Asian survey*, XLIX (1), 59–65.

Wijayapala, R., 2009. Megalomaniac terrorist Prabhakaran killed [online]. *Daily News*, 19 May. Available from: http://www.dailynews.lk/2009/05/19/sec01.asp [Accessed 28 December 2011].

Wingrove, J., Bonoguore, T. and Curry, B., 2009. Tamil protests open political minefield for Ottawa. *Globe and mail*, 12 May [online], Available from: http://v1.theglobeandmail.com/servlet/story/LAC.20090512.TAMILMAIN12ART2253/TPStory/Front [Accessed 26 May 2010].

Workers Vanguard, 2009. *Defend the Tamil people! army bloodbath in Sri Lanka* [online], No. 930. Available from: http://www.icl-fi.org/english/wv/930/lanka.html [Accessed 28 December 2011].

Naked protest: the maternal politics of citizenship and revolt

Imogen Tyler

Department of Sociology, Lancaster University, Lancaster LA1 4YL, UK

This article explores immigrant protest, citizenship and their relationship, through an account of a 'naked protest' by a group of mothers, refused asylum seekers and 'illegal immigrants' at Yarl's Wood immigration removal centre in England and ends with an account of the use of the 'naked curse' in a protest by an indigenous group of mothers against global oil corporations in the Niger Delta. Woven together from activist materials, news reports, interviews, documentaries and historical data, I recount and mobilise these protests to think about 'the scaling of bodies' (Marion-Young 1990) and citizenship under neoliberalism, and the routes through which motherhood is mobilised as a site of political agency and resistance to processes of disenfranchisement. I argue that these maternal protests challenge the 'catastrophic functionalism' of Agamben-inspired accounts of 'bare life', and offer an alternative lens through which to perceive the ethical and political claims made by abject populations (Papadopoulos *et al.* 2008, p. 198). In thinking through and with these naked protests, this article reframes the sexual politics of citizenship and brings questions of maternity and natality to bear on citizenship studies.

'I took my clothes off because they treat us like animals. We are claiming asylum, we're not animals.' (Mercy Guobadia, Yarl's Wood Immigration Removal Centre, 2008)

'We'll go naked. We will do our naked because you people want us to suffer. We're not taking that. Fear will come.' (Lucky Ogodo, Niger Delta, 2005)

Crane Wing, Yarl's Wood Immigration Removal Centre, England, April, 2008

On 10 April 2008, detention officers at Yarl's Wood Immigration Removal Centre moved to deport two detainees, a Burundian mother and her British-born baby. The mother, a refused asylum seeker, took temporary refuge with her baby in a chapel inside the detention centre. In solidarity, a group of fellow African detainees within the removal centre's family unit which is called Crane Wing, confronted the officers, arguing that the young mother and her baby had not had access to adequate legal representation. During the ensuing altercation a pregnant detainee was forcibly restrained, separated from her 6-year-old son and placed into solitary confinement. The following day the Yarl's Wood mothers staged a second protest in a corridor outside a staff office demanding to know what had happened to the women who had been removed. During this gathering several of the mothers proceeded to remove their clothes, some baring their breasts and others stripping to expose their genitals. One of the protestors, Mercy Guobadia, stated in a phone call to an anti-deportation campaigner that this naked protest was a direct response to the inhumane treatment of their children and themselves by the British state: 'I took my clothes off

69

because they treat us like animals. We are claiming asylum, we're not animals' (Guobadia, in Dugan 2008). The mothers followed their naked protest with a hunger strike and released an open letter to the British government, documenting their concerns about the impact of prolonged and indeterminate imprisonment on the health of their children.

There was nothing exceptional about this protest by immigration detainees. On the contrary, since Britain began arbitrarily to detain asylum seekers and other non-documented migrants in the early 1990s, hunger strikes, fires and riots, self-harm, suicides and escape attempts have become regular features of life' within a rapidly expanding immigrant prison estate. This naked protest by 15 mothers at Yarl's Wood is remarkable only because it has been circulated so widely, having leaked out from inside what Liz Fekete has described as 'the European deportation machine' (2005). This protest became public because, unusually, it was reported in national and international newspapers, as well as in online independent news media. As Mercy Guobadia suggests, she and the other mothers took off their clothes as a deliberate (media-oriented) tactic to draw attention to the conditions in which they and their children were being detained. In the context of a Western media gaze, public images of naked and sexualised female bodies are of course routine to the point of banality. However, the idea of a group of protesting naked maternal bodies, particularly those of non-white women, is provocative in the context of long-standing, if now challenged, taboos around the representation of pregnant bodies (see Tyler 2011). The sensationalism of the idea of a group of pregnant women and mothers stripped naked before the detention centre guards transformed this small-scale and unexceptional event into a 'news-worthy' story. Reports of this protest were largely humanitarian in tone, concerned with 'winning sympathy' for the mothers and their children. But in so doing they risked reducing the mothers' political agency, and with it the rage which fuelled their protest. As Joe Rigby and Raphael Schlembach argue in this issue, 'protest on "humanitarian realist" grounds reduces protest to a contest over "the possible" which can only ever mean, at a fundamental level, a conservative acceptance of the existing framework for grasping problems and their solutions' (2013).

Introduction

This article will prise this protest away from the genre of 'humanitarian scandal' and will mobilise it to trouble the conceptual and theoretical frames through which we apprehend the political practices of abject populations who are disenfranchised from citizenship. The intention is to employ this maternal protest, and a naked protest, by mothers in the Niger Delta which I examine in the later sections of this article, as a route into thinking about the significance of immigrant protests as activities which disturb 'the scaling of bodies'[1] through citizenship (Marion-Young 1990, Tyler 2010). More specifically, I intend to recast questions about the sexual politics of citizenship by placing maternal subjectivity and natal politics at the heart of citizenship studies. This article contributes to a growing body of feminist scholarship on gender, migration and citizenship and a critical focus in this literature on the role of native mothers in securing 'the reproduction of the nation' and the identification of migrant and/or other undesirable mothers as a target of border control mechanisms (see for example, Yuval-Davis and Anthias 1989, Yural-Davis 1996, Lentin 2004, 2011, Luibhéid 2004). Developing this feminist scholarship, I will argue that maternal protests are an important site of political revolt against dehumanising and disenfranchising forms of subjugation to sovereign regimes of power.

This article draws on an interview I undertook with one of the Yarl's Wood protestors, conversations with anti-deportation activists, news media reports, British Government policy documents, and, in the case of the Niger Delta protest, published first-hand accounts by activists of their protests against Global oil companies, as well as a documentary film and investigative journalism.[2] Whilst this is a rich archive of data, I am aware that the ways in which I narrate these protests in this article raise a series of larger ethical questions about the routes through which protestors' voices are able, or not, to enter into the theoretical and public debates about citizenship and rights. As Katarzyna Marciniak and I argue in the introduction to this issue, immigrant protests have the capacity to call regimes of citizenship into question in important ways. However, we need to be attentive, in framing the protests of others, to the risks involved in the claims we make for such protests when they are animated and in academic accounts. Indeed, the term 'animation' communicates the sense of *being animated by another* and is a reminder of the partiality of the frames through which 'acts' become perceptible as something we term 'politics' and 'actors' become audible (or not) as political subjects. For disenfranchised populations who, as Rey Chow argues, are 'constantly invoked, apostrophized or ventriloquized by first-world theorists', like myself (in Ngai 2005, p. 99), critical and ethical questions will always remain. Rigby and Schlembach argue that the struggle at the heart of migrant politics is a battle not only over what kinds of protest and protestors can be seen and heard (as politics) but also more fundamentally what kinds of resistance are imagined as possible (this issue). Whilst this article is motivated by a desire to document the fact of these protests, my intention is not to represent the protests in ways which fix the meaning of these acts and I cannot and do not claim to speak on behalf of the protestors. Rather my aim is to *think with* these protests as a means of *speaking back* to theory, troubling existing theoretical paradigms of citizenship by imagining other modes and forms of collective political subjectivity (p. 3). My intention is thus to communicate the epistemic challenge to the Eurocentrism and sexual politics of 'citizenship theory' which is posed by these maternal revolts.

Bare but alive

Legal scholar Stephanie Silverman argues that an 'understanding of refugees as apolitical actors' devoid of agency predominates within legal, charitable and academic discourses about asylum and immigration (2008, p. 1). However, the protests of immigration detainees demonstrate how non-citizens can and do speak in a political voice, claiming agency under crushing social and political conditions. Drawing on interviews with Australian immigration detainees, Richard Bailey argues that:

> When the detainees say 'we are human, not animal', in the course of a protest, it not only suggests that they were demanding that they be treated with more dignity and compassion, it also suggests that they are aware that the camp is attempting to reduce them to a state from which they will not be able to resist; a state in which their politics and their lives will have become indistinguishable. Therefore a key aspect of their resistance involves insisting on this distinction. (2009, p. 121)

As Bailey suggests here, acts of resistance by detainees *enact* a distinction between political life and what Giorgio Agamben terms 'bare life' or 'naked life', enabling them to produce themselves as political actors despite the fact that they are to various degrees severed from public life (Agamben 1998). Practices of protest and revolt can transform the 'non-place' of the detention centre into especially highly politically charged spaces of resistance (Mark Augé 1995). In this context, it is important to remember that the mothers in Yarl's Wood organised their protest autonomously, phoning activists and journalists and releasing a public letter and statements to the press. They were engaged in *doing politics*. As Peter Nyers argues 'in these ways and many others, politicised groups of non-status migrants are enacting themselves as citizens even when the law does not recognize them as such' (2008, p. 179).

Bailey details how for the Australian immigration detainees he interviewed, protest was a central means of drawing themselves out of long depressive periods in which they sank into a state which one detainee described as 'walking death'. Similarly one of the Yarl's Wood protestors, 'Jane', described to me how participation in the naked protest had brought her 'back to life':

> I was nothing...dead inside. Then [when the protest began] I went a bit crazy [laughs]...I was shaking all over [demonstrates this shaking by holding her hands out to me], and I was really crying for my kids and for the others [in detention]... some women pulled their shirts up and some even their skirts... that African curse... do you know it? I was even shouting, maybe my English was not very good but I was so angry [laughs] it is funny. (interview 2010)

Jane's account of 'being dead' in detention is a common theme of interviews with detainees and other kinds of prisoners in a range of national and border contexts. These are in some senses 'deactivated persons', rendered inanimate, inarticulate and without agency (see Ngai 2005, p. 93). It is significant, then, that protests are recalled by detainees as moments when detainees feel themselves *come alive*. In my interview with her, Jane not only describes but also enacts her *reanimation* in the protest, recalling her shaking body, showing me how she shook and impersonating in the interview the sound of her own 'protest voice' crying and shouting. Such accounts of reanimation through protest insist on the capacity of marginalised populations to act as political subjects at the very moment of their abjection by the state. Through this naked protest the Yarl's Wood mothers communicated to their children, family, friends, activist allies, the detention centre guards, the British public, the British government and the international news media, the fact that they are *naked but alive*.

However, I want to explore further the link Jane makes between the naked protest in Yarl's Wood and the deeper historical significance of 'the naked curse' as one of the few routes available to African mothers to wrest power and a political voice in situations of extreme subjugation (Ekine 2009). I interviewed Jane in 2009 as part of a series of interviews with asylum seeker mothers in the UK, a project which is ongoing (see also Tyler 2010), and it was her passing reference to the African history of collective naked protest which inspired this article. As anthropologist and political activist Terisa Turner details, in an African context the threat of the exposure of the naked mother's body carries an ancient, powerful symbolism. As Turner notes:

> [T]he [naked] curse is invoked only under the most extreme of circumstances. Before it is even threatened, women usually take a formal vow to honour the enormity of its symbolism. We all come into the world through the vagina. By exposing the vagina, the women are saying: 'We are hereby taking back the life we gave you,' [...] It's about bringing forth life and denying life through social ostracism, which is a kind of social execution. Men who are exposed are viewed as dead. (Turner in Ekine 2008)

As I will explore in the context of indigenous mothers' protests against oil corporations, the baring of the naked maternal body invokes a 'power to take life that has been given' (Turner in Ekine 2008). Interestingly then, if this naked protest was imagined in the gaze of Western news media as a sensational and/or sexualised act of protest, in an African context this naked protest invokes a radical maternal power which threatens to render that objectifying (male) gaze impotent (see Van Allan 1972). I will return to the African origins of naked protest shortly. For now, I want to note that naked protest has a particular post-colonial resonance which, I shall argue, troubles the conceptual frame of bare life that has frequently been employed to describe the position and disposition of immigration detainees (Agamben 1998).

Drawing on Agamben's concept of 'bare life', Jenny Edkins and Véronique Pin-Fat argue that the use of the body in protests by asylum seekers can be interpreted as 'the assumption of bare life, that is, the taking up one of the very forms of life that sovereign power seeks to impose' (2005, p. 3, see also Darling 2009). Within this interpretative frame, stripping before the detention centre guards might be understood as 'an occupation' by the mothers of their bestowed status as speechless bare life. Edkins goes further in claiming that: 'The ultimate protest against sovereign power's production of its subjects as "bare life" is the unconditional acceptance of that designation. Protests *as "bare life"* are the effective contestation of sovereign power' (Edkins 2001). Edkins and Pin-Fat's account of bare life as a relation of violence which can be contested through appropriation is insightful. I want to develop it further by exploring what it means to understand immigrant protests within the conceptual frame of bare life. Specifically, I want to mobilise the naked protest of the mothers as a means of opening up the rigidity of such a theoretical framing. Certainly, the mothers in Yarl's Wood are not the speechless emissaries of a private and incommunicable dehumanisation but rather come together, if fleetingly, as a community they call 'Family Unite from Crane', in order to stake a claim for their status, and for their children, as *political prisoners*. Moreover, the testimony of the Yarl's Wood protestors suggests that they stripped naked in a deliberate *impersonation* of their dehumanisation. The distinction between accepting their reduction to the status of bare life and impersonating, such a status, is an important one. Impersonation is always a *knowing performance*: 'I took my clothes off because they treat us like animals. We are claiming asylum, we're not animals' (Guobadia, in Dugan 2008). The Yarl's Wood protestors imitate bare life by stripping bare in front of the detention centre's guards. Through this performance they reveal the fabricated and contingent structure of bare life itself, a status which is a consequence not of any essential quality of being, or indeed of any act or crime, but wholly dependent upon the (arbitrary) violence of the state. Their protest is close to what Agamben elsewhere describes as a minor 'biopolitics of reappropriation or riposte' (in Nyers 2004, p. 214). Writing about suffragette hunger strikes in British jails a century earlier, Ewa Ziarek similarly describes how the starving body 'mimics and exposes the hidden irrational violence of the sovereign state' (Ziarek 2008, p. 100). Through their impersonation of bare life the protestors signal their unconditional refusal of their (and their children's) designation as disposable human waste (see Khanna 2009). The mothers' naked protest thus interpreted is not an assumption of bare life but a naked performance which more fundamentally protests and refuses the scaling of life through citizenship. So whilst the naked protest of the Yarl's Wood mothers communicates sovereign abjection, it engenders a defiant agentic maternal subjectivity against bare life. Indeed, the figure of naked motherhood both summons and troubles the concept of bare life in a number of ways: she is not only subject to bare life in Agamben's sense of political desubjectification, and does not protest as bare life, but performs and parodies 'bare life' by stripping bare in order to refute this status. The detained mothers present their naked maternal bodies as a response to bare life: bodies which, particularly in the case of the pregnant protestors, communicate the very possibility of life itself (of beginning) and by extension humanity and generation. As I will suggest, it is the capacity of maternal protest to *materialise* the hidden but constitutive grounds of biopolitical governance, which explains why the securitisation of reproduction is a central plank of state immigration and border control.

The securitisation of reproduction

As I have previously argued, under neoliberalism citizenship has become a pivotal technique of biopolitical governance. Citizenship is designed to fail (Tyler 2010). Indeed, in the contemporary context citizenship is best understood as a 'biological'[3] category, a mutating entity that reproduces endless species of 'citizen being', including abject and failed citizen subjects. The naked protest at Yarl's Wood took place in a biopolitical context in which the bodies of non-citizen pregnant women and mothers have become sites of intensive management, criminalisation and control. As well as the ongoing detention of pregnant women and mothers, there has been a raft of legislation aimed at managing (and excluding) the reproductive bodies of non-citizens within the state by, for example, refusing pregnant women access to free medical care. In 2007, the British government's Border Agency published a report entitled 'Enforcing the rules: a strategy to ensure and enforce compliance with our immigration laws' (Home Office 2007) which outlined measures to improve the implementation of immigration law and identified a series of 'new threats' to Britain's borders. One of these threats was named as 'the health tourist', a figure who had not previously appeared in immigration policy documents. Health tourism was defined in this report as foreign nationals travelling to Britain with the intention of accessing free National Health services. In 2004 a government Health Select Committee reported that there were no empirical data to support claims that health tourists existed in any significant numbers. Nevertheless, in this 2007 immigration enforcement strategy document, the figure of the health tourist was resurrected as a new threat to national security and these 'health tourists' were revealed to be, in fact, 'heavily pregnant women'. As the report notes:

> There is evidence of small-scale but very deliberate abuse of the NHS. For example, a sampling exercise last year at one airport suggested that health tourists were being detected at the rate of about 15 per month. This primarily involved heavily pregnant women arriving in the UK with an intention of using NHS maternity services. (Home Office March 2007)

In 2008, in a series of questions filed under the British Freedom of Information Act (2000), the Home Office was asked for clarification of these 'facts' and admitted that there was in fact no evidence for the claim in its *own* report that 'heavily pregnant women [are] arriving in the UK with an intention of using NHS maternity services'. It also admitted that there had in fact been no 'sampling exercise' at an airport as was claimed. The Home Office nevertheless outlined in some detail the procedures by which foreign women suspected of being pregnant were being vetted for entry to the UK. An extract from these guidelines reads as follows:

> In the case of a female passenger where the Immigration Officer has suspicions from her appearance, that she may be pregnant, the passenger will be asked if she is expecting a child and what her plans are for the birth. If the passenger claims not to be pregnant then the Immigration Officer may refer her to the port medical inspector, who will then examine the passenger and determine the approximate gestation of the pregnancy, if any. If the gestation of the pregnancy suggests that the passenger will be giving birth within the previously claimed period of stay [...] then she may be refused leave to enter. (Home Office 2008)

These extraordinary 'handling guidelines' reveal pregnant women to be a specific target of border controls. Indeed, suspected pregnancy is managed in this immigration policy, in much the same way as smuggling drugs or carrying a weapon. Women are subjected to body searches to ascertain whether or not they are attempting to 'smuggle' unborn foreign nationals into Britain. As Luibhéid argues, 'the pregnant bodies of non-national women provide particularly powerful loci through which the state both extends and legitimises its exclusionary immigration practices' (2006, p. 74). The intensive focus on pregnant women at the border of Britain reveals how citizenship operates biopolitically as a means of managing the undesirable reproduction of non-citizens and thus protecting the 'species life' of the 'native' nation-state.

In *Means Without An End: Notes on Politics* (2000) Giorgio Agamben argues that, '"Nation-state" means a state which makes nativity or birth (that is, naked human life) the foundation of its sovereignty' (20.1). As Agamben argues, there has been until fairly recently, a natural understanding of the relationship between birth-place and citizenship in which 'the natives' of any given place are also, by virtue of their birth, the rightful natural citizens of a territory or state. The fundamental idea of the sovereign state is based upon this myth that 'generations reproducing within an almost unchanging territory in almost stable relationships for centuries have passed on an unchanging essence' (Etienne Balibar in Buckel and Wissel 2010, p. 33). The trinities of 'state–nation–territory' and 'citizen–nation–biological kinship' underpin this mythic conception of sovereignty. However, this trinity has been disturbed by the growing numbers of non-citizens within nation states that cannot be either naturalised or repatriated but have a persistent liminal status. Migrant women represent a specific threat to nativist beliefs. As Martha Escobar argues, 'Ideal migrant labor is frequently defined as sojourner and exploitable, meaning that they migrate, labor for a while, and return to their home countries. The presence of migrant women disrupts this ideal since they represent reproduction and settlement' (2008). The 'reproductive migrant', who threatens to populate 'our country' with 'foreign children', contributes to a rising nativism, by proliferating fears about loss of ancestry, a demise which it is imagined threatens the existence of the nation-state itself.

The 'crisis of sovereignty' described by Agamben effected by nation states themselves, as they sought from the early twentieth century onwards to manage and control their populations more rigorously and intimately. States began passing laws which variously sought to systematically denaturalise specific populations within the state through a scaling of citizenship. In Europe, hierarchal tiers of citizenship emerged and continue to be developed, which distinguish between those with full citizenship rights, those with partial or limited rights, those with limited leave to remain and those who have subcitizen or illegal status. As Agamben notes, 'Such laws – and the mass statelessness resulting from them – marked a decisive turn in the life of the modern-nation state as well as its definitive emancipation from the naive notions of the citizen and a people' (2000, 18.9). An increasing number of nation states have abolished (or have 'scaled') birth right citizenship (Jus soli) so that children who are born in nation-states to non-citizen parents are *de facto stateless* (Blitz 2006). For example, as I have previously detailed in the context of Britain, under the British Nationality Act 1981, children born in Britain to non-citizen mothers are not entitled to British citizenship (Tyler 2010). These children are in the extraordinary position of having entered Britain illegally at birth, and at birth become subject to Britain's border controls, including detention within a rapidly expanding, privately owned, 'for profit' immigration prison estate. These children are the quintessential illustration of the break between nativity and nationality described by Agamben, for they are an indigenous population in all formal senses and yet they are denied the rights of citizenship. The Yarl's Wood mothers are protesting against the aforesaid exclusions of British citizenship and specifically the treatment of their *de facto stateless* children, born in Britain. It is a remarkable fact that British-born children are detained and deported as aliens. While we imagine state borders as 'being somewhere', the cases of pregnant women searched at the borders and stateless children born in British maternity wards reveal borders to be a more complex network of relations (see Nyers 2008, pp. 166–167). Indeed, the specific forms of subjugation experienced by migrant mothers reveals how the bodies of pregnant women, mothers and children are transformed into corporeal border zones, sites of capture by, and correlatively important sites of revolt against regimes of citizenship.

What I want to delineate through my reading of British border control law, policy and practices here, and the animation of this protest against these practices, are the limits of Agamben's theoretical and conceptual framing. This protest is theoretically instructive in several ways. First, the mothers in Yarl's Wood are protesting the break between nativity and nationality described by Agamben: Their children where in many cases born in Britain and as such, these mothers are demanding that these children should have *natural* rights of citizenship. In this respect the mothers mobilise the myth of nativity to stake a political claim on behalf of their children. In order to articulate this demand, they both summon and trouble the concept of bare life in their naked protest. Bare life is a category of being which Agamben argues is a consequence of the break with nativity. However, in their knowing performance, bare life is neither apolitical nor abject (as Agamben suggests), but it is paradoxically claimed as a collective political *maternal subjectivity*. I will explore the deeper theoretical implications of this paradox in the remaining sections of this article.

As I noted above, it was a chance remark in an interview with one of the Yarl's Wood protestors that led me to trace the historical roots of naked protest to West Africa. In what follows I want to examine the connections between the naked protest in Yarl's Wood and a naked protest by indigenous mothers against global corporate oil companies in the Niger Delta in 2003. I do not intend this as a comparative account. Rather, by taking 'naked protest' as a trope, and by restaging these protests together in the space of this article, my aim is to make tangible the existing relationship between these geo-political sites: the common neocolonial economic logic. This logic, albeit in different ways, constitutes these populations of African mothers as disposable, a 'disposability' which their respective naked protests makes audible and refuses (Khanna 2009). As we argue in the introduction to this special issue, the gap between the democratic promise of citizenship and its deployment as a technology of biopolitical governance in local regimes of mobility control is precisely what is being struggled over in immigrant protests. However, the citationality of naked protest, further reminds us that contemporary struggles over citizenship are reconfigurations of long-standing and persistent relations of colonial (and capitalist) forms of injustice and exploitation (see Tyler 2010). As postcolonial theorist Catherine Hall suggests, the same 'sinews of inequality and subordination' and the same commercial interests which shaped previous mobility flows, such as the transatlantic slave trade, are in operation in the design of contemporary regimes of citizenship (Hall, in Ifekwunigwe 2004, p. 400). The environmental degradation, wealth confiscation and forced migration of the colonial period continues unabated, with siphoned wealth and disenfranchised peoples following the same centuries-old routes to the imperial centres of capital.

July 2002, Escravos Oil Facility, Niger Delta

On 8 July 2002, hundreds of unarmed singing and dancing mothers and grandmothers descended on the largest oil-producing facility in the Niger Delta, Escravos Oil Facility, owned by Chevron.[3] This highly organised group of women took control of the facility by threatening to strip naked in front of the male workers. Helen Odeworitse, a representative for the protestors during the 10-day siege stated that 'our weapon is our nakedness' (quoted in BBC News report, 16 July 2002). Mobilising the threat of naked curse, the women held the international workforce of 700 men in a state of lock-down, halting the production of the half a million tons of oil a day. As Sokari Ekine, the International Coordinator of the Niger Delta Women notes:

> The stripping off of clothes particularly by married and elderly women is a way of shaming men – some of whom believe that if they see the naked bodies they will go mad or suffer some great harm. The curse extends not just to local men but also to any foreigner who it is believed would become impotent at the sight of 'the naked mother'. (Ekine 2008)

The Niger Delta has long been an area of intensive and long-standing 'colonial resource extraction': indeed Escravos is a Portuguese word for slave. In the nineteenth century, when a number of European states and corporations juggled for control of the region, it was coined 'the Oil Rivers' due to its economic importance in production of palm oil: This was the oil which lubricated the machines and engines of the industrial revolution in the Global North. In 1884 the British Government granted the British National Africa Company (an amalgam of British commercial interests which was latterly renamed the Royal Niger Company) monopoly control over trading in the area. In the early twentieth century the British Government instigated more direct forms of imperial government in the region, violently subjugating indigenous populations and imposing the ideological and geopolitical structures which laid the ground for what would become the nation state of Nigeria. In the 1950s came the discovery of massive reserves of crude-oil and natural gas in the Delta, and an international scramble for control of 'the black gold' began (Watts 2008). Whilst Nigeria formally gained independence from Britain in 1960, the earlier mechanisms of imperial governance instigated through the chartering of European companies to control resource extraction in the Delta region, where ostensibly reconfigured in the form of the collaboration between the Nigerian government and global oil conglomerates. This relationship takes an institutional form as the Nigerian National Petroleum Corporation (NNPC): A deeply corrupt state-owned company, the NNPC was established in 1977 in partnership with European and North American-owned oil companies. (Its main corporate partners to date have been Royal Dutch Shell, Chevron, ExxonMobil, Agip, Total S.A and the various predecessors and successors of these supermajor energy companies).[4] For many decades, these companies have systematically polluted the land and water in the region (Ekine 2000, 2008, 2009, Watts 2008). As Grace Ekanum, a leader of an indigenous women's movement in Eket, a sprawling urban area in the Delta, notes in a radio interview:

> After 30 years of oil exploration, we still see our people suffering, our children dying day in and day out. Our husbands do not have jobs. Our children do not have jobs. What really brought me to be an activist is because of the oil spill that happened on the 12th of January of 1998. So many things went bad. Our fishes all died in the waters. That made us to fight for our rights. Oil pollution has killed everything and that is why we are suffering. (Ekanum 2000)

Protests by indigenous groups have been brutally suppressed by the Nigerian state with ongoing programmes of mass beatings, executions and rapes in the region by the Nigerian army (Ekine 2000). Nigerian state violence against its own people was highlighted in the international media by the execution of environmental activist, author and political representative of the Ogoni people in the Delta region, Ken Saro Wiwa, in 1995. Whilst the indigenous peoples in this area are legally and formally citizens of Nigeria, any substantive rights of citizenship have been hollowed out by global oil corporations working in cooperation with the Nigerian state, who have in effect militarised the region to maximise the extraction and flow of crude oil. In 2010, for example, WikiLeaks published cables in which Shell officials boast to the US government that they have infiltrated every department of the Nigerian Government and have influence over state decision-making in the Delta region (Smith 2010). In was in the face of this extreme history of colonial, state and corporate violence and corruption, that indigenous women protestors deployed the naked curse *en masse*, demanding compensation, clean water, electricity, jobs and social investment. Anino Olowu, a protestor who led a negotiating team on behalf of the naked protestors at Escravos, insisted meetings with Chevron management which took place in a village in the shadow of the oil facility, so that the company representatives were forced to face the extremity of the environmental conditions facing local people. Olowu noted in a news paper interview at the time, 'I don't know how [Chevron] can allow other human beings to live like this. Why do they treat us like animals?"(in Doran 2002).

In an hour-long documentary film, *The Naked Option: A Last Resort*, a US-based filmmaker Candace Schermerhorn interviewed women and men involved in the protests and explores the meaning and wider international impact of their use of the naked curse. This form of protest also known as 'sitting on a man', includes less shaming types of public ridicule of powerful men through collective acts of singing and dancing, as well as the deeply feared act of naked protest. Schermerhorn's film, and the documentation of the Escravos and many other similar protests by women activists in the Delta region, demonstrates how naked protest is one of the only strategies available to women in this region to expose injustice and 'manoeuvre themselves into a position of power' (Ekine 2009). A naked protest is one which these women do not undertake lightly. As one of the managers of the Escravos oil depot explained, 'it is a taboo in our land for mothers to say that they will go naked. It means every [other] means of protest has failed' (in Schermerhorn, *The Naked Option,* 2010). Over the following two months, thousands of women employed the threat of the naked curse to occupy eight oil facilities in the Delta region. As protestor Lucky Ogodo expressed it, 'We'll go naked. We will do our naked because you people want us to suffer. We're not taking that. Fear will come.' (Figure 1, in Schermerhorn, *The Naked Option,* 2010).

Natal politics

We are all born. Working against a long philosophical tradition that has given primacy to the shared horizon of death, in 1958, Arendt stated that 'Natality and not mortality, may be

Figure 1. Still from *The Naked Option: A Last Resort* (dir, Candace Schermerhorn), with permission.

the central category of political thought' (Arendt 1958, p. 9). What Arendt means by politics is the capacity to speak and act in the public sphere. For her, 'politics occurs when people who are equal come together to discuss and debate their differences without knowing what the material outcomes of political debate will be. In this sense, politics is always a new beginning, an attempt to move into an unknown future, which is always coupled to an originary capacity to begin – a capacity granted by the fact of birth itself' (see Baraitser and Tyler 2011, Tyler 2013). Arendt suggests that without some fundamental understanding of the natality of the human condition, there can be no freedom, no social change and no human future. Arendt suggests that the absence of this primary fact from histories of thought represents a significant lacuna in political and philosophical traditions. Arendt's insistence on thinking natality as the basis for politics is radical in the context of a European tradition so overwhelming preoccupied with death, loss, terror and mourning. *However,* for Arendt, natal politics bears no relation to childbirth and the reproductive sphere. The labours of women (social reproduction) are for Arendt hidden within the private realm of the household, while of course being absolutely foundational to and sustaining the public sphere. Birth, Arendt insists, is an experience 'beyond speech', which is 'antipolitical by definition' (1958, p. 63). Indeed for Arendt, the public sphere depends on the fact that 'man does not know where he comes from' (1958, p. 63). In contradistinction to this claim, the mothers at Yarl's Wood and in the Niger Delta, insist, through the bearing of their naked maternal bodies, that maternal origin is acknowledged. Drawing on another much longer pre-colonial epistemological tradition, they enact natality as a politics of resistance.

What is the relationship between natality and sovereignty? Sovereignty describes the capacity of a state 'to decide on matters of inclusion and exclusion' (Nyers 2003, p. 1069). The forms of abjection, which are integral to the productive work of sovereign power upon populations, delineate not only who is a citizen (or not) but also constitute who counts as 'human' in a given place or time. As Khanna argues, sovereignty is always 'inscribed partly in relation to the state and to the question of species' (2007, p. 258). Françoise Vergès describes the mechanisms of sovereign power, and its creation of waste populations, as 'the transformation of human beings into matter' (Vergès 2001, p. 11 in Khanna 2009, p. 193). It is interesting to engage Arendt's notion of natal politics in the context of the deployment of the naked curse as a protest against sovereign power. The power of the naked curse is dependent on the invocation of the taboo described by Arendt; it confronts men with the fact of their birth, with the natality of the human condition. Again, as one of the male managers of the Escravos oil facility stated: 'They produce us from the wombs of their stomach, they produce us. We cannot see them go naked. Culture does not allow it. Society does not allow it' (in Schermerhorn 2010). If we read against Arendt, and literalise natality, we can see why a revolting maternal body-politic has a particular capacity to unveil the deadly logic and radical inequalities of sovereignty. Communicating with uncanny force the natality of the human condition: *the transformation of matter into human beings* (see Tyler 2000).

In a study of Igbo women in the Delta region, anthropologist Judith Van-Allan argues that British colonialism ushered in forms of gender politics which undermined much of Igbo women's traditional power and autonomy. Imperialism impacted on women's access to high status social roles in public life, and, perhaps more significantly, eroded the Igbo maternal public sphere: a sphere composed of women's autonomous political institutions and spaces (women-only meetings, the marketplace and kinship networks), women's economic independence and the rights of women, as a group, 'to use strikes, boycotts and force' to affect decision making (1972, p. 165, see also Ifi Amadiume 1987, 2000). In more recent work, Allan has described revolts by African mothers against colonial and neo-colonial exploitation as forms of radical political praxis which stake a claim for what she describes as 'an indigenous "counter-constitution" of citizenship against liberal democratic constructions' (Allan 2007). The work of Nigerian sociologist Amadiume is pivotal in developing our understanding of the history and meaning of naked maternal protest. Indeed, Amadiume's account of the 'matrifocality' of African social and political life poses a fundamental challenge, an epistemic challenge, to Eurocentric theoretical accounts of sovereignty. In particular, it insists that we are attentive to the ways in which received understandings of sovereignty, and imagined boundaries between public and private spheres are always already an effect of colonial (economic and sexual) relations of power. Following Amadiume, we might understand the use of the naked curse by the Niger Delta mothers as a form of protest which harnesses older forms of collective matrifocal political subjectivity: a natal politics which read through Arendt's Eurocentric epistemological frame would be unimaginable.

As I noted in the introduction to this article, the struggle at the heart of migrant politics is one over what kinds of protests against a prevailing regimes of citizenship can be seen and heard (imagined as politics), a contest which always concerns the frames of perceptibility in operation, and the extent to which they might be challenged or ruptured. I want to argue that the protests I have examined force an exposure of the theoretical limits of the prevailing epistemological frames of sovereignty. I have suggested that they do this in two connected ways: First, they are a reminder of a persistent colonial lacuna within Eurocentric theories of citizenship and belonging. Protests such as these thus raise the spectre of colonialism in material and theoretical senses, revealing sovereignty to be a contested and diverse trans-national web of relations, in ways which refuse ahistorical and/or state-bound accounts of citizenship and rights. In particular, I hope to have demonstrated how the rich transnational seam of 'maternal politics' enacted through these protests challenges the 'catastrophic functionalism' and Eurocentrism of Agamben-inspired accounts of bare life, and offers an alternative lens through which to perceive the ethical and political claims made by non-citizens and disenfranchised people (Papadopoulos et al. 2008, p. 198). This leads to my second central claim, namely, that whilst (after Foucault) it is widely understood that different epochs and modes of sovereignty generate specific ontologies of the subject, the collective maternal subjectivity enacted in both the Yarl's Wood and the Niger Delta protests challenges Eurocentric models of subjectivity (particularly where 'the subject' has been imagined through the lens of a masculinist, singular and individualistic conceptual frame, see Tyler 2000). This is where my argument becomes complex, for, on the one hand, I am arguing that differential histories (especially the different forms of sexual politics and public/private distinctions in operation in different geopolitical regions and in different historical periods) allow for modes of resistance which are not imaginable within a eurocentric frame: namely, in the case of these protests, collective forms of political maternal subjectivity. On the other hand, following Arendt, I want to also suggest that what this collective maternal subjectivity reveals is the constitutive natality of all subjectivity and politics. This is, as Arendt's account suggests, a radical and universalist claim. Indeed, I want to suggest that through their invocation of 'natality' these mothers introduce a vital 'tension about value and most particularly the value of life itself' (Khanna 2009, p. 195), a tension which has the capacity to trouble sovereignty *and* the theoretical descriptions of sovereignty which dominate in debates about citizenship and rights. Whilst this natalist claim affirms Arendt's re-temporalisation of the political (away from death and towards life), in my preliminary reworking of her account, I mobilise these protests as a means of pushing past what is a Eurocentric and outmoded private/public distinction, in which motherhood (the reproductive sphere) is 'bracketed out' as something akin to 'bare life', the constitutive but unspeakable grounds of public and political life.

Conclusion

When the African mothers in Yarl's Wood Immigration Removal Centre in April 2008 protested their incarceration through a naked protest they knowingly invoked the longer African history of the naked curse (see for example Dike 1995), and the deployment of the curse in the Niger Delta protests against the deathly impact of neo-colonial corporate capitalism. The citational history of the naked protest reveals these populations to be connected by the same historical and transnational networks of inequality, populations made disposable by neo-colonial forces of global corporate capitalism. Through naked revolts, they protested against sovereign and corporate forms of power which constituted them as human waste, using their life-full bodies to constitute alternative, if precarious, political communities. The mothers in Yarl's Wood and the Niger Delta enact political solidarity beyond the bonds of citizenship or statist politics, a form of solidarity which is grounded in what Amadiume describes as '*umunne* or the spirit of shared motherhood' (Amadiume 1987, p. 56). I have suggested that we might understand this collective political subjectivity as a 'natal politics' by drawing on but pushing beyond the Eurocentric and masculinist limits of Arendt's account of natality.

It is important to note that the Yarl's Wood protest did not impact in any perceptible way on the specific regime of citizenship in operation. Indeed, individual protestors were severely punished for this 'act of citizenship': Mercy Guobadia, the Nigerian mother who was instrumental in communicating the events unfolding in Yarl's Wood to activists and journalists outside the detention centre, was moved to another detention centre and shortly after deported with her two young children (see Anon 2008). Furthermore, the scale and significance of these kinds of protests by immigration detainees is diminished in official statements and reports. For example, in the case of the Yarl's Wood naked protest, Serco Limited, the global corporation that is contracted by the British government to manage Yarl's Wood, reported that: 'discussions had taken place between residents and staff, but "no significant protest" had occurred' (in Dugan 2008). Furthermore, the current British Government has, as yet, failed to meet a promise to end the practice of child detention in the UK. For indigenous mothers in the Delta their protests have garnered significant amounts of international attention, including current law suits against oil companies, but as yet their efforts have brought about little material change in the region. However, the 'failure' of these protests does not diminish their significance.

Nyers asks, 'Is there a form of bio-agency capable of resubjectification in a way that does not reproduce the paradoxes of sovereign power?' (2004, p. 212). I want to end by proposing the collective maternal protests of non and disenfranchised citizens as expressions of bio-agency which cannot be recuperated to Eurocentric understandings of sovereignty which are grounded in masculinist understandings of sovereign subjectivity. By making or threatening to make their birthing bodies naked in public, the Yarl's Wood mothers and the Niger Delta mothers, stake a common claim for a 'life-centred political economy' against neoliberalism, an ideology Lauren Berlant has described as 'the capitalist destruction of life in the project of making value' (2007, p. 282). Through their naked revolts, these mothers refused their designation as disposable populations. They forced a disclosure of the radical inequalities and long colonial history of neoliberalism, and in doing so created conditions of possibility for the emergence of a politics which I imagine as a 'maternal commons' (Baraitser and Tyler 2011, Tyler 2013).

Acknowledgements

Thank you to the women who gave up time to be interviewed, especially 'Jane' and Rose McCarthy (Cities for Sanctuary). Thanks to Bruce Bennett, Katarzyna Marciniak, Alison Mountz, the anonymous reviewers and the journal editors for their critical and engaged feedback on drafts of this article. I also gratefully acknowledge the support of a Leverhulme Trust Research Fellowship and an Economic and Social Research Council Small Grant (RES-000-22-3928-A: Making asylum seekers legible and visible).

Notes

1. Iris Marion Young (1990) introduces the notion of 'scaling' to trouble universalist discourses of equality and justice. I am developing her work here as a means of theorising the ways in which citizenship is increasingly 'scaled' along classed, gendered and ethnic lines. In my forthcoming book, *Revolting Subjects* (Zed) I engage with these ideas in depth.
2. An extensive body of research about detained and refused asylum seekers in the UK has been undertaken and collated by activist, charitable and humanitarian organisations. This body of research, particularly as it pertains to the detention of mothers and children, has been an important source of background research for this article.
3. According to Turner and Brownhill (2004) the protestors were mothers and grandmothers whose age ranged from 30 to 90.
4. See G. Ugo Nwojeki's (2007) report on the history of the NNPC.

References

Agamben, G., 1998. *Homo sacer: sovereign power and bare life,* trans. D. Heller-Roazen. California: Stanford University Press.
Agamben, G., 2000. *Means without end,* trans. V. Benetti, C. Casarino. Minneapolis: University of Minnesota.
Allen, J., 2007. *Mothers/workers/citizens: creating embodied citizenship against liberal democracy.* [online]. Unpublished paper. Available from: http://www.allacademic.com/meta/p209993_index.html.
Amadiume, I., 1987. *Male daughters, female husbands: gender and sex in an African society.* London: Zed.
Amadiume, I., 2000. *Daughters of the goddess, daughters of imperialism: African women, culture, power & democracy.* London: Zed.
Anon, 2008. Deportation decision goes against family. *South Wales Evening Post,* 5 May [online]. Available from: http://www.highbeam.com/doc/1P2-16320027.html
Arendt, H., 1958. *The human condition.* Chicago: Chicago University Press.
Augé, M., 1995. *Non-places: introduction to an anthropology of supermodernity,* trans. J. Howe. London: Verso.
BBC News, 2002. 'Deal reached' in Nigeria oil protest. *BBC News,* Tuesday, 16 July. Available from: http://news.bbc.co.uk/1/hi/world/africa/2129281.stm
Bailey, R., 2009. Up against the wall: Bare life and resistance in the camp. *Law and critique,* 20 (2), 113–132.
Baraitser, L. and Tyler, I., 2011. Private view: public birth, In: *Lecture given at 'Birth Rites symposium',* Whitechapel Art Gallery. Unpublished paper.
Berlant, L., 2007. Nearly Utopian, nearly normal: post-fordist affect in La Promesse and Rosetta. *Public culture,* 19 (2), 273–301.
Blitz, B., 2006. Statelessness and the social (de)construction of citizenship: political restructuring and ethnic discrimination in Slovenia. *Journal of human rights,* 5 (4), 453–479.
Buckel, S. and Wissel, J., 2010. State project Europe: the transformation of the European border regime and the production of bare life. *International political sociology,* 4, 33–49.
Darling, J., 2009. Becoming bare life: asylum, hospitality, and the politics of encampment Environment and Planning D. *Society and space,* 27 (4), 649–665.

Dike, Chike, ed., 1995. *The Women's Revolt of 1929: proceedings of a national symposium to Mark the 60th anniversary of the Women's uprising in South-Eastern Nigeria.* Lagos: Nelag.

Doran, D., 2002. Crushing poverty spurs nigerian village women into oil standoff, *Associated Press* [online]. Available from: http://www.waado.org/environment/OilCompanies/Women/Women2002Rebellion/July15.html

Dugan, E., 2008. Mothers detained in immigration centre hold 'naked' protest. *The Independent*, Friday 11 April [online]. Available from: http://www.independent.co.uk/news/uk/home-news/mothers-detained-in-immigration-centre-hold-naked-protest-807802.html

Edkins, J., 2001. *If no story is possible: trauma, testimony and biopolitics after Auschwitz* [online]. Available from: http://isanet.ccit.arizona.edu/paperarchive.html.

Edkins, J. and Pin-Fat, V., 2005. Through the wire: relations of power and relations of violence. *Millennium: journal of international studies*, 34 (1), 1–24.

Ekanum, G., 2000. Delta on fire: Nigerian women's resistance. *Making Contact* [online]. The National Radio Project, Oakland, CA. Available from: http://www.imow.org/wpp/stories/viewStory?storyId=129

Ekine, S., 2000. *Blood and oil: testimonies of violence from women of the Niger Delta.* London: Centre for Democracy and Development.

Ekine, S., 2008. The curse of nakedness: women in Nigeria threaten to bare it all to better their communities [online]. International Museum of Women. Available from: http://www.imow.org/wpp/stories/viewStory?storyId=1098

Ekine, S., 2009. *Women's responses to state violence in the Niger Delta: violence as an instrument of governance.* [online]. Available from: http://pambazuka.org/en/category/features/54174.

Fekete, L., 2005. The deportation machine: Europe, asylum and human rights. *Race and class*, 47 (1), 64–91.

Home Office, 2007. *Enforcing the rules: a strategy to ensure and enforce compliance with our immigration laws* [online]. Available from: http://ukba.homeoffice.gov.uk/sitecontent/documents/managingourborders/enforcementstrategy/enforcementstrategy.pdf?view=Binary.

Home Office, 2008. *Handling of suspected 'health tourists'* [online]. Available from: http://www.homeoffice.gov.uk/about-us/freedom-of-information/released-information/foi-archive-immigration/9707_detection_health_tourism?view=Html.

Ifekwunigwe, J., 2004. Recasting 'Black Venus' in the new African diaspora. *Women's studies international forum*, 27 (4), 397–412.

Khanna, R., 2007. Indignity. *Ethnic and racial studies*, 30 (2), 257–280.

Khanna, R., 2009. Disposability. *Differences: a journal of feminist cultural studies*, 20 (1), 181–198.

Lentin, R., 2004. Strangers and strollers: feminist notes on researching migrant m/others. *Women's studies international forum*, 27, 301–314.

Lentin, R., 2011. Palestinian women from Femina Sacra to agents of active resistance. *Women's studies international forum*, 34 (3), 165–170.

Luibhéid, E., 2004. Childbearing against the state? asylum seeker women in the Irish republic. *Women's studies international forum*, 27, 335–349.

Luibhéid, E., 2006. Sexual regimes and migration controls: reproducing the Irish Nation-State in transnational contexts. *Feminist review*, 83, 60–78.

Ngai, S., 2005. *Ugly feelings: literature, affect, and ideology.* Cambridge, MA: Harvard University Press.

Nyers, P., 2003. Abject cosmopolitanism: the politics of protection in the anti-deportation movement. *Third world quarterly*, 24 (6), 1069–1093.

Nyers, P., 2004. Introduction: what's left of citizenship? *Citizenship studies*, 8 (3), 203–215.

Nyers, P., 2008. No one is illegal between city and nation. *In*: E. Isin and G. Nielsen, eds. *Acts of citizenship.* London: Zed Books, 160–181.

Papadopoulos, D., Stephenson, N. and Tsianos, V., 2008. *Escape routes: control and subversion in the 21st century.* London: Pluto Press.

Rigby, J. and Schlembach, R., 2013. Impossible protest: NoBorders in Calais. *Citizenship studies*, 17 (2), 157–172.

Schermerhorn, C. (director), 2010. The naked option: a last resort. *Trailer.* Available from: http://www.nakedoptionmovie.com/

Silverman, S., 2008. *Redrawing the lines of control: political interventions by refugees and the sovereign state system* [online]. Available from: http://www.law.ed.ac.uk/festivaloflegaltheory/files/silverman.pdf.

Smith, D., 2010. WikiLeaks cables: shell's grip on Nigerian state revealed. *The Guardian*, 8 December [online]. Available from: http://www.guardian.co.uk/business/2010/dec/08/wikileaks-cables-shell-nigeria-spying

Turner, T. and Brownhill, L.S., 2004. Why women are at war with Chevron. Nigerian subsistence struggles against the International Oil Industry. *Journal of Asian and African studies*, 39 (1–2), 63–93.

Tyler, I., 2000. Reframing pregnant embodiment. *In*: S. Ahmed, *et al.* eds. *Transformations: thinking through feminism*. London: Routledge, 69–83.

Tyler, I., 2010. Designed to fail: a biopolitics of British citizenship. *Citizenship studies*, 14 (1), 61–74.

Tyler, I., 2011. Pregnant beauty: maternal femininities under neoliberalism. *In*: R. Gill and C. Scharff, eds. *New femininities: postfeminism, neoliberalism and identity*. London: Palgrave, 21–36.

Tyler, I., 2013. *Revolting subjects: social abjection and resistance in neoliberal Britain*. London: Zed.

Van Allen, J., 1972. Sitting on a man: colonialism and the lost political institutions of Igbo women. *Canadian journal of African studies*, 6, 65–182.

Watts, M. ed., 2008. *Curse of the black gold. 50 years of oil in the Niger Delta*. Powerhouse.

Young, I., 1990. The scaling of bodies and the politics of identity. *Justice and the politics of difference*. Princeton: Princeton University Press, 122–155.

Yuval-Davis, N., 1996. Women and the biological reproduction of 'the nation'. *Women's studies international forum*, 19 (1–2), 17–24.

Yuval-Davis, N. and Anthias, F., eds, 1989. *Woman-nation-state*. London: McMillan.

Ziarek, E., 2008. Bare life on strike: notes on the biopolitics of race and gender. *South Atlantic quarterly*, 107 (1), 89–105.

Medical aid as protest: acts of citizenship for unauthorized im/migrants and refugees

Heide Castañeda

Department of Anthropology, University of South Florida, 4202 East Fowler Avenue, SOC 107, Tampa, FL 33620-8100, USA

This article examines organized efforts by citizens to provide medical aid to unauthorized migrants in Germany. A case study of an activist organization in Berlin highlights how prevailing forms of governance through citizenship are disrupted. Three major themes are explored. First, historical contingencies and policy realities explain why, given examples of grassroots protest by migrants in other settings, efforts in Germany have been driven primarily by citizens. Second, migrants' biolegitimacy shapes specific ideas of relative deservingness. As a result, advocacy for some groups, such as survivors of torture or refugees from specific geopolitical settings, is more highly valued than that which addresses needs of unauthorized labor migrants. Finally, although their sustained efforts have resulted in challenges to policy and called into question prevailing notions of citizenship, medical activist organizations have become increasingly institutionalized, which may jeopardize their goals. As this case illustrates, the distinctive ethics associated with providing medical care has the ability to disrupt the scaling of citizenship by the state by treating noncitizens – especially 'illegal' noncitizens – ostensibly as citizens, thus protesting citizenship as the exclusive organizing principle of German society.

When Gabriela, a 19-year old unauthorized immigrant from Ecuador, became acutely ill and required an appendectomy, she says the first thing that crossed her mind was, 'Where can I go? Not the emergency room, like a normal person, that's for sure. You can end up getting deported that way.' Other family members had been to an organization that assists the uninsured – ostensibly unauthorized migrants, given Germany's system of universal health coverage – and suggested she go there for help. The organization was able to arrange the necessary surgery for Gabriela the next day using volunteer doctors in their network, with no cost and no paper trail. (fieldnotes and interview, 2009)

This article examines organized efforts to provide medical aid to unauthorized migrants like Gabriela. Because they cannot access treatment through regular channels, efforts spearheaded by citizens insure that some level of medical aid is available to them.

In this article, citizenship is understood not simply as legal membership in a state, but rather as a practice of claims-making in various sites and scales that create political subjectivity. A relational definition of citizenship emphasizes that it is a dynamic institution of both domination and empowerment, governing who is citizen, subject, and abject, and how these actors relate to one another in the body politic (Isin 2009). Here, I examine medical aid as an *act of citizenship* (Isin 2008) performed at the site, or field of contestation, of medical treatment. This is related to but also diverges in significant ways from other examinations of acts of citizenship performed by unauthorized migrants and refugees themselves that challenge norms about belonging and political community, contesting formal citizenship as a precondition for political voice (Nyers 2010). Instead, this article examines the disruption of the meaning of citizenship through acts of citizens on behalf of noncitizens.

These acts of citizenship are also acts, or protests, *against* citizenship, utilizing medical aid as a powerful form of dissent. As a 'protest against citizenship' (Derrida 1994, pp. 240–241), these citizens express solidarity with migrants beyond the traditional bounds of political community, and their revised notions of responsibility and resulting actions have the capacity to call into question the fundamentally exclusionary logic of citizenship as an authentic form of political subjectivity (Nyers 2004, p. 203). The medium of protest is medical aid in the face of state disinterest and restriction, with acts of dissent performed by citizen allies rather than migrants themselves. These acts express the desire to live in a just state, and is framed by what Downes (2004) refers to as a human rights discourse that 'regularly articulates a yearning for oneness that repeatedly displaces the ambiguities of democratic citizenship onto narratives of protection and intervention conducted by the free in the name of the bound' (p. 483).

In Germany's system of universal health coverage, as well as for other social services, legal status (but not national belonging) is a precursor for participation. Thus, lack of access to healthcare is a direct effect of exclusion resulting from the state's efforts at illegalization and criminalization. Germany's strict policy environment toward unauthorized migrants is unique in Europe (Laubenthal 2008), and is a combination of laws restricting most legal immigration and a distinct approach toward migrants already living in the country. Despite some positive signs in recent years, unauthorized migrants are not afforded adequate access to healthcare (Castañeda 2011a). Although technically they are entitled to emergency medical services based on provisions in the Asylum Seekers Benefits Act (§ 4 and 6), even these reduced services are often unavailable, since the Social Services Office that handles reimbursements is required by § 87.2 of the Foreigners Act to relay information to the authorities, which may lead to arrest and deportation. This requirement to report remains the central barrier to medical care and has been extensively criticized by human rights organizations.

Access to healthcare is uniquely suited to understanding the biopolitics of citizenship. Migrant 'illegality' is simultaneously a juridical status and a sociopolitical condition (De Genova 2002). Because they interact with poor living and labor conditions to foster increased susceptibility to ill health, these 'pathologizing politics of alienhood' are literally marked on the foreigner's body (Marciniak 2006, p. xiii). The health-related inequalities resulting from exclusion motivate activists to organize on migrants' behalf based on local configurations of legitimacy (Castañeda 2011a, Willen 2011).

This article examines the 'actual practices of intervention and advocacy, together with their potential contradictions, failures, and refusals' (Redfield 2005, pp. 348–349). I begin with a description of the organization founded and staffed by citizen activists that Gabriela visited to arrange her appendectomy, the Berlin Office of Medical Aid for Refugees. It is one of many similar organizations that conceptualize and practice medical aid as a form of protest. Emerging out of this brief case study,[1] I highlight through a series of themes how such practices disrupt prevailing forms of governance through citizenship, arguing that, while powerful, it may also be neither lasting nor complete. Given examples of grassroots protest by migrants and refugees in other settings, the German case is relatively unique in that its pro-migrant movements have been driven primarily by citizens, due to specific historical circumstances and policy preconditions. The distinctive ethics associated with providing medical care has the ability to disrupt the scaling of citizenship by the state by treating noncitizens – and especially 'illegal' noncitizens – ostensibly as citizens. As a consequence, the provision of medical care becomes a protest against citizenship as an exclusive organizing principle of German society.

Case study: the Berlin Office of Medical Aid for Refugees

> When Gabriela's abdominal pain sharpened and she developed a fever, she knew that she could not go to work that morning. She consulted her aunt, who suggested she go to the Berlin Office of Medical Aid for Refugees. Later that afternoon, her aunt and cousin helped her climb two flights of stairs in an old factory building. 'I couldn't walk by myself anymore,' she told me, 'I was buckled over the entire way up those stairs.'
>
> During the late 1970s and early 1980s, this building was one of a complex of squatted buildings in Berlin's Kreuzberg district. Today, it is a revitalized and colorful alternative center, housing collectively owned businesses, a bookstore, infoshop, bicycle shop, theater, pub, Turkish labor organization, and adult literacy program. In a dimly lit hallway, Gabriela and her family sat quietly on wooden chairs waiting for their turn. They thumbed through flyers and pamphlets advertising an anti-racist hotline, an HIV/AIDS support group, a battered women's shelter, a street art show. Finally, a young woman dressed casually in jeans, sweater, and scarf emerged and called for the next person in line. (fieldnotes and interview, 2009)

The Berlin Office of Medical Aid for Refugees, referred to by its nickname 'Berlin MediBüro' in the following sections, assists uninsured migrant patients in locating medical treatment. It is located in Berlin's Kreuzberg district, long considered the epicenter of counterculture and Germany's most prominent multicultural neighborhood. Historically a Turkish enclave, by the late 1960s it was 'already by definition transgressive of Germanness' and a 'space of creative nationalism' (Mandel 2008, p. 90). Open two afternoons a week, the MediBüro facilities consist of a single room located in the multipurpose complex. When patients enter, they are greeted by two volunteers sitting at a desk in an otherwise sparsely decorated room. Their casual dress is a marker that they are not in an authoritative role as medical providers; although they may in fact be doctors, nurses, or students in health professions, they will not be treating the patient right now, nor right here. The patient is invited to take a seat and discuss their complaint with the volunteers, whose role is to match patients to physicians willing to treat them free of charge. Patient anonymity is highly valued: no identification is required, and no records are kept beyond simple counts of symptoms reported and to whom the patient was referred. The lack of facilities to treat patients on-site is purposeful; the Berlin MediBüro attempts to insure equal access to care and opposes the creation of a parallel medical system that a dedicated clinic would imply.

The Berlin MediBüro was founded in 1996 with the goal of 'establishing a practical project and political initiative to combat the racist exclusion of refugees in social policy and regular health care' (Gross 2005, p. 20, my translation). Their work is guided by the principle that access to medical care should not be dependant on legal status. However, at an anniversary event I attended, far from being a joyous event, activists said that they felt they had failed because they had been unable to dismantle the organization. As one founder told me, 'we have been unsuccessful in abolishing ourselves'. This success-as-failure language is typical of many activist organizations (Schmidt 2009), since the ultimate goal is to provoke widespread change and make their efforts unnecessary.

From the very beginning, political advocacy and public awareness have been as integral to their work as practical medical support. The Berlin MediBüro is a part of larger, global anti-racist movements and identifies with the 'No One is Illegal' campaign (Gross and Bieniok 2011). In Germany, these movements emerged in the 1980s and solidified their presence in the mid-1990s, when an informal network of 25 offices called 'MediNetze' (medical networks) or 'MediBüros' (medical offices) were established. The first office was opened in Hamburg in 1994, followed by offices in Bonn and Berlin. They are all autonomous initiatives, loosely linked via personal networks and an annual gathering to coordinate efforts and share information. Each office differs in scope and services; for instance, the Bochum MediBüro also provides social and legal aid, as well as psychotherapy services (Medizinische Flüchtlingshilfe Bochum e.V. 2010).

Volunteers working with the Berlin MediBüro utilized its tenth anniversary to critically reflect upon its history (Büro für medizinische Flüchtlingshilfe 2006). During the early-to-mid 1990s, many groups on the Left faced an orientation crisis with the restructuring of socialist Europe. As part of this new course, groups chose to express their solidarity with refugees by opposing restrictive policies toward foreigners and counteracting increasingly prejudiced public sentiment. A concern with *Überfremdung* ('over-foreignization') had become a dominant discourse in public debates in Germany, and a wave of violence gripped the nation. Brutal attacks and arson strikes led to 17 deaths and 452 injuries in the cities of Hoyerswerda (1991), Rostock (1992), Mölln (1992), and Solingen (1993). Most xeno-racist violence occurred in the states of the former East Germany, where radical Right-wing parties had done especially well since reunification. Although revealing significant xenophobic attitudes in some sectors of German society, these events also provoked profound responses on the Left, including massive demonstrations and the establishment of anti-racist networks. As one practical form of assistance, activists in Berlin organized a system of 'security guards' (*Schutzwachen*) to accompany refugees and protect asylum homes.

At the time, refugees requested medical assistance from their German supporters, but this was initially dismissed by activists for being 'too unpolitical' and short-sighted. Their position reversed with the 1993 asylum law reform, which resulted in drastically reduced benefits for refugees and essentially established two different minimal standards of healthcare – one for residents and one for refugees. At this point, migrants' insistence that access to healthcare was their greatest area of concern began to be viewed in earnest, and a consensus was reached that this could be an effective way to engage with the politics of exclusion. Practical assistance in the form of medical aid thus became a way to establish solidarity with marginalized groups. Notably, unlike other forms of assistance, medical aid requires specialized training, as well as access to material and social resources, and thus can unlikely be provided by migrants themselves.

In 1995, the first organizational meetings were held but the project remained controversial: some argued that by going public, they put themselves, participating physicians, and migrants at risk, and jeopardized exposing clandestine network structures. Furthermore, founders considered that existing migrant networks might be functioning quite well, so that their attempts to set up assistance represented a problematic neocolonialist replacement of these structures (by white, German supporters). Another serious concern was the impact of a law (§ 96 of the Residence Act) stating that 'assisting' illegal persons – including for medical purposes, depending on interpretation – is a crime punishable with a fine or imprisonment up to 5 years. It was not until 2007 that the Ministry of the Interior clarified that medical personnel would not be held accountable under this law. However, for more than a decade, activists suspected that their efforts would attract the attention of the authorities. As a result, the Berlin MediBüro had an elaborate security system when it first opened, including an alarm button to notify staff if the police arrived to raid the facility along with a set of guards at the entrance. Indeed, the larger complex that houses their facilities was raided on at least one occasion in December 1999 as authorities sought members and alleged explosives belonging to the militant group Revolutionary Cells (*Revolutionäre Zellen*). However, over the years, MediBüro staff came to realize that fear of surveillance and repression of *their* work was unfounded. They were not being targeted for surveillance, and in some ways, suspicion was replaced by gratitude on behalf of state authorities, as I discuss below.

Most MediBüro volunteers have some professional experience as physicians, medical students, nurses, or social workers. As in other under-resourced autonomous groups (Wright 2003), volunteer continuity is a challenge, with the number of engaged individuals fluctuating between 10 and 30 at any time. Regular meetings to discuss specific cases and a bottom-up, acephalous organizational structure encourage that the organization's goals are kept in view. However, despite attempts to include them, migrants themselves have rarely been part of the organizational structure (more on this below). One founder also noted with some frustration that collaborators who had grown up in East Germany did not have the same 'intellectual background' as their West German colleagues, having been 'exposed to a very different educational system and political literature'. The organization has remained concerned about these challenges of representation.

Today, the Berlin MediBüro assists up to 1000 persons a year, who are referred to approximately 100 healthcare providers within its network (Gross and Bieniok 2011). Medical issues range from simple colds to pregnancy, vision problems, serious infections, deafness, malignant tumors, chronic joint pain, mental illnesses, and complex fractures. In the past, the majority of patients were of Latin American origin; their clientele has shifted over the years, with an increase in individuals from Eastern Europe. Many physicians in their network have begun to set limits (e.g., only two patients per month). Although it has a good working relationship with a local hospital, limits to services offered have had to be negotiated, e.g., no more than two patients per day or two births per month. Occasionally, one volunteer reported that they have received invoices from doctors, 'as if we were an alternative health insurance'. In these cases, they remind physicians that any services rendered are voluntary and any materials can be considered tax-deductible donations. Money is a factor in treating more complex illnesses and operations, in which case the Berlin MediBüro draws upon donations.[2] One founder told me that they are constantly 'operating at their limits' financially, but while some patients might be covered through government programs (technically, unauthorized persons are entitled to emergency medical services based on provisions in the Asylum Seekers Benefits Act § 4 and 6, and are also eligible for some services provided by public health departments), the Berlin MediBüro does not probe into issues of actual legal status or income level to make this determination, recognizing that other access barriers may exist, specifically, fear of being reported to the authorities.

Situating medical aid as protest: the mobilization of activist citizens

Pro-migrant movements and their campaigns, such as medical aid, provide an occasion for the critical reexamination of the privileges and practices of citizenship. Using the example of the Berlin MediBüro, the remainder of the article explores themes related to the refusal of citizenship viewed through the lens of medical need.

Social movement research has sought analytical models to explain the emergence of movements within particular contexts, commenting both on political opportunity structure

– that is, the specific features of national systems that can shape differences in the action repertoire of movements and in interaction with authorities (Tarrow 1996) – and on the importance of framing or the relevance of discursive factors for movement emergence (Snow and Benford 1988). Since the mid-1990s, unauthorized migrants in several European countries – most notably France, Spain, and Switzerland – have displayed collective action and robust pro-regularization movements. Notably, these protest efforts have required those people who are 'not supposed to exist' or 'do not count' to become political actors (Laubenthal 2007, Nyers 2010). A number of umbrella organizations arose in the late 1990s to channel these efforts, including No-one is Illegal *(Kein Mensch ist Illegal)* and the no border network, which hosts international bordercamps to strengthen solidarity by providing a 'laboratory of creative resistance' (Alldred 2003, Rigby and Schlembach this volume, Walters 2006). Strong networks and joint protests across borders have led some scholars to consider the transnational nature of this movement as an 'imagined community', despite a primacy of national-level interests (Guiraudon 2001, Uggla 2006). Different cultures of contention have emerged based on issues relevant for each country, ranging from wage disputes, unsafe working conditions, housing discrimination, or medical needs. Some organizations, such as the Platform for International Cooperation on Undocumented Migrants (PICUM), consultant to the European Union (EU) Commission, mediate between the grassroots and the policy level. These European-wide efforts directly question the notion of citizenship as linked to state-based identities, further emphasized by the fact that many issues have been directed at the EU – calling, for instance, for an 'open Europe' with removal of barriers to free movement as part of the regularization of unauthorized foreigners.

Within this larger movement, actions in Germany are interesting because they have relied more heavily on citizen activists rather than on noncitizens. Refugees and unauthorized migrants have been less likely to organize themselves in comparison to other settings (Laubenthal 2007). Some have argued that neighboring countries – such as France – have historically been more accepting of social movements than has Germany (Hartmann 1999). Germany lacks large communities from former colonies (unlike, e.g., France, the UK, or the Netherlands), resulting in dispersed public voice and less immediate base for political organizing. Another barrier is the legal restriction that forbids the formation of (formal) organizations if the majority of members are noncitizens.[3] In general, Germany's policy environment toward unauthorized migrants is considered the strictest in Europe (Laubenthal 2008, Hoff 2009). Particularly telling is the fact that residence without a valid permit is a felony, rather than a simple breach of administrative procedures. In addition, the Residence Act *(Aufenthaltsgesetz)* contains a section (§ 87), which imposes penalties for failure to report persons residing in Germany illegally.

Finally, the legacy of the Holocaust has resulted in a political culture shaped by a particularly profound ambivalence about the state's treatment of foreigners (Ellermann 2006). In recent history, the right to asylum held a special place in West German political life and in the consciousness of postwar society, and it is the only nation in the world to enshrine this right in its constitution. As noted earlier, the state severely limited the right to asylum in 1993, still considered the critical juncture of German immigration law. Today, although restrictive immigration policies are generally valued, there is occasional large-scale public resistance to their implementation. For instance, impending deportations are often met with grassroots resistance and media attention, and labor unions, once defiantly protectionist, have recently argued for both better management of skilled labor migration and the protection of rights for migrants with precarious residence status. Tolerance of minorities reflects positively on postwar, democratic Germany and is part of the 'heightened self-consciousness of German efforts to be seen as a "normal nation among nations"' (Mandel 2008, p. 13).

As a result of these historical contingencies and legal barriers, the majority of efforts consist of citizens acting on behalf of migrants. There are many qualified individuals willing to step in to provide medical care out of political conviction and humanitarian concern. Nevertheless, as noted earlier, they often lamented the fact that they were viewed as mere 'service providers' and that few migrants were willing to participate in decision-making and leadership roles within organizations. Despite consistent attempts to include them, they felt there was little interest, citing language, the voluntary nature of the work, the majority presence of Germans, and unfamiliar structures (especially acephalic committees) as barriers to participation. One Berlin MediBüro founder said they have continually attempted to include migrants in their structure, to no avail. Migrant collaborators would often volunteer at the biweekly office hours, but not attend planning meetings and did not always see eye-to-eye with some of the organization's activities. Although she attributed this to their different cultural backgrounds, she also noted that it appears to work well in other places, 'like France'. The place of unauthorized migrants in the politics of their own liberation and the proper role of citizen advocates representing and working on their behalf remain a central dilemma (Nyers 2003).

In addition, not all citizen activists share the same points of reference. Some efforts can be characterized as secular/activist while others are more faith based/charitable in orientation, based on philosophical foundations in either a human rights or a humanitarian orientation (Castañeda 2011a). The work of the Berlin MediBüro is firmly situated in the notion that health is a human right and it is openly acknowledged to be of more a symbolic character, since they are not neither capable nor intend to provide sufficient medical care for unauthorized migrants (Schmidt 2009, Verbruggen 2001). Their emphasis on integration into the regular system rather than on the creation of parallel structures is an important distinction from other humanitarian-based efforts in Berlin (Hoff 2009). Faith-based initiatives in Germany have championed the rights of refugees since the 1980s and are a natural source of assistance for people in need, often with sufficient resources and infrastructure to provide medical aid. Many of these efforts have grown out of the church asylum (*Kirchenasyl*) movement, which encourages parishes to harbor individuals facing deportation. In many large cities, medical clinics that run through faith-based organizations have been set up to specifically aid unauthorized migrants. Unlike activist organizations such as the Berlin MediBüro, they provide on-site treatment and have become increasingly professionalized. One example is the Catholic relief organization run by the Order of Malta, which runs the Berlin *Malteser Migranten Medizin* clinic and has recently expanded to include nine additional clinics in major cities.

There have been many attempts to bridge the two models described above and advocate jointly for migrants through umbrella organizations. However, each side also retains fundamental critiques of the other's approach. In Berlin, faith-based organizations fault activists for being 'too radical' in their calls for full inclusion of unauthorized migrants and refusing to dialog with the government for attainable solutions. Activist organizations, on the other hand, charge charity organizations with establishing a system of parallel or second-class medicine, keeping patient records that authorities could easily confiscate, colluding with the Church and other power structures, and not politicizing their activities. Ideological differences were generally characterized by participants in this study as 'political' versus 'pragmatic'.

Biolegitimacy and a 'hierarchy of aid work'

Beyond the tensions between the types of organizations offering medical aid, there is also differentiation based on the validity of the migrant body. One physician talked about this in the following way:

> You could say there is a hierarchy of aid work among us. At the very top are those who work with refugees who are victims of torture – they get lots of acknowledgment and respect. Then there are people who work with rejected asylum seekers. Finally, at the very bottom are those who work with the 'illegals.' Because of all the talk about 'economic migrants' they are not put on the same level as refugees, and people don't like to talk about them.

As this quote illustrates, social prestige and satisfaction is gained by providing support for the 'right' kinds of migrants, such as those who are traumatized or have fled geopolitical settings that evoke specific ideas of deservingness, e.g., Sudan or Cuba. These groups' implicit biolegitimacy (Fassin 2009) remains in stark contrast with the situation faced by labor migrants who are driven to leave their countries for less socially validated reasons, such as Gabriela and her family who arrived from Ecuador seeking work. In other words, although a focus on 'human' as opposed to simply 'citizen' rights frames the work of physicians, some bodies in need are viewed as more legitimate, more valued, or imbued with specific meanings compared with others.

At a physicians' conference I attended on the topic of medical aid for 'persons without papers', there was an interesting reaction to a scholar's overview on illegal labor migration to Germany. In his transition to the next speaker, one of the organizers (who works with refugees) noted that he 'was surprised to learn about all this...we usually only think of rejected asylum seekers when we talk about people without papers'. This comment led me to wonder if this was what most attendees considered people 'without papers'. Indeed, the majority of the conference presentations centered on political refugees (and e.g., the need for language-appropriate services for torture victims), rather than on labor migrants, who are more numerous and more blatantly without access to services. This value judgment reflects larger discussions on who, exactly, is considered a refugee: is someone facing political persecution a 'true' refugee, in contrast to those seeking economic opportunity?

A more recent phenomenon has been the influx of EU citizens from the newer member states, especially Poland and Romania. While permitted to travel freely, at the time of this study individuals from these states were not authorized to work in Germany because of transitional measures curbing access to national labor markets for 7 years. As a result, they faced many everyday forms of exclusion, including unequal relationships in the labor and housing markets and difficulties accessing medical care (Castañeda 2011b). Although not technically 'illegal', without health insurance coverage they regularly turned to organizations such as the Berlin MediBüro. However, at the same time, physicians in their network began to refuse these patients, erroneously believing that as EU citizens they surely must have access to the full range of healthcare services (Gross and Bieniok 2011).

Interpreting this hierarchy of 'appropriate' migrant bodies and the more or less legitimate responses to them aid requires context. Legitimacy depends on changing and historically produced notions of relative deservingness and emulates distinctions made between citizens, 'real' others, and 'other' others in different national settings (Willen 2010). Over the years, this has been evident in the contrast between not only guestworkers and ethnic German resettlers, but also between 'true refugees', especially asylum seekers, and unauthorized labor migrants, who are considered illegal felons at worst or 'economic refugees' at best. These forms of relative deservingness offer a powerful window into specific ideologies of inclusion and exclusion.

Further, to understand the conflation between 'refugees' and 'other' migrants, it is necessary to recall that the organized efforts of citizens described earlier were initially in response to severely restricted access to asylum and reduced benefits for political refugees. Since the mid-1990s, however, there has been a decrease in the number of asylum seekers and a concomitant increase in unauthorized labor migrants. With the calculated removal of legal entry options, especially asylum opportunities, unauthorized migration has increased. Nonetheless, debates over all forms of migration continue to be strongly linked to the topic of asylum. Today, a large number of Germany's unauthorized migrants are either (1) people who would have qualified as refugees before the 1993 change in asylum law; (2) rejected asylum seekers who decide to remain or (3) people who might qualify as refugees but, discouraged by the low approval rate, do not bother to apply (Castañeda 2010). Furthermore, neoliberal reforms since reunification have led to a high demand for flexible labor in certain sectors, especially construction, home healthcare, agriculture, and domestic fields. Some organizations and activists are perhaps still ambivalent about their role in providing assistance to these migrants, and may have not fully adjusted to the implications for their political missions. For example, the Berlin Office of Medical Aid for Refugees is now more frequently referred to as the Berlin MediBüro ('Medi-Office'); although the nickname is certainly less unwieldy, it also diminishes the specific focus on refugees.

Activists often refuse the distinction between 'economic' and 'political' refugees in order to highlight the causes of displacement globally, especially national and supranational economic policies, through an explicitly anticolonial perspective (Wright 2003). However, *refugee* is a category with a unique history and meaning in Germany. First, as noted earlier, the postwar state has enshrined the fundamental right to asylum in the constitution. This comparatively liberal policy attracted refugees from across the world, and the severe limitations produced by the 1993 revision provoked substantial debates about Germany's commitment to justice. Furthermore, although refusals to distinguish between refugees and unauthorized migrants indeed underscore the role of structural economic violence, it is important to note that refugees and asylum seekers have (limited, but guaranteed) access to healthcare. This distinction is crucial in understanding the distribution of rights and resources. Some activists interviewed felt that indiscriminate use of the term 'refugee' further delegitimized the unique forms of suffering for those who had experienced forced migration due to political violence. Finally, I desire to challenge the implicit assumption that all unauthorized migrants desire to legalize themselves, especially through the mechanism of asylum. That process involves subjugation to the German regime of legality, surveillance, and often sustained deportability, without the options for work and freedom of movement that staying 'invisible' permits (Castañeda 2010). This is part of the dual nature of citizenship, as 'both domination and empowerment separately or simultaneously' (Isin 2009, p. 369). Ultimately, most unauthorized labor migrants in the German setting do not view the concept of 'refugee' as interchangeable with their situation, although many are keenly aware of the benefits associated with refugee status.

Co-optation and institutionalization?

The MediBüro organizations described here have positioned themselves as overtly antagonistic toward the state and its policies, with the goal of challenging existing power structures. However, some have suggested that organizations providing medical aid to vulnerable populations play a 'convenient role' in the EU (Romero-Otuño 2004). Thus, while organizations purport to defend the rights of the disenfranchised, an equally persuasive argument is that they essentially protect national institutions by shouldering the costs so that the state is not encouraged to change anything.

The citizen activists from the Berlin MediBüro openly recognize this dilemma. In interviews, staff noted that they have become (or are becoming) 'Lückenbüsser', which translates as 'stopgaps', for the social welfare system. They have always wanted to 'avoid becoming mere humanitarians', as one of the founders told me. As they themselves note, 'the threat of falling into the "stopgap trap" is immanent to our project and is continually, heatedly debated' (Gross and Bieniok 2011, my translation). One of the founders – no longer active with the organization – said the situation became

> ... too frustrating. The goal was always to create change – change policy and change the way things are done. But years later, they're still doing the same thing and nothing has changed! If anything, the laws are getting stricter and they are just legitimizing them.

As noted earlier, the initial fear of repression and surveillance was not realized in the case of the Berlin MediBüro, which had initially set up an elaborate early warning system to notify staff if the police were to arrive. Quite the contrary, their efforts have been used overtly to discourage state responsibility. In an official statement, politician Barbara John (of the center-right CDU party) argued that because such aid was being provided, there was 'no need for the government administration to intervene, thus effectively relinquishing her office from any further responsibility in the matter' (Verbruggen 2001). Consider also the following quote from an activist working with the Berlin MediBüro:

> As it turns out, the State offices were quite satisfied when we set up. The repression and surveillance we had feared at the beginning never happened and over time, more and more State offices started to rely on the availability of medical aid through [our Office]. Here we were, critiquing their policies, demanding change, and they were actually referring people to us for treatment! We even started receiving Christmas cards from them, thanking us for our efforts!

Despite this institutionalization, the organization continues to struggle for an abolishment of the parallel structures of which it has became part, as activists continually reshape the movement in response to various events. Public and political awareness has increased through organized summits, reports by entities such as the German Institute for Human Rights, and sustained pressure on politicians at the municipal levels. In recent years, the Berlin MediBüro has successfully engaged government officials in debate, leading to policy changes. These include longer and more favorable temporary residency permits for pregnant unauthorized women; an official statement regarding the legal situation for hospitals and doctors, clarifying that neither are required to pass information on to the authorities; clarification that physicians will not be held liable for treating unauthorized patients (as a result, inpatient treatment for emergency care is now possible); and continuing talks regarding the implementation of an anonymized insurance card as a solution that does not rely on a parallel system of care (Gross and Bieniok 2011, Misbach et al. 2009). However, experiences from Berlin have shown that despite political will, finding adequate solutions is difficult. Even through these successes, activists worry about further bureaucratization and distraction from the 'real issues', recognizing that the more they engage with local political structures, the less they are able to criticize them.

Discussion

This article has presented a case in which the medium of immigrant protest is medical aid, an everyday act of citizenship for physicians and other German supporters. According to

Isin (2008), acts of citizenship can be interpreted according to three principles. First, their grounds and consequences must be examined in order to arrive at an interpretation of subjects becoming activist citizens. An 'activist' citizen is contrasted with 'active' citizens, where the former are creative in writing scripts and creating scenes, while the latter follow scripts and participate in scenes already created (2008, p. 36). The case presented here described medical professionals who are not only active citizens but also activist citizens and who create new interactions and attempt to transform the meaning of citizenship altogether. Second, theorizing acts of citizenship recognizes that the acts produce actors answerable to justice against injustice. In the sections above, justice is invoked in the form of right to medical care, as well as through the actors' explicit rejection of the language of 'illegality' and utilization of the term 'refugee' to describe many varieties of exclusion. Notably, unlike other examples of such social movements, efforts in Germany do not focus on pro-regularization campaigns. The goal is not the acquisition of formal citizenship (via regularization or naturalization) but of substantive citizenship (Isin 2008); in this case, social rights and access to medical care. The final principle for interpreting acts of citizenship is the recognition that they do not need to be founded in law, nor enacted in the name of law; 'to be acts at all they must call the law into question and they may, sometimes, break it' (Isin 2009, p. 382). In the case presented here, the provision of medical aid is often portrayed as potentially illegal, and it is physicians' willingness to break the law that creates effective protest. These powerful forms of dissent go beyond what might on the surface appear to be the regular lobbying efforts by civil society, and are instead potentially transformative as a 'protest against citizenship'.

This case is unique because dissent is performed by citizens motivated to step in on behalf of noncitizens; here, subjects claim rights not for themselves, but for others. As Nyers notes, 'citizens can speak with an assured voice and assume an audience within civil society (2010, p. 141)', whereas unauthorized migrants cannot. These activist citizens are more than simply supporters or allies; their citizenship status allows for a powerful refusal of governance by those privileged enough to be included. However, alliances between citizens and noncitizens are also contradictory. Relationships of medical aid necessarily create relationships of dependency, and migrants are rarely active agents in this form of protest. The central dilemma of representation remains; Nyers asks, 'Should advocates relate to non-status immigrants as clients or allies? Should they speak on behalf of the non-status or in conversation with them?… What place is there for abject migrants in the politics of their own liberation?' (2003, p. 1081) In the case presented here, historical factors and a uniquely strict policy environment limit the place for migrants themselves but motivate others to speak for them.

For physicians, these are small and ordinary acts of resistance, since they do not entail radical action but an extension of their professional duties – only, directed at individual bodies designated as 'illegal'. Physicians become a particular variety of 'moral spectator' (Redfield 2005), combining prestige and social status with the capacity for public intervention. The distinctive ethics associated with providing medical care has the ability to disrupt the scaling of citizenship by the state by treating 'illegals' ostensibly as citizens. Medicine – like illness to which it responds – makes no distinction between citizen and noncitizen, but simply between an ailing body and a whole body. As a consequence, the provision of medical care to this population is a protest against citizenship as fundamental organizational structure of German society. The emphatic acknowledgment of a common humanity through bodily experience challenges legally prescribed borders between citizen and migrant.

However, although these acts have the capacity to function as a catalyst for social transformation, they may also fail to produce citizens or effect long-term change. For the most part, as this case study has illustrated, these are contestations of citizenship at the local, rather than at the national level (Gross and Bieniok 2011). Such short-term, localized strategies are embedded in a historically particular ideological environment that simultaneously condemns yet relies upon 'illegal' immigration. The general absence of debates on unauthorized migrants in Germany hints that no major improvements related to their healthcare exclusion can be expected anytime soon (Laubenthal 2008).

Nonetheless, these activist citizens dynamically structure the terms of debate – or refashion the scene (Isin 2008) – by emphasizing the right to medical aid through their acts, by bringing awareness to the issue, and even by critically examining their role in reproducing the structures they are attempting to replace. These sustained efforts allow them to, on some level, challenge their own complicity by questioning shared constructs of citizenship. It is a step in the process of inventing new forms of subjectivity and connection, perhaps even of 'resubjectification in a way that does not reproduce the paradoxes of sovereign power' Nyers (2004, p. 214). For a moment, the meaning of this framework is disrupted by, for example, the surgery provided to Gabriela, the young woman from Ecuador. There are no clear traces of her as a patient at the hospital, where she remembers the kindness of the nurses who assisted her after the surgery and the Berlin MediBüro volunteer who helped to arrange it. Gabriela returned to her job cleaning houses a few short weeks after her appendectomy. Her life and body back to 'normal', she likely would not have recognized the powerful yet intimate protest the event provoked. These protests by citizens have the effect of opening new possibilities and generating new political subjectivities, rather than simply representing 'moral pleas' for more humanitarian treatment of migrants (Nyers 2010). 'Without such creative breaks', Isin (2008, p. 18) writes, 'it is impossible to imagine social transformation or to understand how subjects become citizens as claimants of justice, rights, and responsibilities'.

Notes

1. This paper draws upon ethnographic data collected in Berlin, including participant observation in a clinic serving unauthorized migrants, interviews with migrants, physicians who treat them, and volunteer staff from 24 organizations. Information on the Berlin Office of Medical Aid for Refugees' history is derived from interviews with five women working with this organization over the past 14 years and supplemented by a report written by the organization. The information was also reviewed by two participants who provided helpful feedback on an earlier version of the article. Finally, I systematically collected and archived German-language media coverage on unauthorized migration between 2004 and 2011.
2. Although there are a variety of donation drives, two are worth mentioning here. First, the left-leaning daily newspaper *Die Tageszeitung* (or *taz,* as it is known) regularly publishes articles on undocumented persons and deportation scandals, and often includes information on donating to the Berlin MediBüro. A second source of donations is '*Soli-Partys*' (solidarity parties) in which proceeds go to a particular cause.
3. Paragraph 92 abs 1 Nr 7 AuslG.

References

Alldred, P., 2003. No borders, no nations, no deportations. *Feminist review*, 73 (1), 152–157.
Büro für medizinische Flüchtlingshilfe, 2006. *10 Jahre Büro für medizinische Flüchtlingshilfe – Eine Erfolgsgeschichte?* Berlin: Büro für medizinische Flüchtlingshilfe.
Castañeda, H., 2010. Deportation deferred: 'illegality,' visibility, and recognition in contemporary Germany. *In*: N. de Genova and N. Peutz, eds. *The deportation regime: sovereignty, space, and the freedom of movement.* Durham: Duke University Press, 245–261.
Castañeda, H., 2011a. Medical humanitarianism and physicians' organized efforts to provide aid to unauthorized migrants in Germany. *Human organization*, 70 (1), 1–10.

Castañeda, H., 2011b. Effects of transitional measures associated with EU integration on medical care access for Central and Eastern European migrants in Germany. *Anthropological journal of European cultures*, 20 (2), 68–86.

De Genova, N.P., 2002. Migrant 'illegality' and deportability in everyday life. *Annual reviews of Anthropology*, 31, 419–447.

Derrida, J., 1994. Nietzsche and the machine: interview with Jacques Derrida by Richard Beardsworth. *Journal of Nietzsche studies*, 7, 7–66.

Downes, P., 2004. Melville's Benito Cereno and the politics of humanitarian intervention. *The South Atlantic quarterly*, 103 (23), 465–487.

Ellermann, A., 2006. Street-level democracy: how immigration bureaucrats manage public opposition. *West European Politics*, 29 (2), 293–309.

Fassin, D., 2009. Another politics of life is possible. *Theory, culture, and society*, 26 (5), 44–60.

Gross, J., 2005. *Möglichkeiten und Grenzen der medizinischen Versorgung von Patienten und Patientinnen ohne legalen Aufenthaltsstatus*. Berlin: Flüchtlingsrat Berlin e.V, Büro für medizinsche Flüchtlingshilfe Berlin, PRO ASYL, IPPNW Deutschland.

Gross, J. and Bieniok, M., 2011. Büro für medizinische Flüchtlingshilfe Berlin – Praktische Erfahrungen und politische Lösungsansätze. *In*: M. Mylius, W. Schmalz, A. Frewer, *et al.* eds. *Medizin für Menschen ohne legalen Aufenthaltsstatus. Menschenrechte und Ethik in der Praxis des deutschen Gesundheitssystems. Medizin und Menschenrechte*, Band 4. Göttingen: V & R Unipress.

Guiraudon, V., 2001. Weak weapons of the weak? Transnational mobilization around migration in the European Union. *In*: D. Imig and S. Tarrow, eds. *Contentious Europeans: protest and politics in an emerging polity*. Lanham: Rowman & Littlefield, 163–185.

Hartmann, B., 1999. *Illegal in Berlin. Momentaufnahmen aus der Bundeshauptstadt*. Berlin: Erzbischöflichen Ordinariat Berlin.

Hoff, B.-I., 2009. Gesundheitliche Versorgungen von Menschen ohne Aufenthaltsstatus in Berlin. *In*: T. Borde, M. David and I. Papies-Winkler, eds. *Lebenslage und gesundheitliche Versorgung von Menschen ohne Papiere*. Frankfurt am Main: Mabuse, 35–67.

Isin, E.F., 2009. Citizenship in flux: the figure of the activist citizen. *Subjectivity*, 29, 367–388.

Isin, E.F., 2008. Theorizing acts of citizenship. *In*: E.F. Isin and G.M. Nielsen, eds. *Acts of citizenship*. New York: Zed Books, 15–43.

Laubenthal, B., 2007. The emergence of pro-regularisation movements in Western Europe. *International migration*, 45 (3), 101–133.

Laubenthal, B., 2008. *Two steps forward, one step back: recent trends in German migration policy*. Rome: CeSPI Country Paper.

Mandel, R., 2008. *Cosmopolitan anxieties: Turkish challenges to citizenship and belonging in contemporary Germany*. Durham: Duke University Press.

Marciniak, K., 2006. *Alienhood: citizenship, exile, and the logic of difference*. Minneapolis: University of Minnesota Press.

Medizinische Flüchtlingshilfe Bochum e.V, 2010. *Jahresbericht 2010*. Bochum: Medizinische Flüchtlingshilfe Bochum e.V.

Misbach, E., Bartholome, B. and Groß, J., 2009. Integration in die Regelversorgung statt Entwicklung weiterer Parallelsysteme: eine aktuelle Perspektive für Berlin? *In*: C. Falge, A. Fischer-Lescano and K. Sieveking, eds. *Gesundheit in der Illegalität. Rechte von Menschen ohne Aufenthaltsstatus*. Baden-Baden: Nomos, 81–87.

Nyers, P., 2004. Introduction: what's left of citizenship? *Citizenship studies*, 8 (3), 203–215.

Nyers, P., 2003. Abject cosmopolitanism: the politics of protection in the anti-deportation movement. *Third world quarterly*, 24 (6), 1069–1093.

Nyers, P., 2010. No one is illegal between city and nation. *Studies in social justice*, 4 (2), 127–143.

Redfield, P., 2005. Doctors, borders, and life in crisis. *Cultural anthropology*, 20 (3), 328–361.

Romero-Otuño, R., 2004. Access to health care for illegal immigrants in the EU: should we be concerned? *European journal of health law*, 11, 245–272.

Rigby, J. and Schlembach, R., Impossible protest: noborders in calais. this volume.

Schmidt, S., 2009. Gesundheitliche Versorgung von Papierlosen in Deutschland aus Sicht der Medizinischen Flüchtlingshilfen. *In*: C. Falge, A. Fischer-Lescano and K. Sieveking, eds. *Gesundheit in der Illegalität. Rechte von Menschen ohne Aufenthaltsstatus*. Baden-Baden: Nomos, 63–80.

Snow, D.A. and Benford, R.D., 1988. Ideology, frame resonance, and participant mobilization. *International social movement research*, 1, 197–217.

Tarrow, S., 1996. States and opportunities: the political structuring of social movements. *In*: D. McAdam, *et al.* eds. *Comparative perspectives on social movements. Political opportunities, mobilizing structures, and cultural framings*. Cambridge: Cambridge University Press, 41–61.

Uggla, F., 2006. Between globalism and pragmatism: ATTAC in France, Germany, and Sweden. *Mobilization: an international quarterly*, 11 (1), 51–66.

Verbruggen, N. ed., 2001. *Health care for undocumented migrants: Germany, Belgium, the Netherlands, United Kingdom*. Antwerp: PICUM: Platform for International Cooperation on Undocumented Migrants.

Walters, W., 2006. No border: games with(out) frontiers. *Social Justice*, 33 (1), 21–39.

Willen, S.S., 2010. Citizens, 'real' others, and 'other' others: governmentality, biopolitics, and the deportation of undocumented migrants from Tel Aviv. *In*: N. de Genova and N. Peutz, eds. *The deportation regime: sovereignty, space, and the freedom of movement*. Durham: Duke University Press.

Willen, S.S., 2011. Do 'illegal' im/migrants have a 'right to health?' Engaging ethical theory as social practice at a Tel Aviv open clinic. *Medical anthropology quarterly*, 25 (3), 303–330.

Wright, C., 2003. Moments of emergence: organizing by and with undocumented and non-citizen people in Canada after September 11. *Refuge*, 21 (3), 5–15.

Gagging orders: asylum seekers and paradoxes of freedom and protest in liberal society

Deirdre Conlon[a] and Nick Gill[b]

[a]Department of Sociology and Urban Studies, Saint Peter's University, Jersey City, NJ, USA;
[b]Department of Geography, College of Life and Environmental Sciences, University of Exeter, Exeter, UK

The detention of non-status migrants is now commonplace in developed countries. Detention has been justified on such grounds as security, the welfare of non-status migrant populations, and as a way to speed up processing asylum claims. Drawing from the artist Krzysztof Wodiczko's sustained interest in themes of migration and belonging, this article examines the relationships between technologies of government in detention and accommodation facilities, and the possibilities and constraints of protest that these settings and practices give rise to. The analysis highlights paradoxes of freedom as well as opportunities for protest that imbue these spaces. Using Foucault's discussion of technologies of government, we draw on empirical research to highlight how orientation booklets, classes, and legal self-representation manuals are technologies that compel asylum seekers to become ideal detainees in hopes of being understood as 'liberal subjects' worthy of inclusion in a small number of evermore tightly policed Western European states. We conclude with the suggestion that asylum seekers' paradoxical encounters with technologies of liberal government deliver a challenge to the accepted framework of citizenship within liberal societies.

Introduction

Burchell (1996) defines the key liberal problem space of government as follows: liberal thinkers have long held that government should be held in check so as to minimize the economic inefficiencies and socially undesirable consequences of an over-bearing state. A challenge arises, however, because the market – understood by liberal thinkers as a 'natural' result of the absence of government – turns out to be profoundly artificial. It requires that individuals conduct themselves in ways that are entrepreneurial and develop habits that secure the survival of 'the market' through conduct such as 'saving and providentialism [. . .] cleanliness, sobriety, fidelity, self-improvement, responsibility and so on' (Burchell 1996, p. 26). The dilemma of liberal government, then, is to develop ways to maintain individual freedom, on the one hand, since the state should be limited, but, on the other hand, guarantee that autonomous individuals play their part in reproducing the less-than-natural market system. Liberalism is, therefore, best understood as a problem and 'not a theory, an ideology, a juridical philosophy of individual freedom, or any particular set of policies adopted by government' (Burchell 1996, p. 21). To understand liberal government and society, we need to appreciate that their relationship is constructed around the central dilemma of 'what techniques, what procedures, what regulations and laws' (Burchell 1996, p. 25) are most effective in producing a society that must, at once, be governed and a partner in its own governing. As described by Foucault (1991), this delicate task gives rise to the practice of 'the art of government'. Liberal societies, for their part, can be interpreted as the outcome of a long history of attempts and experiments to fine-tune the techniques or technologies of government that constitute this art.[1]

The delicate nature of the compromise between rules and self-rule that has emerged renders liberal societies sensitive to outsiders. What has been painstakingly calibrated as a detailed apparatus of techniques of liberal government suitable for one population may not be fitting for another. Immigrants, therefore, represent a threat to such liberal governments because they hold the possibility of disrupting liberal society. They may be less susceptible to the technologies of government that produce characteristics required for the members of liberal society or they may be unschooled in liberal values and expectations. It should come as no surprise, then, that Western European states police their meticulously constructed societies with elaborate 'initiation' procedures, designed, on the one hand, to screen those who are not suitable to the liberal order and, on the other hand, to train others in the appropriate modes of conduct that liberal societies expect and depend upon. Building upon the work of several scholars who detail these screenings, trainings, and 'responsibilizing strategies' (Inda 2006, p. 40, see also Nevins 2002, Sales 2002, Pyykkönen 2007, Mountz 2010), this article is concerned with the experiences of migrants who undergo such initiations into 'liberal' society. Consonant with this special issue's focus on immigrant protest, we highlight how this induction into liberal society also invites protest in the form of critique and questioning the rules and the art of government. We argue that through this process, migrants expose conceits and paradoxes of the liberal order in ways that call into question the freedoms and 'rights' of all citizens in liberal society.

Figure 1. Krzysztof Wodiczko *Mouthpiece* [Porte Parole] 1995. Operated by Boubacar Diallo & Vu-Thi-Hau, Helsinki, Finland. © Krzysztof Wodiczko. Courtesy Galerie Lelong, New York.

Apropos of the dilemma migrants present within this context, the artist Krzysztof Wodiczko's *Mouthpiece (Porte Parole)* vividly portrays the paradoxical predicaments that migrants confront and also lay bare in liberal societies. Wodiczko, a Polish-born, US-based artist, has long been concerned with the political and relational dynamics that mark immigrants as outsiders in Europe and the USA. His projects include projections on monuments and in public spaces such as *The Tijuana Projection* (2001) and *Sans Papiers* (2002) as well as performative interventions that engage the members of the public in urban spaces such as *Xenology: Immigrant Instruments* (1992).[2] Wodiczko's work deals with the ambiguous place that migrants occupy as socially invisible strangers who, nonetheless, fulfill vital roles in western societies as well as the equivocations between curiosity and suspicion that migrants encounter. Connected with these concerns, Wodiczko examines questions of citizenship and alienhood in contemporary society (see Deutsche 2002, Wodiczko 2009, Marciniak and Turowski 2011).

Our deliberations resonate with Wodiczko's *Mouthpiece (Porte Parole)*, which is part of the *Xenology: Immigrant Instruments* series. This series began in the early 1990s coinciding with an outbreak of xenophobia that has been recurrent across Europe and the USA ever since. The *Mouthpiece (Porte Parole)* evolved from an earlier instrument, *Alien Staff (1992)*, which is a technological tool – literally a staff – into which photographs and recorded narratives that represent the immigrant's story are programmed. The immigrant carries the staff around with them in public, inviting attention and the possibility of dialog with strangers. Like Alien Staff, the *Mouthpiece (Porte Parole)* is a technological instrument designed to mediate and facilitate communication between immigrants and non-immigrants; it is distinguished from the former because, as a kind of prosthesis, the mouthpiece is worn on the body and, as such, the technology is integrated with the immigrant's body and becomes integral to their identity and visibility (Figure 1). Wodiczko describes the *Mouthpiece (Porte Parole)* as:

> A device that attaches directly to the face of the immigrant, as an extension of their body. [The] object encircles the jaw with a small video monitor and loud speakers placed directly over the wearer's mouth, showing the lips moving in sync to the prerecorded narrative. [Its function is] to empower those who are deprived of power. It is designed to replace the hesitations and fearful silence of an immigrant's personal voice with a fully formed version of the immigrant's story. It functions both as a conduit of one's voice and image as well as a gag that blocks the mouth and prevents the individual from speaking freely. (Wodiczko 1996)

Like several other of Wodiczko's 'instrumentation' projects, the *Mouthpiece (Porte Parole)* engages politics, technology, and public audiences in everyday urban spaces. Between 1994 and 1997, immigrants, refugees, and other displaced individuals wore variants of this mouthpiece in seven European cities including Amsterdam, Warsaw, and Paris. These performative events took place at sites and situations not typically associated with the presence of migrants and thus represented visual and political interruptions to public perception and space (Wodiczko 1999). The artist explains that the mouthpiece is both strange and fascinating; as an esthetic, it marks difference and simultaneously invites curiosity and attention. It is intended to give immigrants 'a possibility of developing their capacity to speak [a]nd also for [those] who are strangers to them to become close and to open their ears without so much fear, out of curiosity and entertainment' (Wodiczko 2009, p. 10). In other words, in addition to enabling the immigrant to speak, in a kind of way, the instrument is intended to inspire an exchange between strangers and thus to cross social, political, and semantic boundaries despite the strangeness of the device and the unfamiliarity of such an encounter.

The politics and esthetics of the *Mouthpiece (Porte Parole)* provoke reflection on several aspects of immigrant encounters with liberal society, understood in Burchell's sense, and with our research, which focuses on the situations that asylum seekers navigate in their initiation into the liberal order. The device allows the immigrant to speak but not with his or her own voice; instead, they speak through the technology in a way that makes the individual legible to non-immigrant interlocutors. In this sense, the instrument exposes a paradoxical freedom; it liberates the individual by allowing them to speak yet their speech is also constrained by the device. The *Mouthpiece (Porte Parole)* thereby symbolizes a contradiction between assertions of the right to free speech – common in liberal society – and immigrants' experiences. It also identifies the potential to resolve this contradiction by empowering immigrants, in a certain way.

Although Wodiczko's project uses material and digital forms of technology, in this article, we draw on Michel Foucault's concept of 'technologies of government' to highlight how asylum seekers are encouraged to be 'free' in specific ways (Rose 1999). Technologies of government include procedures and practices as well as specific tools such as diaries, interviews, manuals, and brochures that form an ensemble through which governmental power is materialized. From empirical research with asylum seekers residing in detention centers in the UK and accommodation centers in the Irish Republic,[3] we note that asylum seekers are under pressure to produce themselves as 'liberal subjects'. These pressures come in the form of techniques and procedures through which asylum seekers may come to apprehend the necessity of conducting themselves in ways that accord with the expectations of citizenship within liberal society. Akin to the *Mouthpiece (Porte Parole)*, we argue that the technologies that operate within residential centers for asylum seekers expose paradoxes of freedom, constraint, and protest embedded within technologies of government and in liberal society more broadly.

The *Mouthpiece (Porte Parole)* is comprised of a small video monitor that barely covers the speaker's lips yet the apparatus encircles the speaker's mouth and jaw. This 'forces viewers to come close to the user's face in order to see the image of the speaking lips and to hear the voice clearly' (Wodiczko 1999, p. 118). This technology thus empowers the immigrant to speak but becoming audible demands proximity. In this manner, the characteristics of the device are intended to encourage closer contact between immigrants and non-immigrants. In an exchange, it is hoped that the non-immigrant – as much as the immigrant – confronts the process of subjection and the contradictions this entails. As a result, each party encounters the strangeness, limits, and commonalities of their respective subject positions. The intention here is not only to increase familiarity between migrant and non-migrant subject positions, it is also to demonstrate that the immigrant's position – what he or she experiences, sees, and voices – has the potential to interrupt the order of things. Wodiczko notes that his instrumentation projects invoke the ancient practice of *parrhesia* where those without citizenship exercise a kind of fearless speech (2009, p. 11). As a tool in this process, the *Mouthpiece (Porte Parole)* empowers migrants, giving them the possibility to 'disrupt and make a scandal [. . .] and [to] make us think and feel [perhaps] for the first time that something is profoundly wrong' (Wodiczko 2009, p. 14).

This resonates with a facet of Foucault's discussion of the 'art of government' (1991), namely the interrelated concepts of counter-conduct and critical attitudes, wherein subjects invoke a right to question how they are governed. As we will see further on, and as Foucault argues, this right inheres within liberal government. From our research on asylum seekers' experiences in residential centers, we highlight some of the ways migrants speak freely as they become versed in liberal self-government. We view such actions that simultaneously enact and critique such conduct as forms of protest that demonstrate migrant autonomy, understood as action that 'confounds systems of [social] political and economic control' (Walters 2008, p. 189). These practices illuminate paradoxes of freedom and protest that are immanent with liberal government and also invite a broader critique of understandings of citizenship in liberal society.

The analysis begins at the early stages of the asylum process with an examination of orientation booklets received by asylum seekers as they are 'dispersed' to accommodation centers. These booklets espouse liberal values as they guide asylum seekers self-conduct toward 'suitable' and 'acceptable' uses of their freedom. Following this, we turn attention to educational classes that are frequently available for individuals in these centers. We examine staff perspectives on how these classes help to train asylum seekers as reflective entrepreneurs of the self. Finally, we examine self-representation notebooks. These are a legal orientation tool, developed by non-governmental organizations, to guide asylum seekers through processes including the asylum claim, interview, appeal, and bail-hearing procedures. We highlight how technologies such as these expose paradoxes of freedom, constraint, and protest as they produce responsible, liberal, and autonomous asylum seeker subjects. The conclusion draws on recent critical attention to the intersections between migration, security, and citizenship (De Genova 2007, Isin and Nielsen 2008, Lister 2008, Walters 2008, Tyler 2010) to examine the implications of asylum seekers' initiation into and protests against liberal government for understanding how citizenship is limited in liberal society. Linking Imogen Tyler's (2010) observations about how citizenship is designed to produce a range of precarious subjects to experiences in accommodation and detention centers, we argue that asylum seekers act autonomously to disrupt, destabilize, and also potentially transform notions of liberal citizenship. In this respect, asylum seekers' actions echo Wodiczko's views about his role as an artist who creates conditions where migrants and non-migrants can cross boundaries and may recognize one another's 'common strangeness' (1999, p. 120) and where migrants 'critical speech activity' (2009, p. 11) along with related forms of protest, highlight the potential for moments of interruption that can alter how each one of us is governed through citizenship in liberal society.

Secure facilities in Ireland and the UK

In examining the ways in which asylum seekers are invited, coaxed, and encouraged to adopt the habits and conducts of good and proper citizens as well as the challenges and opportunities this poses for protest, we draw on research with asylum seeker communities in Ireland and the UK. Although these are distinct geographical and political contexts, there are a number of overlaps related to the demographics of asylum as well as parallel policies and practices of government.

Asylum and detention in Ireland

Until the mid-1990s, the number of asylum seekers arriving in Ireland was relatively small with fewer than 100 applications received annually [Refugee Integration Agency (RIA) 2009]. Between 1996 and 2004, there was a significant increase in the number of applications for asylum in Ireland; asylum requests peaked at 11,364 in 2002. Since then, coinciding with the reversal of constitutionally enshrined birthright citizenship provisions

Table 1. Time spent in direct provision system in Ireland.

Time in direct provision system	Number of residents total = 6674*	Percentage of total number of residents
3 + years	2156	32%
2–3 years	1248	19%
1–2 years	1623	24%
Less than 1 year	1590	24%

*Total as of October 2009.
Source: www.ria.gov.ie

in 2004 (see White and Gilmartin 2008, Conlon 2010) as well as the tumultuous freefall of Ireland's economy in recent years, the number of asylum applications has declined considerably.

In general, Ireland's policies and provisions for asylum seekers mimic those instituted in the UK. For example, following on the heels of UK policy, in 2000, when the number of asylum seekers arriving in the Irish state began to increase, a program of 'direct provision' and housing dispersal was implemented. Direct provision means that individuals whose asylum claims are pending are provided board and meals in what are referred to as 'accommodation centers'; these include former nursing homes and convents, hostels, a caravan park, and a former holiday camp. The centers are semi-secure residential spaces where asylum seekers must sign in with management staff daily; they are also required to eat meals at scheduled times but, in general, they are free to have visitors during the day and to come and go independently. However, prohibitions on employment, restrictions on participating in third-level education, combined with a meager allowance of €19.10 per week,[4] and living in isolated rural locations mean that asylum seekers' freedoms are, in effect, quite curtailed. Over half of those living in accommodation centers remain there for over 2 years. Consequently, as Table 1 indicates, even though asylum applications have declined in recent years, the number of asylum seekers living in accommodation centers has actually increased.

Currently in Ireland, there are no dedicated immigration detention centers for 'non-status' migrants and, if detained, asylum seekers are held in one of nine prison facilities in the country. Although the detention of asylum seekers remains comparatively rare in Ireland, it is expected to increase with current government proposals to overhaul and streamline immigration enforcement and securitization (O'Halloran 2010).[5] With this, the Irish state is poised to follow the UK and other European states in instituting detention as routine policy for a range of non-status migrants.

Detention in the UK

Like Ireland, the UK also operates a system of dispersal and direct provision for asylum seekers; this system has been in place since early 2000.[6] In contrast to Ireland, however, the use of detention centers for asylum seekers and other non-status migrants has been commonplace in the UK for several years. Detention centers facilitate the incarceration of men, women, and children without trial, often for indefinite periods, in prison-like conditions. The capacity to detain asylum seekers in the UK increased rapidly from 250 in 1993 to over 2500 in 2005 (Bacon 2005). As Table 2 illustrates, most European Union (EU) states have established maximum limits over the length of time asylum seekers can be detained. The UK stands out among EU states, however, because no such limit exists.

Table 2. Limits for periods of detention in select EU-states.

EU state	Limits for periods of detention
France, Cyprus	32 days
Italy, Spain	40 days
Ireland	56 days
Portugal	60 days
Greece, Luxembourg	3 months
Hungary, Czech Republic, Slovakia, Slovenia, Romania	6 months
Belgium	8 months
Austria	10 months
Poland	12 months
Germany, Malta	18 months
Latvia	20 months
UK, Sweden, Denmark, Finland, Netherlands, Estonia, Lithuania	Unlimited

Source: Phelps (2009, p. 11).

Even the EU has adopted a maximum limit of 18 months in the 2008 Returns Directive. 'Although this period has been widely criticised as excessive', writes Phelps, 'the UK derogates and will not implement it' (2009, p. 11). The UK also uses so-called 'fast-track' procedures whereby applicants whose claims are deemed 'manifestly unfounded' have their entire legal process completed within detention. Detention of women and children is routine, and the movement of detainees around the detention estate – apparently 'to demoralize or curtail complaints about abuse and to deter asylum seekers from getting help with their immigration case' (Source A, Gill interviews)[7] – is a regular practice (Gill 2009).

These contexts and policies are not merely indications that accommodation centers and detention often work to subjugate asylum seekers and migrants generally. In addition, they are bound up with discourses on securitization within liberal society and must also be viewed as serving strategic and conceptual purposes. Weber and Bowling (2008), for example, argue that the regulation of movement and control of status are key metrics of power in late modernity. Adapting Wacquant's (2001) observations about how the mass incarceration of criminal prisoners reproduces racialized ghettos and other historical forms of partition, Weber and Bowling note that a similar strategy is now being rolled out within migration regimes. As part of this process, the imprisonment of migrants and criminals merges. This causes confusion over classifications and legitimates the punitive use of immigrant detention as well as the double punishment of foreign criminals who are incarcerated in the mainstream prison estate and also as they await deportation. All this occurs despite the fact that 'detention of irregular migrants is not equivalent to criminal incarceration. It is detention without court trial and is thus called 'administrative detention'' (Schinkel 2009, p. 785).

Methodology

Our analysis draws from discrete studies in these distinct geographic but overlapping social and political contexts. Research in Ireland included a thematic analysis of orientation booklets disseminated to asylum seekers by the RIA, the institution responsible for overseeing and managing accommodation centers, and interviews with 25 asylum seekers, who, at the time of the study in 2004–2005, were either living or had recently lived in accommodation centers.[8] Research in the UK involved 13 interviews, conducted in 2005 and 2006, with activists, former detainees, and employees in and around Campsfield Immigration Removal Center (Figure 2), a facility in rural Oxfordshire that

Figure 2. Campsfield House Immigration Removal Center. Photograph by N. Gill 2009.

ostensibly houses 'failed' asylum seekers who have reached the end of their legal process in the UK.[9] Campsfield has the capacity to intern 198 detainees. Although the composition of the detainee population varies according to Home Office targets, the center houses men exclusively.

Rose *et al.* note that using governmentality as a methodological framework involves examination of 'the mundane business of governing everyday economies and social life [and of] the shaping of governable domains and governable persons in the new forms of power, authority, and subjectivity being formed within these mundane practices' (2006, p. 101). Our analysis focuses on practices within detention and accommodation centers. Specifically, we analyze three examples of the technologies of government that asylum seekers encounter in these centers. Migrants are, of course, subject to myriad checks, classifications, and orderings intended to sort so-called 'deserving' from 'undeserving' claims (Sales 2002) and to encourage 'suitable' conduct and liberal self-government (Inda 2006, Mountz 2010). The three examples presented here combine with a focus on both accommodation and detention centers to represent the span from initial contact to the end point of – and possible rejection from – the asylum process, and, as such, serve to convey how asylum seekers' everyday lives are thoroughly immersed in, and bound up with, paradoxes of liberal society.

Becoming oriented

Writing about the intersections between migration and citizenship, Lister (2008) notes the ascension of liberal values in European states, not merely as a normative *goal of*

106

citizenship but also in *a priori* perceptions of who may or may not be eligible for entry and residence within a given state. Similarly, Bigo observes that migrants are imagined 'by inverting the image of a good citizen' (2002, p. 70) and linked to religious fanaticism or apparently deviant social practices in the effort to delineate between liberally governed citizens and migrant outsiders. Given this, the capacity of asylum seekers to express and demonstrate allegiance to liberal ideas is crucial.

At the outset of their encounter with liberal society, asylum seekers are often dispersed to accommodation centers where they must wait for a review of their refugee request. In Ireland, in preparation for this, individuals are given an orientation package compiled by the RIA. Orientation booklets provide general information about social norms, cultural practices, and resources that asylum seekers can expect to find in communities surrounding their residential center. Booklets include sections on accommodation, policing in Ireland, culture, money matters, welfare, and related amenities in the area. Table 3 presents excerpts from these booklets, detailing information about accommodation and Irish culture.[10]

The guidelines convey the need for order, peacefulness, cleanliness, and fitting in, as well as extending an invitation to asylum seekers to participate with area residents in maintaining the security and stability of the local neighborhood. With few exceptions, the guidelines emphasize individual choice and responsibility. Thus, they serve to 'fashion and guide the bodily comportment and inward states of others and of the self' (Huxley 2007, p. 187) within a liberal context.

Orientation booklets combine with implicit and explicit rules within accommodation centers with requirements such as 'signing in' with center management on a daily basis and taking meals with other residents at specified times. Individuals who do not adhere to

Table 3. Excerpts from 'accommodation' and 'culture' sections of orientation booklet for asylum seekers

---

Accommodation

- Irish people will, in general, make you feel welcome and many areas have groups, which monitor the activities of those in the area to ensure areas are safe from crime and general vandalism.
- There are a number of small organisations such as Residents Association, Neighbourhood Watch, Community Alert, and you are welcome to join such groups. A primary aim of resident's associations is to ensure estates, roads and green areas are kept tidy, and that litter, rubbish, loitering and general nuisance activities are prevented.
- Keep your accommodation tidy, avoid unsightly objects such as broken-down vehicles, etc.
- Do not engage in unsocial activities.
- It is the norm in Irish society to keep curtains/ blinds in your accommodation open during the day - having curtains/ blinds constantly drawn can arouse suspicion and can also attract adverse attention to your accommodation.
- It is important to build up a working, respectful relationship with your landlord.

Culture

- Being respectful of other people in your living environment leads to a happy and more pleasant environment. Constant loud noise early in the morning or late at night is considered to be disturbing the peace and can therefore cause residents to feel disrespected and resentful.
- Use of rubbish bins- where bins are provided. Please use them and ensure that they are not left on footpaths and roads where they may cause a nuisance.
- Gathering in large groups can cause a lot of fear amongst other residents, and can be seen as a form of intimidation.

Source: Galway Orientation Booklet, Jan 2004, www.ria.gov.ie

these rules are reprimanded. One interviewee explained that failure to comply with 'the law of the RIA' leads to punishment, and if someone does not follow the guidelines, 'if they return to the center late or stay out all night, they are reprimanded or moved to centers where conditions are not as good and freedoms are fewer' (Source B, Conlon interviews). These rules are expressed through practices where asylum seekers' monetary allowances are withheld if they fail to sign in or if they are absent for 3 days or more, as this is taken to indicate that the individual has made the autonomous decision to remove himself or herself from the asylum process.

For asylum seekers in detention centers in the UK, similar rules and expectations prevail. One interviewee outlined the expectations that staff have of the detainees in their care:

> Staff expects politeness. Certain items may be borrowed (hair clippers, TV remote, DVDs, table tennis bats and ball) and the detainee's card is handed in as suretee. Smoking is only permitted in certain places. Detainees may not have matches, but must ask an officer for a light. Looking too long at the fence is considered a risk and the detainee is likely to be called an escape risk and moved into the segregation cells. (Source A, Gill interviews)

Expectations about what constitutes suitable self-conduct extend to where one looks and how one addresses detention center staff. Following these rules is not merely an expectation but also becomes indispensable to avoiding sanctions such as segregation. A discourse of choice, responsibility, moral order, and self-managed conduct pervades these settings. At times, disciplinary measures, such as rules and punitive measures, overlap this discourse as a reminder that 'liberalism in no way disputes [. . .] the importance of discipline in the production and maintenance of good order' (Hindess 2001, p. 2).

Through the policies and practices that they encounter daily, asylum seekers become oriented to the significance of liberal conduct through a rhetoric of free choice. Although the guidelines espoused in booklets and detention center routines are extended as free choices, asylum seekers are not quite at liberty to decide to follow or disregard them. Instead, these technologies are designed to bring order, to encourage appropriate behavior and use of time, and to further a specific relation to one's self. These processes chime with Lippert's (1999) observations about refugee camps in the global South where refugees 'were not assumed to be liberal citizens capable of exercising choice [and a] well-administered camp promised to bring them into line with requirements of such citizenship' (1999, p. 9). Similarly, in initial encounters with European society, it is often assumed that asylum seekers neither espouse nor embody liberal values. The guidelines, routines, and procedures that operate within detention and accommodation centers exemplify 'techniques and procedures for directing human behavior' (Foucault 1997, p. 82) in accordance with liberal government. In this way, as Tyler indicates, citizenship – or the prospect thereof – entails the governance of populations within the state and the production of 'some subjects as successful citizens and others as variously precarious or failed' (2010, p. 66). On the whole, the technologies of government asylum seekers encounter are analogous to Wodiczko's *Mouthpiece (Porte Parole)*. They extend to asylum seekers the opportunity to participate in liberal society but in ways that actually block asylum seekers' personal voice and autonomous choice. Thus, they exemplify a paradox of liberal government, simultaneously offering a conduit to freedom and a gag that prevents asylum seekers from conducting themselves freely.

The tension between freedom and constraint encountered by asylum seekers does not preclude possibilities for expressions of autonomous critical viewpoints, however, and just as Wodiczko's *Mouthpiece (Porte Parole)* allows migrants to engage in a kind of 'fearless speech', in our research several asylum seekers critically reflected and questioned the notions of liberal freedom extended to them. Individuals living in accommodation centers in Ireland observed:

> I can't go anywhere, and this is awful because what we wanted, we wanted freedom in this country, but because of the circumstances I'm more trapped that even in my country, I can't move anywhere. (Source C, Conlon interviews)

> I feel like a caged bird, waiting to be free. (Source D, Conlon interviews)

One former detainee and hunger striker, who had fled his country of origin because he feared persecution following his association with political parties that opposed the incumbent government, made an explicit comparison between the circumstances that drove him to flee and his experience of detention in the UK, noting:

> [The] detention system is very hard because you know the people they left, they left our country because of problem and when they come here it's like same, same treatment so I mean, like me, I been in my country, I been in prison and here I been in detention. I think almost it's the same, almost is [the] same so I think detention is very I think is very hard yeah is very hard. (Source E, Gill interviews)

Statements such as these illustrate how migrants often confront protracted periods of immobility. These experiences contrast with the rhetoric of freedom of movement and mobility associated with European liberal society, and they have been critically documented by Schuster (2011) and Bayart (2007), among others.

Such statements are also imbued with a paradox of protest within liberal society. Asylum seekers avail themselves of the right to speak, thus exercising a liberal freedom, in order to call into question opportunities that – apparently – extend to everyone in liberal society. We can account for this paradox from a governmentality perspective with reference to the related concepts of counter-conduct and critique. According to Foucault, liberal government is not a unidirectional process where well-governed subjects uncritically accept the terms of government. Instead, problematization, dissent, and objections to being governed in particular ways are consistent with the rationality of government and values of freedom and autonomy that characterize liberal society (Cadman 2010). As such, questioning why one is governed in a particular way, as these asylum seekers did, is a form of protest that is always already incorporated within liberal society.

Moreover, Foucault argued that such questioning advances a 'positive' form of critique, which is distinct from understanding it as a practice focused primarily on identifying errors and flaws (Lemke 2011). On this view, critique is related to, if not derived from, counter-conducts, which Foucault refers to as forms of struggle that emerged with pastoral power. Counter-conducts and critique involve 'questioning the processes implemented for conducting [the self and] others' (Foucault 2007, p. 201) not as an outright negation of such practices but instead in an effort to open up possibilities to govern and be governed differently. As Foucault notes, the objective of counter-conducts is 'a different form of conduct, that is to say: wanting to be conducted differently, by other leaders [. . .] towards other objectives [. . .] and through other procedures and methods' (2007, pp. 194–195). These interventions are positive in the sense that they interrupt technologies of government in an effort to expose their limits and transform them. In this regard, counter-conducts and critiques operate like Wodiczko's *Mouthpiece (Porte Parole)*; they potentially disrupt situations and may, perhaps, provoke everyone involved to question their relation to these situations. The critical reflections and attitudes expressed by asylum seekers in accommodation and detention centers enact paradoxes that are immanent with liberal government. Their actions affirm individual freedom while also exposing the highly constrained ways in which they are free, and, yet, their counter-conducts simultaneously invite questions that interrupt the order of things and suggest the possibility of governing conduct as well as citizenship in other ways.

Subjection through release and strategies of freedom

Lippert argues that governmentality works by creating spaces within which the volitional individual can come to rule himself or herself; it also relies upon an opposition of public and private space: 'Liberal government establishes limits on political intervention and presumes a realm of freedom and action outside the acceptable reach of politics' (1999, p. 2). Observations and interviews at the Campsfield detention center in the UK show that efforts are made to create such spaces in classes, which, within the context of asylum, are designed to encourage self-re-discovery after trauma. These spaces include a busy schedule of arts, language, and computer classes, as well as opportunities for drama and music. The officer responsible for coordinating Campsfield's education program describes the program as follows:

> [The classes are] nice and light and set apart from the rest of the building which is nice because it's nice and quiet. Actually, we had an inspection about three years ago by the prison inspectors and they referred to it as a 'little oasis' which was nice; people actually come over there and sit in the corner and listen quietly to the books and things we have audio books or do a language course and 'em it's just a chance to get away from everyone else as there are so many people here. (Source F, Gill interviews)

Once again, these classes highlight the paradoxes of freedom within liberal society and lead us to question, from a governmentality perspective, both the motivation and the effect of these pedagogical 'oases'. First, there is valorization of specific characteristics. 'Quietness', in particular, seems to be encouraged as an opportunity to reflect and complete the detailed work on the self that is appropriate in order to achieve the necessary personal, attitudinal changes that will render the individual suitable for inclusion into liberal society. On the other hand, self-expression is not only valorized but also seen as necessary. It is expected that asylum seekers will lay bear their inner thoughts to the 'compulsory visibility' (Foucault 1979, p. 187) of the state apparatus and government representatives. This surveillance through the encouragement of self-expression is especially effective because as Rose argues, it 'binds subjects to a subjection that is the more profound because it appears to emanate from our autonomous quest for ourselves' (1990, p. 256).

The encouragement to participate in creative arts classes also illustrates what Salter (2008) describes as the 'confessionary complex'. This idea follows from *The History of Sexuality* (1981) where Foucault details how confession has been pried from exclusive use in religious spheres and, now, is deeply ingrained in many facets of individual life as well as throughout society. Classes, where self-expression is encouraged, provide a 'private' space where asylum seekers can recount traumas and conflicts they have experienced. Through these practices, they enact and re-enact vigilant self-examination or acts of confession, which are fused with secular society. These scrutinizing practices are not merely a way to produce one's own truth and one's subjectivity on an individual scale; they also ensure that asylum seeker subjectivity is legible to non-immigrants (Conlon 2013). In addition, these 'releases' are useful to authorities when scrutinizing asylum seekers as a population. They provide a means of categorization and comparison that may be put to use in attempts to establish the legitimacy of other asylum seekers' confessions. In this manner, as Burchell (1996) notes, freedoms, including opportunities for self-expression and self-discovery, are put to work under a liberal framework; they are enlisted as a necessary technique in the construction of autonomy, and then become a site of governmental power.

Yet, another aspect of this technology – that we are referring to as subjection through release – is the acquisition of skills that are valued in liberal society. These skills are typically ones that would facilitate individuals' participation in productive circuits of capital and liberal society, regardless of the outcome of their claim for refugee status. As a staff member at Campsfield explained when describing the classes they coordinate:

> [W]hen they leave Campsfield they're ready to slot into education should they be released into the community or be sent home [...] we award a certificate which is at the level they're studying at so that they can go to a higher education college and start at the right level. We also have computer studies; that's mainly Microsoft office. [...] The computer certificates are [...] awarded by 'em, it's OCR [Oxford, Cambridge and RSA examinations] I think, so they are recognized all over the world so they can use those. (Source F, Gill interviews)

Hindess notes that 'education and training are required in order to realize the capacity for autonomy' (2001, p. 3). For asylum seekers, this is achieved by inserting them into systems and circuits that will benefit global economies. Classes also help to classify and condition the asylum seeker subject, acting as an informal means to distinguish detainees in terms of their willingness to be 'useful' and to pursue something that they can 'show for their time'.

In some cases, as asylum seekers realize this capacity, they also enact counter-conducts. Among those interviewed in Ireland, one group of women questioned the value of 'craft' classes, such as knitting and crochet, offered to them and, instead, successfully petitioned for access to secretarial and computer certificate courses in adult education programs within the local community. Interestingly, these individuals took seriously the encouragement to 'join community associations' articulated in orientation booklets. Rather than participating in neighborhood watch associations for example, they conducted themselves as autonomous entrepreneurs who elected to be governed in a manner that was, perhaps, unanticipated but nonetheless consistent with the opportunities extended to them as part of their orientation into liberal society.

Writing about *The Mouthpiece (Porte Parole)*, Wodiczko suggests the 'mouthpiece points to the absurdity of any attempt to deprive people of speech rights in a democratic society. It responds to the actual political process of this deprivation, while at the same time it helps to translate this disadvantage into a new advantage' (1999, p. 119). The classes and opportunities extended to asylum seekers are analogous in that they expose a tension around how liberal freedoms are proffered and constrained for certain groups. They also demonstrate how this tension creates situations that enable asylum seekers to innovate and turn their subjection into 'a new advantage'. Walters describes such practices as 'acts of demonstration' where 'an injustice is revealed [and] a relationship of power is contested' (2008, p. 194). Or, in keeping with Foucault's discussion of counter-conducts, Cadman argues, 'the governed may – indeed should – strategically use governmental technologies, which are supported by transactional realities [...] against governments themselves' (2010, p. 552). The actions described in this section enact productive acts of demonstration and counter-conducts that not only critique but also interrupt and potentially transform government and, all the while, produce asylum seekers as entrepreneurial *and* autonomous subjects in liberal society.

Self-representation and responsibility

Citizenship within liberal society is generally defined in opposition to that which is not considered citizenly, and asylum seekers are one of several groups who occupy a space of excluded inclusion that serves this function, paradoxically attracting heightened state resources in order to maintain their status as subjects officially outside the state's legal and geographical jurisdiction (Agamben 2005, Hyndman and Mountz 2007). As we have seen, throughout their experience in accommodation and detention centers, asylum seekers are exposed and invited to participate in practices considered appropriate for members of liberal society. This continues even to the end point when claims are deemed to have 'failed' and asylum seekers are on the verge of being rejected from liberal states although, in fact, fully 57% of long-term detainees in the UK are released, illustrating if nothing else the profound wastefulness of the detention process (LDSN 2010).

Our final example examines a formalized practice of protest that is made available to individuals whose claims for refugee status have been denied. Consistent with discourses of choice and empowerment that prevail in liberal society, individuals whose applications have failed are invited to partake in formal channels of protest ranging from complaints to appeals. In the face of shortcomings of these systems to provide a voice to detainees, one strategy has been to school detainees in their legal rights and in the obligations of the legal system so that they can represent themselves at their own legal hearings. Bail for Immigration Detainees (BID) is one of several organizations in the UK that work to win irregular migrants, including asylum seekers, bail. Like other legal advocacy organizations, BID has developed self-help 'notebooks' that accompany individual asylum seekers and allow them to represent themselves at legal hearings pertaining to their status such as bail hearings or denial of an asylum claim. The notebooks orient detainees to issues such as what to expect at an immigration or bail hearing, what the individuals' rights are within this context, and also provide guidelines for presenting a legal argument or responding to questions about the individual's status. One interviewee, who had helped to circulate these notebooks, explained how trainings for legal self-representation work:

> We go into Campsfield from BID on the first Wednesday of every month to do a whole morning of legal advice and people can book one of us to talk to, and we go in on the third Thursday of every month to do a workshop with whoever wants to come down, it may be 20 or 30 people, to explain to them the process of doing their own bail hearing. We have so many clients we can't possibly do even a small fraction of them so BID has devised a system, we call it the notebooks, which explain to people the process of bail and how they can run their own bail hearing [. . .] we actually help them make the arguments [. . .] we draft out, em, what their best arguments are.

> *Interviewer:* and then they do it themselves?

> They don't have a barrister; they go into the court on their own [and represent themselves]. (Source G, Gill interviews)

What are we to make of these notebooks, which allow asylum seekers to represent themselves at their own legal hearings? On the one hand, there is a clear need for this type of support. The interviewee cited here estimated that as many as one-third of those detained at Campsfield rely on BID for assistance with their appeal and to secure bail. This number is increasing as the staff at Campsfield refers more and more detainees to this organization.

Yet, it is also possible to mount a series of objections to these self-help notebooks. Pyykkönen notes how technologies of government 'call people in marginal positions to be self-responsible through actions that are considered acceptable for them in order to advance their participation in the fields of "normal society"' (2007, p. 198). Self-representation notebooks have similar effects, so that even when failure and possible deportation is impending, asylum seekers are expected to be responsible, autonomous, and entrepreneurial participants in liberal government. Self-representation notebooks thus produce a form of empowerment that, in the end, delivers more responsibility to detainees, renders them more exposed to institutional demands, and ameliorates the responsibilities of institutions to provide legal representatives for asylum seekers. Above all, this technology seeks to produce an entrepreneurial, yet subjugated, detainee who 'identif[ies] their own desires and aspirations with those of others, so that they [. . .] become allies in governing' (Rose *et al.*, 2006, p. 89).

The possibility of dual contradictory functions is one that faces not only BID but also a range of activist organizations working on behalf of asylum seekers as well as other third-sector, non-governmental organizations (see Katz 2005). Like Wodiczko's *Mouthpiece (Porte Parole)*, the technologies and strategies employed by these organizations, while attempting to intervene and disrupt prevailing modes of governance, may facilitate projects that work in partnership with the state apparatus, and in so doing, further exploit and marginalize those who are subjugated. This is not to undermine the importance of these organizations and the provocation to technologies of government that self-representation by asylum seekers present but, instead, to point out that the effects of formal protests, counter-conducts, and critical attitudes are by no means certain; at times these forms of protest are captured in and replay problematic relational systems of power in liberal society.

Conclusion

We have been concerned with understanding accommodation and detention centers as an extension of the original problem of liberal government, that is, how citizens are produced so that they are free from the state and yet predisposed toward conducting themselves in ways that support the functioning and reproduction of 'free' markets and society. We have also been concerned with how counter-conducts and related forms of protest are immanent with the technologies that produce liberal citizens. Our findings indicate that asylum seekers in accommodation and detention centers in Ireland, the UK, and beyond undergo elaborate initiation procedures before being admitted into societies where this liberal order prevails. Technologies of government are put to use in this process and range from orientation booklets that promise to 'guide', to classes that promise 'release', and to notebooks that promise to 'empower'. Each fuses the delivery of such promises with the distribution of norms, rules, and codes that distinguish between migrants on the basis of their suitability for inclusion into the liberal order. Asylum seekers and irregular migrants generally are charged with the responsibility to adhere to these norms or face the consequences of contravention. Yet, amidst this initiation process, a number of paradoxes operate. Asylum seekers are compelled to become liberal subjects who govern themselves as self-examining, self-expressive, and self-responsible entrepreneurs. Contradictions exist because expectations of self-responsible conduct simultaneously invite forms of protest – fearless speech and critical attitudes – that invoke questions and confound the system of government of which we are all part. In Foucault's terms, these 'counter-conducts' are immanent with liberal government. That is to say, the possibility of protest imbues liberal society and is part and parcel of asylum seekers' initiation into the liberal order.

There are myriad different ways to protest within the centers where asylum seekers reside or are detained. Some strategies – such as the demand for classes to develop individuals' entrepreneurial skills – turn governmental techniques 'into a new advantage' (Wodiczko 1999, p. 119). Some – such as legal orientation and self-representation programs – reluctantly and unwittingly collude with liberal regimes of governance. Other protests – including refusals to participate in activities, refusals to eat, or falling silent –

firmly reject the invitation to self-rule and, therefore, may be seen as a political rejection of liberal society and its conditions. Even though these protests ostensibly align with freedoms extended to liberal subjects and citizens, such actions can immediately be constituted as evidence of the need for harsher forms of policing. Protests may also be taken as confirmation of the unsuitability of certain individuals and groups of asylum seekers, thus as grounds for their exclusion, disenfranchisement, or expulsion from the state. Alternatively, as we have shown, many of these forms of protests are also productive. In the process of becoming liberal, asylum seekers also conduct themselves autonomously, thereby revealing the limits as well as the possibilities for transforming practices of government.

Given these paradoxes of freedom and protest that asylum seekers encounter, in the end, we must ask what are the implications of these techniques of liberal government not only for asylum seekers but also for all subjects and citizens of liberal societies? As previously noted, Wodiczko's *Mouthpiece (Porte Parole)* is intended to inspire exchange, to serve as a point of recognition of 'common strangeness'. In a similar vein, as asylum seekers enact and protest their subjection, the paradoxes of liberal government that are laid bare extend beyond the individual scale to the subjects of liberal government *en masse*. Moreover, although we concur with Wodiczko's observations about how the forms of protest represented in the *Mouthpiece (Porte Parole)* are unlikely to achieve changes on a large scale, these 'small moments, these small disruptions' (2009, p. 14) are important because they destabilize the very notion of a 'liberal subject' and categories of belonging within liberal societies.

The encounters with technologies of government we have described also highlight the 'security continuum' (Bigo cited in Walters 2004, p. 240) that links migration, citizenship, and the state. As previously noted, Tyler (2010) observes that in the current era of security and societies of government, internal and domestic problems and populations, rather than external threats, are an increasing focus of attention. In this paper, we have seen that asylum seekers are thoroughly scrutinized from the very first moment of entry into liberal society through to the point of possible inclusion in or expulsion from the state. Tyler also demonstrates that techniques for monitoring, controlling, and separating out potential trouble makers extend all the way through to citizenship, and thus play a central role in securing the state. In this way, citizenship, premised upon individual responsibility to 'earn, demonstrate, or buy their "right" to state protection and care' (Tyler 2010, p. 71), is designed to produce various subjects who are either successful or failed citizens. We can trace a very clear line from the technologies of government that asylum seekers encounter in residential and detention centers to the production of other failed or marginal citizen-subjects such as the old, infirm, homeless, and addicted. With this, the proximity and 'common strangeness' between migrants and non-migrants in liberal society are once again highlighted.

Finally, this continuum, coupled with the paradoxes of freedom and constraint that asylum seekers encounter, raise questions about liberal society and citizenship more broadly: How do we understand liberal society and belonging therein? Exactly who is free in this context? And, why govern through citizenship in this way? Writing about the ways monitoring, self-surveillance, and the securitization of migrants in the US 'Homeland Security State' (2007, p. 440) is inextricably linked to the securitization of citizenship, De Genova calls for 'an unrelenting interrogation of the liberal conceits and complacencies that adhere to the very notion of citizenship as the presumptive framework for our practices of freedom' (p. 441). In the process of their induction into the liberal order, asylum seekers enact this interrogative task by engaging in fearless speech and forms of protest that expose the Janus-face of 'liberalism' where freedom is at once conditional, mandatory, and a problem. In so doing, they issue what Foucault describes as a 'permanent provocation' (1994, p. 342) to the achievement of liberal government and to citizenship as a basis for liberal freedoms.

Acknowledgements

We are grateful to Imogen Tyler and Katarzyna Marciniak for assiduously nurturing this article. We are indebted to Stephanie J. Silverman and Evelyn Massa, organizers of *The Theory and Practice of Immigration Detention* workshop held in May 2010 at Oxford; Alison Mountz, Jenna Loyd, Tina Catania, and participants in the Fall 2010 *Political Geographies of Violence* seminar at *Syracuse University*; and to organizers – Elizabeth Cullen Dunn and Carole McGranahan – and participants at the *Humanitarianism and Migration* conference held at *University of Colorado at Boulder*, March 2011 for insightful feedback on earlier drafts. Thanks to three anonymous reviewers, whose constructive comments are greatly appreciated. We are also grateful to the Economic and Social Research Council for financial support [project reference: RES-000-22-3928].

Notes

1. In so far as European and North American governments, as well as a range of other states grapple with the classical problem of liberal government described, the arguments outlined here apply equally to these contexts.
2. For a detailed catalogue and discussion of the artist's exhibitions, projections, and instrumentations, see Wodiczko (2009).
3. Hereafter referred to as 'Ireland'.
4. Equivalent to $3.60 (US) or £2.30 (UK) per day, exchange rate calculated on 10 April 2010.
5. In 2008, 961 'non-status' migrants were detained in prisons in Ireland with the majority (83%) detained for 10 days or less (http://www.globaldetentionproject.org).
6. The UK system commenced on 3 April 2000 and was first administered under the National Asylum Support Service (NASS) Dispersal Programme. NASS has since been renamed Asylum Support.
7. Interviews with asylum seekers in accommodation centers in Ireland are listed as 'Conlon interviews' and with detention center staff and affiliates in the UK as 'Gill interviews'; specific interviewee details are subject to anonymity.
8. The category 'asylum seeker' comprised women whose refugee claims were pending, women who had been granted refugee status, humanitarian leave to remain, or had been granted residency in accordance with family reunification policies.
9. There is evidence that applicants are often detained earlier in the determination process.
10. The orientation booklet for 2004 coincides with the data collection period in Ireland. The RIA published an updated orientation booklet focused on 'rules, regulations, and procedures' in 2009.

References

Agamben, G., 2005. *State of exception*, trans. K. Attell. Chicago, IL: University of Chicago Press.
Bacon, C., 2005. The evolution of immigration detention in the UK: the involvement of private prison companies [online]. *Refugee studies center.* Working Paper 27. Available from: http://www.rsc.ox.ac.uk/publications/working-papers-folder_contents?all=1 [Accessed 18 August 2010].
Bayart, J.-F., 2007. *Global subjects: a political critique of globalization*, trans. A. Brown. Malden, MA: Polity.
Bigo, D., 2002. Security and immigration: toward a critique of the governmentality of unease. *Alternatives: global, local, political*, 27 (1), 63–92.
Burchell, G., 1996. Liberal government and techniques of the self. *In*: A. Barry, T. Osborne and N. Rose, eds. *Foucault and political reason: liberalism, neoliberalism and rationalities of government*. London: University College London Press, 19–36.
Cadman, L., 2010. How (not) to be governed: Foucault, critique, and the political. *Environment and planning D: society and space*, 28 (3), 539–556.

Conlon, D., 2010. Ties that bind: governmentality, the state, and asylum in contemporary Ireland. *Environment and planning D: society and space*, 28 (1), 95–111.

Conlon, D., 2013. Becoming legible and 'legitimized': subjectivation and governmentality among asylum seekers. *In*: P. Kretsedemas, J. Capetillo and G. Jacobs, eds. *Migrant marginality: a transnational perspective*. New York: Routledge.

De Genova, N., 2007. The production of culprits: from deportability to detainability in the aftermath of 'homeland security'. *Citizenship studies*, 11 (5), 421–448.

Deutsche, R., 2002. Sharing strangeness: Krzysztof Wodiczko's aegis and the question of hospitality. *Grey room*, 6, 26–43.

Foucault, M., 1979. *Discipline and punish: the birth of the prison*. New York: Vintage.

Foucault, M., 1981. *The history of sexuality, volume I: an introduction*, trans. R. Hurley. Hammondsworth: Penguin.

Foucault, M., 1991. Governmentality. *In*: G. Burchell, C. Gordon and P. Miller, eds. *The Foucault effect: studies in governmentality*. Hempstead: Harvester Wheatsheaf Hemel, 87–104.

Foucault, M., 1994. The subject and power. *In*: P. Rabinow, ed. *The essential works of Michel Foucault: volume IIII: power*. New York: New Press, 326–348.

Foucault, M., 1997. *The politics of truth*. Los Angeles, CA: Semiotext(e).

Foucault, M., 2007. Security, territory, population: lectures at the Collége de France 1977–78. M. Senellart, ed. trans. G. Burchell. New York: Palgrave.

Gill, N., 2009. Governmental mobility: the power effects of the movement of detained asylum seekers around Britain's detention estate. *Political geography*, 28 (3), 186–196.

Hindess, B., 2001. The liberal government of unfreedom. *Alternatives: global, local, political*, 26 (2), 93–111.

Huxley, M., 2007. Geographies of governmentality. *In*: J. Crampton and S. Elden, eds. *Space, knowledge, and power: Foucault and geography*. Aldershot: Ashgate, 185–204.

Hyndman, J. and Mountz, A., 2007. Refuge or refusal. *In*: D. Gregory and A. Pred, eds. *Violent geographies: fear, terrorism and political violence*. New York and London: Routledge, 77–92.

Inda, J.X., 2006. *Targeting immigrants: government, technology, and ethics*. Oxford: Blackwell.

Katz, C., 2005. Partners in crime? Neoliberalism and the production of new political subjectivities. *Antipode*, 37 (3), 623–631.

Lemke, T., 2011. Critique and experience in Foucault. *Theory, culture, society*, 28 (4), 26–48.

Lippert, R., 1999. Governing refugees: the relevance of governmentality to understanding the international refugee regime. *Alternatives: global, local, political*, 24 (3), 295–329.

Lister, M., 2008. Introduction: Europeanization and migration: challenging the values of citizenship in Europe? *Citizenship studies*, 12 (6), 527–532.

London Detainee Support Group, 2010. No return, no release, no reason: challenging indefinite detention, London [online]. Available from: http://www.ldsg.org.uk/files/uploads/NoReasonReport0910.pdf [Accessed 12 December 2010].

Marciniak, K. and Turowski, K., 2011. *Streets of crocodiles: photography, media and postsocialist landscapes in Poland*. Chicago, IL: Chicago University Press.

Mountz, A., 2010. *Seeking asylum: human smuggling and bureaucracy at the border*. Minneapolis, MN: University of Minnesota Press.

Nevins, J., 2002. *Operation gatekeeper*. New York: Routledge.

O'Halloran, M., 2010. Amended immigration bill expected before autumn. *The Irish Times*, 1 June 2010 [online]. Available from: http://www.irishtimes.com [Accessed 6 January 2010].

Phelps, J., 2009. Detained lives: the real cost of indefinite immigration detention [online]. London: London Detainee Support Group. Available from: http://www.ldsg.org.uk/files/modules/content/index.php?id=11 [Accessed 12 December 2010].

Pyykkönen, M., 2007. Integrating governmentality: administrative expectations for immigrant associations in Finland. *Alternatives*, 32 (2), 197–224.

Refugee and Integration Agency (RIA), 2009. *Monthly statistics report, December 2009*. Dublin: Department of Justice, Equality and Law Reform.

Rose, N., 1990. *Governing the soul: the shaping of the private self*. London: Routledge.

Rose, N., 1999. *Powers of freedom: reframing political thought*. Cambridge: Cambridge University Press.

Rose, N., O'Malley, P. and Valverde, M., 2006. Governmentality. *Annual review of law and social science*, 2, 83–104.

Sales, R., 2002. The deserving and undeserving? Refugees, asylum seekers and welfare in Britain. *Critical social policy*, 22 (3), 456–478.

Salter, M., 2008. When the exception becomes the rule: borders, sovereignty, and citizenship. *Citizenship studies*, 12 (4), 365–380.

Schinkel, W., 2009. Illegal aliens and the state, or: bare bodies vs. the zombie. *International sociology*, 24 (6), 779–806.

Schuster, L., 2011. Dublin II and Eurodac: examining the (un)intended(?) consequences. *Gender, place and culture*, 18 (3), 401–416.

Tyler, I., 2010. Designed to fail: a biopolitics of British citizenship. *Citizenship studies*, 14 (1), 61–74.

Wacquant, L., 2001. Deadly symbiosis: when ghettos and prisons meet and mesh. *Punishment and society*, 3 (1), 95–133.

Walters, W., 2004. Secure borders, safe haven, domopolitics. *Citizenship studies*, 8 (3), 237–260.

Walters, W., 2008. Acts of demonstration: mapping the territory of (non-)citizenship. *In*: E. Isin and G. Nielsen, eds. *Acts of citizenship*. London: Zed Books, 182–206.

Weber, L. and Bowling, B., 2008. Valiant beggars and global vagabonds: select, eject, immobilize. *Theoretical criminology*, 12 (3), 355–375.

White, A. and Gilmartin, M., 2008. Critical geographies of citizenship and belonging in Ireland. *Women's studies international forum*, 31 (5), 390–399.

Wodiczko, K., 1996. Porte-parole exhibited in *Xenology: immigrant instruments, 1992* [online]. Available from: http://interrogative.mit.edu/projects/1993/porte-parole [Accessed 25 August 2010].

Wodiczko, K., 1999. *Critical vehicles: writings, projects, interviews*. Cambridge, MA: MIT Press.

Wodiczko, K., 2009. *Guests\goscie*. Warsaw: Zachęta National Gallery of Art.

Legal/illegal: protesting citizenship in Fortress America

Katarzyna Marciniak

Department of English, Ohio University, Athens, OH 45701, USA

This article examines the issue of legality and illegality, focusing on U.S. citizenship, anti-immigrant rage, and pro-immigrant protests. The central case study is an analysis of what I call digital rage, namely, the rhetorical strategies present in anti-immigrant online activism. I argue that online performance of rage invests in acts of bordering (Nyers 2008) which propel a discourse of white supremacist pure nation and neurotic citizenship (Isin 2004). The final part of this article explores *No Human Being is Illegal*, a protest art exhibition. Imaginatively refusing forms of citizenship grounded in legal/illegal axis, the exhibition exposes U.S. citizenship itself as illegal, rooted in the colonization of indigenous people and in current neocolonizing practices of exploitation.

> Spivak: Getting drivers' license is not an epistemic project.
> Butler: It is if you are an illegal immigrant.
> –Judith Butler and Gayatri Spivak, *Who Sings the Nation-State?*

Memory

On 1 May 2006, I attended the immigrant protest march in Los Angeles, one in the series of marches that year and the most public display of immigrant rage[1] in the contemporary history of the USA. Passionate about the cause, I was nonetheless consumed by ambivalent feelings about taking part in the march. When I shared this uncertainty with a colleague, she first responded with silence. My ambivalence must have felt terribly ironic to her: I sensed she had in mind my own 'alien' experiences and my work on the discourses of alienhood. Perhaps she considered me to be a sell out, a double-crosser. At the close of our conversation, she teased me jokingly: 'You know, since you are now a U.S. citizen, you have to do at least one march'.

I foolishly assumed that my colleague would immediately capture the context of my resistance. This resistance is visceral, deeply lodged in my bones. Marching catapults me back to my behind the Wall years in Poland, where, every year, 1 May, a public holiday honoring the working class of the nation, was a visual extravaganza of state socialism performed through compulsory marches. Everyone involved as a student or employee in the life of a particular institution was obligated to participate in the annual 1 May parades. Hence, children, high school students, and adults employed in various venues – engineers, journalists, construction workers, educators, and so on – were mandated to march. Children were considered especially valuable marchers because their waving of flags and flowers was promoted as charming and convincing in its 'pure' emotionality. The culmination of every march in my hometown of Łódź, took place in the city center where, behind the podium, stood the municipal authorities for whom the marching spectacle was performed. The authorities, typically male figures, waved at the marchers below, smiling. The overall structure of such nationalist performances – men in power waving back to the gratefully marching citizens – was a miniature version of the spectacular Soviet Red Square May parades, images of which were often shown on television and were secretly mocked by viewers in Eastern Europe.

The intricate web of hypocrisy behind this forced marching is a compelling metaphor for the twisted intricacies of the socialist era, which even after so many years living in the USA, I instinctively respond to with irritation. On the one hand, 1 May was showcased as a national holiday, a day free from work, a celebratory and flamboyant display of socialist ideals. On the other hand, these marches were mandatory and closely surveilled. Although my mother bitterly complained about the preposterous facade of those marches, feeling disdain and anger, every year she had to go. I marched through my elementary school and high school years, accumulating my own resistance.

Because of this troubled history of marching, I was surprised to feel pulled by the Los Angeles protest, by its performative power, its sheer emotional force. All the way to the horizon, Wilshire Boulevard was filled with thousands of women, men, children, and babies carried or wheeled in strollers by adults. The marchers, overwhelmingly Latinos and Chicanos, carried banners, posters, and placards with such phrases as 'legal', 'illegal', and 'we are all immigrants – stop the hypocrisy!' The dominant visual motif was the American flag in different sizes and shapes; many participants had their bodies wrapped in the fabric of the flag.[2]

Encounter

In this context, I recall a marginal yet revealing incident, when, right after the immigrant marches, I encountered another immigrant academic from Eastern Europe with whom I chatted about our work and life in Los Angeles. Answering the new acquaintance's question about my current research, I mentioned that I was working on a new project, 'Immigrant Rage', and that I took part in the recent march. She thought of my participation in the march as a 'research activity': 'Surely, you are not one of those immigrants who needs to march'. Even though her comments were deeply problematic, I instinctively knew what she meant. Having gone through the U.S. legalization process years earlier, I remember many remarks from sympathetic Americans who all, in a variety of forms, said that 'I was lucky to be white.'

But never did it occur to me that someone who had gone through the process of obtaining U.S. citizenship might not at least acknowledge the inequalities of this system, never mind the frustration, anger, or humiliation generated by its often condescending, arduous, uncertain, long, and costly meanderings. My interlocutor kept asking pointedly, 'Why rage? Have you been angry? I don't quite understand why'. We both looked at each other in disbelief; I was as intrigued to meet an unangry immigrant as she was surprised to meet an angry one.

Ultimately, this encounter revealed how limited we both were in our ways of thinking about immigration and legality. As much as I was invested in the discourse of anger, an emotionality that has been an integral part of my immigrant claims for the rights of citizenship, she took for granted the fact that the legalization process may be a relatively easy exercise in cosmopolitan mobility, if only for *the select* ethnically desirable newcomers. It was when she mentioned her own immigrant experience – a direct transfer from one academic institution in her country to another one in the USA, which was legally handled by the academic administration and which only required her to 'sign various papers' – that I realized why her passage to U.S. citizenship was cleansed from anger and why my anger over the process I went through was genuinely bewildering to her. Experiencing the privilege of 'global academics', as Zygmunt Bauman might say (1998, p. 89), resulted in her going through the legalizing process without having to submit to it. Although she obviously completed the process, she did so in a shielded, institutional manner, which protected her from often intense vulnerabilities and from scrutinizing her own legitimacy. Quite sensibly, as she explained to me, she always thought of herself as 'legal'.

Inflamed passions

> Are you fed up with illegal aliens marching in the streets? Demanding a reward for crashing the border and breaking our law? (FAIR, Federation for American Immigration Reform http://www.fairus.org, May 2006)

In the wake of the 2006 and 2007 marches which ignited powerful emotional responses, heated debates about (il)legality and citizenship have been placed center stage, and even more so in the course of the 2008 presidential campaign during which the candidates were inevitably asked the 'immigration question'. During his visit to the Aspen Institute, CO, Senator John McCain, then widely unpopular in the Republican Party for his 'radical' views on immigration, opened his talk:

> I have never seen an issue that has *inflamed the passions* of the American people the way the issue of immigration reform has. Ever. Including Iraq. I have never seen anything like it. I have never heard such rhetoric. We have never received death threats before like I received. It's unbelievable....There is a fear among some people, particularly the further you get from the border, about invasion they are experiencing....I believe with all my heart we need a comprehensive approach to immigration reform. (2007, my emphasis)

It is to the territory of the 'inflamed passions' in discourses on immigration that I turn in this article, showing how these passions have been vigorously developing in digital culture. I hope to contribute to the debates about the politics of citizenship by focusing on material that remains undertheorized, that is, the rhetorical strategies of various online anti-immigration groups whose texts are widely available, yet rarely studied closely. The online campaigns I bring into focus are galvanizing forces behind the commonly accepted understandings of legality and illegality; they participate in shaping cultural imaginings and national consciousness about the sanctioned boundaries of citizenship. The dissection of the supposedly straightforward 'anti-immigrant', pro-legality position these groups collectively advocate reveals ambivalences, contradictions, and contingencies that, upon a closer scrutiny, disclose how these groups invest in the notion of a 'pure' nation, activating in the process the idea of 'the neurotic citizen' (Isin 2004). This desirable purity is reinforced by a particular cultural investment in what I call a *visuality of illegality*, that is, a persistent imagining of 'illegal aliens' as nonwhite, dangerous, and poor (see also Michael C. Williams on the concept of 'image-rhetorics' 2003). As a counter-narrative to the anti-immigrant digital culture, I end this article with a brief analysis of an art exhibition, *No Human Being is Illegal*. I read it as a political intervention into the hegemonic practices of citizenship in 'Fortress America' – a historical construct emphatically reasserted in the post-9/11 era alongside the xenophobic rhetoric of 'immigration reform' and the criminalization and abjectification of undocumented workers whom De Genova, for example, refers to as 'racially subordinate and legally vulnerable migrant labour . . . confronting the spectacle of security' (2010, p. 92). *No Human Being is Illegal* directly addresses the 'visuality of illegality' by imaginatively refusing forms of citizenship rooted in the legal/illegal axis.

The two marches with which I opened my discussion are very different, speaking to the power of the nation-states. It is their difference that subtly points to the need to destabilize the meaning of marching as a progressive performance: 'to march . . . implies a progressive and forward-moving action' (Nyers 2008, p. 175). Clearly, if, as Peter Nyers claims, 'the act of marching is deeply political' (2008, p. 175), a right-claiming performance, then the Los Angeles march, the highly organized protest against the exclusionary model of citizenship, might be thought of as akin to what Engin F. Isin and Greg M. Nielsen refer to as 'acts of citizenship', 'collective or individual deeds that rupture social-historical patterns' (2008, p. 2). It was certainly an event 'when subjects constitute themselves as meriting recognition *as* citizens' (Walters 2008, p. 193) while, simultaneously, creating a space of ambivalence in that it is possible to read the protest as *critically aporetic* – as both performance in the name of citizenship *and* its refusal. That is, the LA protests were about opening up the boundaries of citizenship to include non-status peoples who participate in society *as if* citizens. In that sense, the protest can be read as a demand for inclusion. But it can also be understood much more ambiguously through the trope of immigrant rage as for many Mexicans the U.S. citizenship is historically contentious, recalling the history of the Mexican–American War of 1846, a point to which I will return later.

The socialist march, a forced if 'deeply political' performance of national allegiance, does not fit within the frames of understanding marching as a progressive and 'forward-moving action'. If the Los Angeles voluntary march was about solidarity, visibility and audibility of communal anger, and the need for change – enacting 'collective affects of belonging' (Papadopoulos and Tsianos, this issue) – the Łódź marches were a government-orchestrated compulsory promotion of socialist ideals and the reaffirmation of the totalitarian regimes in Eastern Europe under the banner of 'proletarians of all countries, unite!' If the Los Angeles immigrant march was enacting freedom of assembly and dissent by performing protest, the Łódź marches enacted 'imprisonment' of its participants who were denied the right to dissent and who, by marching, had to perform the communal happiness of the working class in the Soviet block, carrying banners proclaiming 'Long live the Polish–Soviet friendship'.

Judith Butler's notion of 'performative contradiction' (Butler and Spivak 2007, p. 63) is useful here: the annual requirement to march in the name of the Polish–Soviet friendship took place during the Soviet occupation of Eastern Europe and the 1 May marchers who chanted 'Long live the international working class' themselves had no access to 'becoming international' because the government did not allow its citizens to own passports and easily cross borders.[3] Unlike many of the marchers in Los Angeles, whether legal, illegal, or of liminal status, the legal citizens of socialist Poland were deprived of some of the key privileges of citizenry: freedom of assembly, the right to protest, and freedom of movement. These two acts of citizenship, incongruous and incompatible because of their different historical contexts, form a complex connection with the anti-immigrant material I analyze in the core section of this article. Like the totalitarian, Soviet-imposed socialist government in Poland, the U.S. online groups perform 'acts of bordering' (Nyers 2008, p. 168) which enact what Michel Foucault describes as 'rituals of exclusion' (1979, p. 198). The Soviet-imposed government masqueraded as legitimate, caring for the well-being of the nation. The online groups, too, act in the name of protecting the U.S. citizenship, validate their own questionable legitimacy by delegitimating others.

Immigrant insults: legal/illegal

Calling the 2006 marches in the USA 'May Day illegal alien protests', many anti-immigrant commentators argued that these marches were an insult not just to American citizens but to every immigrant who resides in the USA legally. Rhetorically, it is a shortcut to divide those who have come to the USA into two clear-cut, impermeable, groups: there are those newcomers who are praised for having followed the path of law, for 'doing it the right way', and there are those other 'bad ones' who have chosen to avoid legality and whom, in turn, this culture envisions as unwanted trespassers and criminals. At the heart of such statements, lies a particular understanding of legality as moral and just making illegality immoral and condemnable. Jocelyn Solis, a psychologist who undertakes research with undocumented Mexican immigrants in New York, confirms this point:

> Illegality as an identity serves as a political and moral divider, one that validates some as insiders, or people who 'belong' in the United States, while identifying others as outsiders who have committed an illicit act. It also serves as a racial divider because illegal immigration is generally associated with nonwhites. (2008, p. 184)

Furthermore, such divisive proclamations presume a straightforward understanding of 'legality' and rely on the idea that all – 'natural' citizens, immigrants, and guest workers alike – immediately tap into a singular notion of legality which does not have to be interpreted because we all know the definition that is implied.[4] Like many public figures who commented on immigrant protests after 1 May 2006, Jett Williams, country music singer, articulated this 'transparent' idea of legality:

> It is a disgrace when those who have benefitted from what this country has to offer, then wail up in protest. Illegal is illegal; you are not an undocumented immigrant; you are an illegal alien period....*Legal is legal and illegal is illegal.* (Williams, my emphasis)

How to pierce through such an unnerving reductionism that forcefully circulates in the U.S. culture? In order to destabilize the presupposed *fixity* of legality/illegality, citizen/noncitizen, it is important to consider the myriad processes of 'coming to legality', brushing against illegality, and the possibility of upgrading one's illegal status to a legal one if one is a desirable worker and finds a proper support (see Nyers 2008).

In her study of the historical origins of the 'illegal alien' in American law and society, *Impossible Subjects: Illegal Aliens and the Making of Modern America*, Mae M. Ngai claims that, contrary to conventional thinking, the line between alien and citizen is soft:

> ...illegal alienage is not a natural or fixed condition but the product of positive law; it is contingent and at times it is unstable. The line between legal and illegal status can be crossed in both directions. An illegal alien can, under certain conditions, adjust his or her status and become legal and hence eligible for citizenship. And legal aliens who violate certain laws can become illegal and hence expelled and, in some cases, forever barred from reentry and the possibility of citizenship. I suggest that shifts in the boundary between legal and illegal status might tell us a lot about how the nation has imagined and constructed itself over time. (2004, p. 6)

These nuances, however – the intermixed valence of legality and illegality and the complex experiences they produce *vis-à-vis* the acquisition of citizenship – are often concealed by silence, and understandably so. Those who do go through an immigration process often implicitly understand that the unspoken assumption in delicate legal negotiations is that these volatile issues of (il)legality are not to be discussed openly with others so as not to reveal the intricacies of the process and vulnerabilities of the applicant's tenuous position. Thus this delicacy, or perhaps even secrecy, of the legalization process is something a lot of immigrants are trained to guard: these are matters of high stakes and of a highly confidential nature whose successful handling depends on tacit agreements, implicating the applicant as fully cooperative and silent.

My own experiential reality of being processed as an 'alien', 'the ins and outs of immigration control', to use Ali Behdad's apt phrase (1998, p. 143), revealed to me what those who undergo the immigration process know quite intimately: there is no universal immigrant experience and there is no universal experience of legalizing one's status. One's specific context of race, class, sexuality, education, nationality, and, above all, economic privilege dictates the way the process shapes itself and its subject. For example, 'green card marriage', that is, a marriage with an American citizen, even though not free from scrutiny and potential humiliation, produces a very different experience of legalization than the one in which a person changes status without the help of a 'native'. One of the multiple immigration legalization venues is winning the 'green card lottery' through an 'Official U.S. Government Diversity Lottery Program'. Even though this lottery may sound like any other gamble dependent on the luck of the draw, access to the prize is carefully orchestrated, starting with the restriction on participation (among many factors, the applicant must be a native of a 'qualifying country' and, upon winning, must demonstrate adequate sponsorship in the USA). A venue that tops the lottery concept in terms of its originality and speed in bypassing all immigration complexities and uncertainties is the option known as the 'immigrant investor' program, allowing wealthy foreigners to invest in the U.S. economy. These 'alien investors', as U.S. Citizenship and Immigration Services webpage calls them, who can document 'their engagement in a new commercial enterprise' through a million dollar investment in the USA, are able to effectively 'purchase' U.S. residency ('Immigration Through Investment'). It is an interesting legal detail that is hardly publicized, which shows how corporate capitalism is deeply intertwined in access to citizenship.

However, the populist rhetoric of legality does not concern itself with such details and very much hinges on the 'clarity' of the dictum that 'legal is legal and illegal is illegal'. This clarity, however, is contingent upon a specific concealment, that is, the fact that this supposedly lucid rhetoric of (il)legality hides the implicit racial and ethnic hierarchy of immigrant 'illegal' identities and the fact that raging against the 'illegals' is mainly directed at a specific class of Mexicans (and Latino/as in general) as well as Arabs and other nonwhite newcomers from economically disadvantaged or 'failed' states. As many have argued, this specific class of often undocumented Latinos occupies a profoundly ambivalent position in the U.S. economy as they are, as Ngai refers to them, 'impossible subjects', simultaneously wanted and unwanted, welcomed and unwelcomed, as labor that is cheap and disposable (2004, p. 2).

To probe these complex issues through the analysis of online anti-immigrant activism raises obvious questions. What can we learn from these sites knowing *a priori* that they rely on rhetoric of racist hate and patriotic righteousness? Why study them at all? What might be their pedagogical use? First, the close reading of these online discourses allows one to trace the ways in which hate is formed discursively, to see how it shapes itself through language, and to recognize voices and identities that are given prominent space to fuel this activism and perform 'a passionate symbolic cohesion' of a nation (Kintz 1997, p. 4). Second, if we think about what Nicholas De Genova terms 'spectacles of increasingly militarized border policing' (2010, p. 91) (recent punitive legislatures in Alabama, Arizona, and Georgia), we also have to acknowledge that this discourse has been effectively translated into political power that impacts public policy and overall institutional politics. It also works as a conceptual and rhetorical ground for civilian border patrol groups such as the much publicized Minuteman, a group which, interestingly, operates both online and offline (see Doty 2007). It is thus precisely through their material power that these discourses have the political significance.

Digital rage: white racial extinction

> America is beautiful. Why spoil it?
> – Americans for Immigration Control

Anti-immigrant organizations have been developing rapidly and the web is by now their most vigorous field of activism, expanding readership, accessibility, and impact, offering an array of interactive activities and materials. The list of these organizations is extensive, including such groups as National Organization for European American Rights (run by the former Klan leader, David Duke); California Coalition for Immigration Reform; American Immigration Control Foundation; ProjectUSA; NumbersUSA; Grassfire.org; The Social Contract Press; and Voices of Citizens Together (also known as American Patrol). Many of these organizations are interwoven as their writers/leaders publish in each other's webzines and newsletters and advertise each other's books, pamphlets, booklets, and videos.

For scholars following the contemporary anti-immigrant movement in the USA, perusing the digital rhetoric of these sites feels like an experience of anxious, 'daemonic repetition' of a stereotype that Homi Bhabha identifies as central to a construction of colonial discourse and its ideological constructions of otherness through fixity (1983, p. 18). The stereotype for him is a 'form of knowledge and identification that vacillates between what is already 'in place', already known, and something that must be anxiously repeated' (1983, p. 18). Indeed, this rhetoric is reminiscent of the 1990s anti-immigrant raging expressed by such authors as Lawrence Auster (1990), Peter Brimelow (1995), or Patrick Buchanan (2002). As I have analyzed elsewhere (Marciniak 2006), the overall elegiac, alarmist, and even apocalyptic tone and statements such as Auster's that 'open immigration and multiculturalism constitute a mortal threat to American civilization' (1990, p. 53) permeate these publications; the metaphors of 'pollution' and 'peril' are dominant tropes meant to assert the need to invest in the logic of racial purity. 'Death', 'invasion', 'mortal menace', 'alien nation', 'cultural wasteland', and 'end of the West' convey the calamities that await the American nation if it does not stop this 'path to national suicide'.

With the legacy of this performative 'nation narration' (Bhabha 1990) that enacts the need for racial homogeneity over and over again, predictably, the discursive registers of the anti-immigrant online groups reveal a skillfully concerted effort to construct unwanted immigrants, once again, through the rhetoric of othering, dehumanization, and fear, as nonwhite usurpers of 'our' national space and polluters who want to steal what is rightfully 'ours'. The myth about 'illegal aliens' mercilessly draining the welfare system is perhaps the most enduring in the American imagination, despite the fact that those who are undocumented have no access to welfare benefits, while they do have access to public schools and public health care. In 'The Truth about the Illegal Invasion', Steve Elliott, the president of Grassfire.org, contends: 'Illegal immigration is inundating our borders with mountains of garbage. And illegal immigration is undermining American culture and threatening our future' (2006). The rhetoric of 'garbage' and the implied 'dirt' and 'defilement' is accompanied by the rescue narratives of the nation, which is typically represented as in great jeopardy and in need of 'cleaning', 'repair', and reinstated 'security'.

Run by John Vinson, the American Immigration Control Foundation (AICF), one of the nation's oldest immigration reform organizations, as it describes itself, advertises its mission: 'Representing many different ethnic groups and backgrounds, AIC Foundation supporters have a deep commitment to preserving *our common heritage as Americans*, and to helping AIC Foundation educate our fellow citizens on the disastrous effects of uncontrolled immigration' (AIFC, my emphasis). What is perhaps most stunning in the proud tone of the mission is a claim to an unquestioned rightful ownership of the nation and a complete erasure of Native Americans as if 'our common heritage as Americans' has always legitimately and solely belonged to a postcolonial imaginary. Also, 'uncontrolled immigration' needs to be apprehended historically, as it refers to the abolishing of the so-called racial quotas in the 1965 Immigration Act, which, prior to the Act, legitimized the influx of selected groups of white Western European immigrants while restricting Asians and Eastern and Southern Europeans. In this logic, the past practices of 'controlled immigration' were perceived as the lawful tactics, whereas the present-day arrival of mainly nonwhite immigrants (even if legal) is perceived as 'uncontrolled immigration'.

The discursive battleground staged by these various organizations is energized less by what these groups say about immigrant overpopulation and its purportedly fatal effects on a long list of 'ills' (poverty, environmental degradation, school congestions, welfare rip-offs, and crime) than by issues that are elided. What lurks underneath such statements is the performed anxiety over a threat of white racial extinction and thus the 'end of American civilization' as we know it – 'the passing and death of America as waves of foreign people and cultures submerge our land' (Vinson 2000, 1). In 'Immigration Out of Control: The Interests Against America', Vinson comes close to articulating this fear openly: 'Within 50 to 60 years, "Anglo-American" . . . will become a minority of slightly less than 50 percent of the population. . . .[A] country with multiple cultures will be as confused as a psychologically disturbed person with multiple personalities' (14–17). Even though the USA has always been a nation of multiple cultural strands, this logic sees non-Anglo cultures as only adjacent to the dominant one whose core is unquestionably Western and white.[5]

Undoubtedly, the fear of white racial extinction is an underlying sentiment in anti-immigrant raging. Vinson, for example, claims that Americans are 'fighting a war' with an 'unseen enemy' who is rapidly ravishing our land. This carefully chosen language casts immigrants as germs and bacteria that, outside the realm of visibility, infest the nation. A 'raging flood' of Latins, Haitians, and other 'Third Worlders' – 'the greatest wave of immigration the world has ever witnessed' – threatens America's 'generally European' core with 'foreign domination'. 'America is beautiful', says the narrator in one of the videos distributed by AICF, 'why spoil it?'

Such a strong emotional appeal subtly shifts the performance of righteous patriotism toward anger and violence against nonwhite immigrants.[6] In 'It's Righteous Indignation, Not Hate', Vinson writes:

> Agreed upon standards and values, derived from Western culture, have been the source of American success and freedom. Communities of Americans, working in harmony, have achieved impressive civic and material goals. . . .Sadly this harmony is fading, as community after community falls victim to the kind of diversity which destroys common purpose. Even when immigrants are hard-working, this does not mean that they share all American values and sentiments. . . .Many natives, feeling like foreigners in their own country will experience a deep sense of alienation, a psychological condition characterized by anger and sadness. *Such anger is entirely appropriate, and is justified further by the undemocratic manner through which 'diversity' comes about.* (2000, my emphasis)

The perception that many natives now feel like foreigners in their own country echoes Buchanan's earlier claim that, because immigrant invasions turned 'America' into a 'moral sewer', millions of rightful Americans 'feel like strangers in their own land' (2002, p. 5).

But, unlike Buchanan's often inflammatory rhetoric, Vinson's language is more nuanced, acknowledging, in fact, that many immigrants do contribute to the nation's economy through their 'hard work'. The twist offered here is thus not about the immigrants' productivity but about their allegedly inherent *inability* to contribute to the (white) *harmony* of the nation.

To fully comprehend Vinson's paradigm of 'righteous indignation, not hate', it is crucial to consider his other pamphlet, 'Immigration and Nation: a Biblical View', where he argues that nations 'are not arbitrary human creations, but divinely ordained entities' (1997, p. 8): 'As God is the author of nationhood, the ethnic make-up of a nation is not an arbitrary human choice, but a reflection of divine providence' (1997, p. 19). The biblical vision of nationhood fully justifies U.S. ethnic nationalism and the logic of racial purity, ominously reminding us of the Nazi's genocidal tactics of 'cleaning up' the 'lesser' races to save the Aryan nation from the 'pollution' by Jews, Slavs, Gypsies, and homosexuals, as well as of the 1990s wars in the Balkans under the banners of nationalist ethnic purity.

Thus, the performativity of 'legality' and 'illegality' I have been probing in this essay, that is, the 'reiterative power of discourse' (Butler 1993, p. 2), loses its supposed 'clarity' if we consider the specific Christian nationalism that often implicitly underpins the logic propagated by many of these online organizations. The biblical take on immigration is all about the undisputed superiority and the right of white Westerners to the American nation, a right, which does not have to be argued for because it is a result of 'divine providence': 'God does not view all nations and their respective cultures as equal' (Vinson 1997, p. 8). Thus, 'diversity', 'pluralism', 'multiculturalism', or any notion that strays from the logic of cultural homogeneity is deemed ungodly, dangerous, and in need of eradication.

How does one theorize this anxious performance of domination, which, under the guise of a godly culture, deeply invests in an ideology of contempt and resurrects the specter of white supremacy? The linguist, Nancy Dorian, introduced the notion of an 'ideology of contempt' to argue that colonizers brought with them the assumed superiority of Western standardization: 'Europeans who came from polities with a history of standardizing and promoting just one high-prestige speech form carried their "ideology of contempt" for subordinate languages with them when they conquered far-flung territories, to the serious detriment of indigenous languages' (1998, pp. 9–10). Though Dorian approaches the issue of contempt from the position of linguistic mastery, the attitude she describes – the claimed right to unquestioned white Western superiority most powerfully articulated in Vinson's arguments – is historically ingrained in national consciousness.

This point leads me to 'emotions', an element that should not be underestimated in any effort to unravel the magnetic appeal of the online anti-immigrant groups. In *Between Jesus and the Market: The Emotions That Matter in Right-Wing America*, Linda Kintz studies both religious and secular traditionalist conservatism to analyze its powerful attraction. She asks to consider emotions seriously, outside the confines of the binary logic that separates emotionality from rationality. Such an insistent separation impedes any nuanced discussion of political identity, whether religious or secular, left or right, and forecloses 'the fact that politics are not only about abstract reasoning or economic interests but also about belief, which combines the rational and the irrational, the conscious and the unconscious, thought and feelings, the abstract and the physical' (1997, p. 5):

> While [. . .] the emotions have been trivialized, at another level, men have powerfully drawn on emotions in their own interests, in the media construction of a cultural imaginary, as well as in the emotions of masculinity in relation to patriotism, property, the frontier, and guns. (1997, p. 4)

Such a contention allows us to recognize that the success of anti-immigrant online activism indicates the triumph of a particular kind of patriotic, God-created white masculinity, given the fact that all the leaders and most visible members of those groups are men of 'pure whiteness' (Kintz 1997, p. 759) who occasionally usher in women's voices as their aid. One such voice is Yeh Ling-Ling's whose pamphlet, 'U.S. Immigration: Viewed by an Immigrant', is advertised by AICF as particularly valuable because Ling-Ling is an immigrant herself – a native of Vietnam of Chinese descent and a naturalized U.S. citizen who works as an executive director of Alliance for a Sustainable America (AS-USA). She claims that a number of immigrants are restrictionists because they 'don't want their adopted country to lose the unique character and appeal which attracted them in the first place' (1999). The preservation of the uniqueness of the USA, a point which permeates many of Ling-Ling's texts, reveals a desire to uphold the exceptional character of the nation, even if, paradoxically, it is supported by a nonwhite 'foreign' woman who, writing from the expected position of a properly grateful yet concerned immigrant, argues that an anti-immigrant stance is actually pro-immigration: 'Advocating immigration reduction is not only pro-environment, but pro-immigrant and pro-minority as well' (2004).

But what should not be overlooked in such discursive twists is the issue of economic privilege discreetly obliterated in Ling-Ling's writing but visible in her profile, which states that Ling-Ling had approximately 20 years of education abroad in Cambodia, Taiwan, and the University of Paris-Sorbonne (AS-USA). Through this description, she herself emerges as an 'exceptional' immigrant, worthy of being listened to and one who deserves to be added to the national make-up, confirming Bonnie Honig's well-known formulation that 'American xenophilia and xenophobia both operate in service of American nationalism' (2002).

Stop the Invasion!: 'The Hispanic Challenge'

> We chose the words very carefully. We think this is actually an invasion.
> – Steve Elliott, President of Grassfire.org: Real Impact Online

On 7 June 2006, local Los Angeles TV station, KTLA, reported that a new billboard was unveiled in California: 'A controversial billboard is triggering a new debate on the issue of immigration reform here in Southern California. The billboard calls illegal immigration–and I am quoting–an invasion of America'.

The billboard, washed in colors of the U.S. flag and proclaiming, 'Stop the Invasion! Secure our Borders', is an example of an online activism moving into a public space. The signature is Grassfire.org: Real Impact Online, a group which describes itself as 'grassroots conservative online citizen networking' (Grassfire). The reporter explains that the group chose this high visibility area: 'Over the next thirty days that the billboard is up, they [the group] estimate some five million people will get to see their message'. The Stop the Invasion campaign is a nationwide effort. The billboard also appeared in Dallas, Atlanta, Miami, Phoenix, and San Diego. In addition, the organization's webpage discusses how 'ordinary' citizens can participate in the campaign, how they can personalize it and make it local by purchasing smaller versions of the giant billboard.

While other anti-immigrant online campaigns I have been discussing offer similar tools and use similar tactics, what distinguishes Grassfire.org are its carefully crafted discursive registers. Unlike IllegalAliens.US, Vdare.com, Fairus.org, or saynotoillegals.org, whose organizations often use aggressive tone, mocking tonality, belligerent exclamations, and racist statements, Grassfire.org's rhetoric is deliberately dressed in the language of politeness and concern for the well-being of the nation. As Elliott appears onscreen during the KTLA news report, the audience hears the punchline: 'Grassfire.org . . . is made up of residents against amnesty for immigrants. Grassfire's president says his group doesn't fault immigrants but instead blames citizens for causing the invasion' (KTLA). In the realm of conventional anti-immigrant rhetoric, this argument – not faulting the immigrants but instead blaming the citizens – is undoubtedly a novel and bold discursive strategy, turning traditional sentiments on their head. As Elliott claims, 'This is an invasion that American citizens *have brought upon themselves* by not demanding that our laws be enforced, by not demanding that our borders be secured' (KTLA, my emphasis).

The discourse of 'invasion' refers to the 'illegal' crossings of the U.S.–Mexico border. But how does one dissect such an *inverted* logic of invasion that the rhetoric propelled by Grassfire pretends to be unaware of? In pondering such a question, Guillermo Gómez-Peña's point feels indispensable: 'the social and ethnic fabric of the U.S. is filled with interstitial wounds, invisible to those who didn't experience the events that generated them, or who are victimized by historical amnesia' (1989, p. 21). The 'wounds' refer to the fact that the concept of the border for Mexicans living on the borderlands and, more broadly, for the Chicano communities evokes, as Linda Rosa Fregoso sums up, conflicted history: 'the border figures as an intrusive or invasive border; the division established after the Mexican-American War of 1848, that is, an illegitimately imposed separation' (1993, p. 65). Samuel P. Huntington, a political scientist and a frequent commentator on immigration, further explains the particular 'historical presence' of Latinos, which he refers to as 'the Hispanic challenge'. The notion of a challenge singles out Mexican Americans as a particularly troubling group in the U.S. immigration history, one that feels 'increasingly comfortable with their own culture and often contemptuous of American culture' (Huntington 2004, p. 44). According to Huntington, these historical circumstances result in a large-scale Latino immigration, which poses a cultural threat to the dominant 'national identity':

> No other immigrant group in U.S. history has asserted or could assert a historical claim to U.S. territory. Mexicans and Mexican Americans can and do make that claim. Almost all of Texas, New Mexico, Arizona, California, Nevada, and Utah was part of Mexico until Mexico lost them as a result of the Texan War of Independence in 1835–1836 and the Mexican-American War of 1846–1848. Mexico is the only country that the United States has invaded, occupied its capital . . . and then annexed half its territory. (p. 36)

Situating the Los Angeles immigrant marches in the context of a difficult legacy of the border, in the structures of 'wounds' Gómez-Peña talks about, reveals these protests as having an emotional tonality of exceptional significance, resonating with the critique of historical amnesia. Behdad's *A Forgetful Nation: On Immigration and Cultural Identity in the United States*, directly engages these issues, arguing that 'the forgetful representation by the United States of its immigrant heritage is part of a broader form of historical amnesia about its violent formation. Both the benign discourse of democratic founding and the myth of immigrant America deny that nationhood has been achieved, at least in part, through the violent conquest of Native Americans, the brutal exploitation of enslaved Africans, and the colonialist annexations of French and Mexican territories' (2005, p. xii).

Read in this context, the Los Angeles marches took place on the protest ground whose ambivalence 'haunts the idea of the nation' (Bhabha 1990, p. 1). This ground draws attention to the particularly volatile issues of (il)legality and citizenship in relation to Latino communities, the ground that, as Lalo Alcaraz's 1998 playfully sarcastic cartoon reminds us, has never been 'ours': 'Welcome to America the Illegal Immigration Country. Don't Let This Happen to Your Country. Call 1(800) NO PILGRIMS' (see Figure 1).

Figure 1. *Welcome to the Illegal Immigration Country*, 1998. Courtesy of Lalo Alcaraz.

No human being is illegal

> You who are so-called illegal aliens must know that no human being is 'illegal.' That is a contradiction in terms. Human beings can be beautiful or even more beautiful . . . they can be right or wrong, but illegal? How can a human being be illegal?

> – Elie Wiesel

Elie Wiesel's statement – no human being is illegal – particularly evocative because it comes from a Holocaust survivor and U.S. immigrant, has been functioning as a title of a traveling exhibition organized by the Center for the Study of Political Graphics (CSPG): *No Human Being is Illegal: Posters on the Myths and Realities of the Immigrant Experience.* Los Angeles-based CSPG is an archive that preserves and exhibits domestic and international posters relating to historical and contemporary movements for peace and social justice. In newsletters, CSPG advertises its mission by displaying Vladimir Mayakovsky's well-known saying that 'Art is not a mirror held up to reality but a hammer with which to shape it' and states that 'CSPG is reclaiming the power of art to educate, agitate and inspire action'. Carol Wells, founder and executive director of CSPG, writes: 'A poster is not just an informative piece of paper. It is art that grabs your attention and gets in your face. It is designed for a specific moment, a distinct cause, and with an explicit message. We use posters to teach new generations the history of struggle and resistance that they don't learn in school' (Poli-Grafiks 2007). Wells explicitly stresses the issue of histories of political resistance missing from institutional discourses which shape the official version of History.

No Human Being is Illegal premiered in 1988 as a graphic response to the escalating deportations of Central Americans and it was updated 5 years later, when Proposition 187 was on the ballot. Although the ensuing events – 9/11, the Patriot Act, the Iraq War – have profoundly affected the entire nation, immigrants undoubtedly remain the most vulnerable to the resulting rise in racism, discrimination, and patriotic vigilantism. Wells claims that, especially in such a repressive climate, art posters are central to educational and organizing efforts.[7]

The exhibition stands as a powerful opposition to the anti-immigrant campaigns I have been analyzing. It historicizes migration, highlights a multitude of reasons behind it – escaping war, apartheid, seeking political asylum from persecution, or pursuing better economic opportunities – and shows complexities of immigration experiences without romanticizing, victimizing, or demonizing migrants. Through a multivocal tonality – anger, empathy, playfulness, poignancy, sarcasm, irony – the exhibition counters the prescribed visuality of illegality by exposing the U.S. citizenship itself as 'illegal' – rooted in the colonization of indigenous people and in neocolonizing practices of exploitation.

One of the most well-known images in the exhibition is Yolanda Lopez's 1978 drawing, reissued in 1994 in response to California's Proposition 187 (see Figure 2). While many of the posters are designed to evoke empathy – a father being separated from a son, a family looking through a chain-link fence – Lopez alters this mood by showing an Aztec in a provocative posture who holds 'Immigration Plans' and demands, 'Who's the illegal alien, PILGRIM?' Challenging the time-honored immigrant narrative of the nation, her work reminds the viewer that everyone in the USA, except for indigenous people, is descended from immigrants. She appropriates the figure's pointing finger and frontal stare from James Montgomery Flagg's famous World War I recruiting poster 'I Want You for U.S. Army', the

Figure 2.   Yolanda Lopez. *Who's The Illegal Alien, Pilgrim?* 1978. Courtesy of the artist and CSPG.

Figure 3.   THINK AGAIN. *Admit None*, 1999. Courtesy of the artists and CSPG.

alteration that strikingly defamiliarizes the previous image, shifting the alien coding onto those who only know how to imprint others with the stamp of alienhood.

Many of the posters in the exhibition use the Statue of Liberty. 'Admit None', by artist collaborative THINK AGAIN, is another particularly memorable example (Figure 3). Focusing specifically on California, it showcases what this culture, despite all its denials, fully understands in its tenacious pretense, particularly when it comes to the *usefulness* of migrants: 'Welcome to America. Wash Our Dishes, Clean Our Clothes, Now Go Home'. The central image is a movie ticket displaying the Statue and the words 'Admit None', a design that skillfully links Hollywood cinematic culture to migrants whose labor supports the economy, enticing the viewer to think about 'our' dependence on immigrant labor and everyone's complicity in the exploitation of these workers. The image evokes a paradoxical tension in the discourses of inclusion and exclusion: 'the more the anti-immigrant frenzy of right-wing politics howls ... for "exclusion", and the more border is militarized, the more the inclusion of these "illegal" workers continues – *inclusion as labor subordination*' (De Genova and Borcila 2011, my emphasis).

Importantly in this context, THINK AGAIN has also co-authored 2006–2007 *Salt in the Wound* (*The NAFTA Effect*), a multimedia art project, which uses video and outdoor projection to expose contradictions in the debates about free trade, immigration, and increased border security. According to the group's press release, 'The title references the gratuitous infliction of additional misery on those in an already grueling situation ....This project acknowledges the contribution and participation of immigrant laborers in our daily

Figure 4.   Xico González, *Welcome to Gringolandia*, 2006. Courtesy of the artist and CSPG.

lives. On the level of policy, *Salt In The Wound* highlights how international treaties like NAFTA, in concert with national anti-immigration efforts like a 700-mile border fence, insidiously reshape the ways that families live and work on both sides of the border' (Think Again n.d.).

Xico González's 'Welcome to Gringolandia' echoes both Lopez's message and THINK AGAIN's multilayered imagery by employing the Statue of Liberty, but in a mode of playful yet poignant mockery (Figure 4). The Statue is a smiling Mickey Mouse and next to it there is an image of Speedy Gonzalez, 'the fastest mouse in all Mexico' from the Warner Brothers' *Looney Tunes* animation series. The image of a speedy mouse is counterpoised by the well-known 'Caution' sign depicting a running 'alien' family. The poster is signed, 'Welcome to Gringolandia: Where Racism and Exploitation Officially Started in 1776'.

Inviting us to be mindful of complex historical circumstances of migration, this alternative visual imaginary compels the viewers to 'think again' about the so-called immigration question, a cliché meant to suggest that immigration is forever a national wound, a problem in need of solution, whether this solution emerges from the aggressive vigilantism practiced by Arizona's Minuteman or from the benevolent rhetoric expressed by both Senator Clinton and Senator Obama during the Democratic Debate in January 2008 in Hollywood. Though using slightly different language, both Senators basically suggested the same solution, one based on a capitalist logic of domination. Carefully avoiding the controversial issue of amnesty, they claimed that the best remedy at present would be for the 'illegals' to 'pay fines' (to pay monetarily for illegality) and 'learn English' (to pay for it linguistically), after they have 'come out from the shadows' (a trope which de-ontologizes them before 'inviting' them to ontology). These penalties speak to the need to discipline the unruly 'aliens' and, in the process, make them pay for national belonging with both money and language.

Finally, it is crucial to consider how *No Human Being Is Illegal*'s alternative visualizations resonate locally and transnationally through a No One Is Illegal politics at large via various oppositional forms of social activism that attempt to effect policy change (No One is Illegal networks, the Solidarity Across Borders coalition, No More Deaths/No Más Muertes, No Border camps, DADS campaigns (Don't Ask, Don't Tell)). It is clear that the exhibition is not a singular act of art protest but rather it is conceptually linked to multiple efforts to undo phobic nationalisms in the USA and beyond. Referring to the insidious power of national homogeneity *vis-à-vis* the 2006 immigrant marches, Butler explains the notion of 'performative contradiction': 'They have no right of free speech under the law although they're speaking freely, precisely in order to demand the right to speak freely' (2007, p. 64). She claims that the effects of such acts 'unfold in time': 'there can be no radical politics of change without performative contradiction' (2007, p. 66).

It is especially in this context that the exhibition dislodges the concept of 'legality' from its supposedly unshakable moral anchoring and universal righteousness, disclosing such contradictions. It creates a nuanced visual landscape that helps us read anti-immigrant activism by pointing to its euphoric discourses of patriotism as grounded in the ruthless practices of nationalism in Fortress America. These anxious acts of citizenship, the 'neuropolitics' propelling 'the neuroticization of the border' (Isin 2004, pp. 231–232), indeed, 'the Border Spectacle' itself (De Genova and Borcila 2011), guard privileges of mobility and inclusion reserved for only some of its members. Ultimately, these two political efforts, anti- and pro-immigrant one, return me to the two marches and their incommensurability. In conclusion, it is clear that the online groups rely on historical amnesia and, like the colonizing Soviet-imposed government in Poland, proclaim the desire to protect the nation and celebrate its power. The full significance of the Los Angeles immigrant protest can only be realized if this amnesia is exposed as a strategic erasure masking layers of colonial pasts. *No Human Being is Illegal* exposes the immigrant roots of the nation and, with emotive fierceness and without necessarily eliciting pity for the migrants, it asks the viewers to consider the profound ironies that enmesh (il)legal human bodies in the sustenance of the 'legal' body of the nation.

Acknowledgements

The author would like to thank Áine O'Healy, Marguerite Waller, Imogen Tyler, and the anonymous reviewers for their engaged feedback. The author shows her gratitude to Lalo Alcaraz, THINK AGAIN collective, Yolanda Lopez, and Xico Gonzalez for allowing her to showcase their art and to Carol Wells for helping her secure the images from the CSPG collection.

Notes

1. I am using the notion of 'rage' evocatively; the marches and protests, at least in Los Angeles, were peaceful, though guarded heavily by the LAPD whose members accompanied the protesters on motorcycles, on horseback, and in patrol cars.
2. On nationalism, immigration advocacy, and the use of the flag, see Bauder (2006).
3. In order to travel abroad, one had to apply for a temporarily issued passport and go through interviews, explaining and documenting one's desire for mobility as well as signing declarations promising a scheduled return. After the return, one had to return the passport to the authorities.
4. My questioning of the 'clarity of legality' is indebted to Linda Kintz who, in her discussion of right-wing visual culture and virtual whiteness, defines this clarity as one that shuts down complexities and denies 'messiness of interpretation' (2002, p. 761).

5. As I have discussed in *Alienhood*, the notion of whiteness *vis-à-vis* the U.S. immigration policy needs to be de-universalized, as the logic of racial whiteness has been historically fluctuating and slippery, contingent upon changing politics of race (see, e.g. Haney-López 1996, Jacobson 1998).
6. The massacre at a youth summer camp in July 2011 in Norway by Andreas Breivik, propelled by his desire to return Christian Europe to its white 'native' glory, certainly urges us to take online white supremacy seriously.
7. Conversation with Carol Wells at CSPG in Los Angeles, 7 February 2008 (quoted by permission).

References

Alliance for a Sustainable America (AS-USA), [online]. Available from: http://www.asustainableusa.org/asusa_leaders.html [Accessed 3 May 2008].

American Immigration Control Foundation (AIFC), [online]. Available from: http://www.aicfoundation.com/ [Accessed 7 March 2008].

Auster, L., 1990. *The path to national suicide: an essay on immigration and multiculturalism.* Monterey, VA: AIC Foundation.

Bauder, H., 2006. And the flag waved on: immigrants protest, geographers meet in Chicago. *Environment and planning A*, 38 (6), 1001–1004.

Bauman, Z., 1998. *Globalization: the human consequences.* New York: Columbia University Press.

Behdad, A., 1998. INS and outs: producing delinquency at the border. *Aztlán*, 23 (1), 103–113.

Behdad, A., 2005. *A forgetful nation: on immigration and cultural identity in the United States.* Durham, NC: Duke University Press.

Bhabha, H., 1983. The 'other' question. *Screen*, 24 (6), 18–36.

Bhabha, H. ed., 1990. *Nation and narration.* New York: Routledge.

Brimelow, P., 1995. *Alien nation: common sense about America's immigration disaster.* New York: Random.

Buchanan, P., 2002. *The death of the west: how dying populations and immigrant invasions imperil our country and civilization.* New York: Thomas Dunne Books.

Butler, J., 1993. *Bodies that matter: on the discursive limits of 'sex'.* New York: Routledge.

Butler, J. and Spivak, G.C., 2007. *Who sings the nation-state? language, politics, belonging.* London: Seagull Books.

Center for the Study of Political Graphics (CSPG), [online]. Available from: http://www.politicalgraphics.org/home.html [Accessed 7 June 2008].

De Genova, N., 2010. Alien powers: deportable labour and the spectacle of security. *In*: N. De Genova and N. Peutz, eds. *The deportation regime: sovereignty, space, and the freedom of movement.* Durham, NC: Duke University Press, 91–115.

De Genova, N. and Borcila, R., 2011. An image of our future: on the making of migrant 'illegality', AREA Chicago [online]. Available from: http://www.areachicago.org/p/issues/immigrations/image-our-future/ [Accessed 12 July 2011].

Dorian, N., 1998. Western language ideologies and small-language prospects. *In*: L.A. Grenoble and L.J. Whaley, eds. *Endangered languages: language loss and community response.* Cambridge: Cambridge University Press, 3–21.

Doty, R.L., 2007. States of exception on the Mexico-U.S. border: security, 'decisions', and civilian border patrols. *International political sociology*, 1 (2), 113–137.

Elliott, S., 2006. The truth about the illegal invasion [online]. *Grassfire.org Alliance*. Available from: http://web.archive.org/web/20060915071949/http:/www.grassfire.org/ [Accessed 15 April 2008].

Foucault, M., 1979. *Discipline and punish: the birth of the prison.* New York: Vintage Books.

Fregoso, L.R., 1993. *The bronze screen: Chicana and Chicano film culture.* Minneapolis, MN: University of Minnesota Press.

Grassfire.org: Real Impact Online, [online]. Available from: http://www.grassfire.com/ [Accessed 9 May 2008].

Gómez-Peña, G., 1989. The multicultural paradigm: an open letter to the national arts community. *High performance*, 12 (3), 17–27.

Haney-López, I.F., 1996. *White by law: the legal construction of race.* New York: New York University Press.

Honig, B., 2002. A legacy of xenophobia [online]. Boston review: a political and literary forum 27, Available from: http://www.bostonreview.net/BR27.6/honig.html [Accessed 9 May 2008].

Huntington, S.P., 2004. The Hispanic challenge. *Foreign policy*, March/April, 30–45.

Immigration Through Investment, [online]. Available from: http://www.uscis.gov/portal/site/uscis/menuitem.eb1d4c2a3e5b9ac89243c6a7543f6d1a/?vgnextoid=facb83453d4a3210VgnVCM10 0000b92ca60aRCRD&vgnextchannel=facb83453d4a3210VgnVCM100000b92ca60aRCRD [Accessed 7 June 2008].

Isin, E.F., 2004. The neurotic citizen. *Citizenship studies*, 8 (3), 217–235.

Isin, E.F. and Nielsen, G.M., 2008. Introduction: acts of citizesnhip. *In*: E.F. Isin and G.M. Nielsen, eds. *Acts of Citizenship*. London: Zed Books, 1–12.

Jacobson, M.F., 1998. *Whiteness of a different color: European immigrants and the alchemy of race*. Cambridge, MA: Harvard University Press.

Kintz, L., 1997. *Between Jesus and the market: the emotions that matter in right-wing America*. Durham, NC: Duke University Press.

Kintz, L., 2002. Performing virtual whiteness: George Gilder's techno-theocracy. *Cultural studies*, 16 (5), 735–773.

KTLA TV News, 2006. June 7 *KTLA TV News*.

Ling-Ling, Y., 1999. U.S. immigration: viewed by an immigrant [online]. Available from: http://www.aicfoundation.com/pamphlets.htm [Accessed 10 June 2008].

Ling-Ling, Y., 2004. Close our borders: advocating immigrant reduction is pro-environment and pro-immigrant [online]. *Asian week*. Available from: http://diversityalliance.org/docs/article_asianweek_2004jun11.hmtl [Accessed 7 July 2008].

Marciniak, K., 2006. *Alienhood: citizenship, exile, and the logic of difference*. Minnesota, MN: University of Minnesota Press.

McCain, J., 2007. Talk at the Aspen Institute (Aspen, CO) [online], Available from: http://www.youtube.com/watch?v=1sIEAD_sVF0 [Accessed 5 June 2008].

Ngai, M.M., 2004. *Impossible subjects: illegal aliens and the making of modern America*. Princeton, NJ: Princeton University Press.

Nyers, P., 2008. No one is illegal: between city and nation. *In*: E.F. Isin and G.M. Nielsen, eds. *Acts of citizenship*. London: Zed Books, 160–181.

Papadopoulos, D. and Tsianos, V.S., 2013. After citizenship: autonomy of migration, organisational ontology and the mobile commons. *Citizenship studies*, 17 (2), 178–196.

Poli-Grafiks, 2007. *Newsletter of the Center for the Study of Political Graphics*. Los Angeles: Center for the Study of Political Graphics.

Solis, J., 2008. No human being is illegal: counteridentities in a community of undocumented Mexican immigrants and children. *In*: B. Oers, E. Elbers and R. van der Veer, eds. *The transformation of learning: advances in cultural-historical activity theory*. Cambridge: Cambridge University Press, 182–200.

Think Again, n.d. [online]. Available from: http://saltinthewound.org/ [Accessed 15 June 2008].

Vinson, J., 1997. *Immigration and nation: a biblical view*. Monterey, VA: AIC Foundation.

Vinson, J., 2000. It's righteous indignation, not hate [online]. The Virginia Land Rights Coalition, Available from: http://www.vlrc.org/articles/128.html [Accessed 7 May 2008].

Walters, W., 2008. Acts of demonstration: mapping the territory of (non-) citizenship. *In*: E.F. Isin and G.M. Nielsen, eds. *Acts of citizenship*. London: Zed Books, 182–206.

Wells, C., 2007. *Letter to readers*. Los Angeles: Poli-Graphics Newsletter of the Center for the Study of Political Graphics.

Williams, M.C., 2003. Words, images, enemies: securitization and international politics. *International studies quarterly*, 47 (4), 511–531.

Williams, J., 2006. Jet Williams on immigration protests [online]. Available from: http://truecountry.com/forums/showthread.php?4588-Jett-Williams-On-Immigration-Protests [Accessed 20 June 2008].

'I am an American': protesting advertised 'Americanness'

Cynthia Weber

Department of International Relations, University of Sussex, Brighton BN1 9RH, UK

How are citizenships and nationalisms constructed, connected, and contested in the post-9/11 USA – performatively, affectively, and visually – and how do their relationships figure 'Americanness'? This article takes up this question (1) by tracking how Americanness was advertised in the American Ad Council's 'I am an American' campaign and (2) by introducing the multimedia project *'I am an American': Video Portraits of Unsafe US Citizens*, which engages the Ad Council's campaign as a practice-based protest of the Ad Council's advertised 'Americanness'. The article traces how the Ad Council's campaign advertises what Evelyn Alsultany calls 'diversity patriotism'. It also constructs a complex, mobile system of differentiation that marks some citizens as 'safe' and others as 'unsafe', which runs counter to the idealized notion of a unified 'Americanness' that it advertises. The article then examines how the practice-based protest project 'I am an American' takes these 'unsafe citizens' – US citizens who either will not or cannot make their differences normatively conform to the national ideal of the 'One' composed of the 'Many' propagated by the Ad Council's campaign – as its point of departure to reflect upon how citizenship protests function for and against citizenship, nationalisms, and various figurations of Americanness.

Introduction

How are citizenships and nationalisms constructed, connected, and contested in the post-9/11 USA – performatively, affectively, and visually – and how do their relationships figure, 'Americanness'? This article suggests that among the ways citizenships and nationalisms figure Americanness is through public service advertising campaigns.

As Alsultany (2007) has pointed out, advertising was a strategy used not just by the American Advertising Council but also by other nonprofit groups such as the Council on American–Islamic Relations (CAIR) to figure patriotic post-9/11 US identities as racially and ethnically diverse, yet nationally unified. Taking Alsultany's work as its points of departure, this article tracks how Americanness was advertised in the American Ad Council's 'I am an American' campaign. It does this by focusing specifically on how the Ad Council's 'I am an American' Public Service Announcement (PSA) attempts to 'not so much represent society *as it is* but society as it *should* be' (Cronin 2004, p. 113) through its advertising of what Alsultany calls 'diversity patriotism', a patriotism that makes the celebration of diversity its foundation for affecting feelings of national unity. For a nation that envisions itself as a melting pot in which individual differences melt into insignificance when US citizens identify with the US nation, diversity-patriotism is a highly charged affective technology of patriotism.

Yet running counter to the idealized notion of a unified Americanness that it advertises, the PSA also uses visual, aural, and editing techniques to construct a complex, mobile system of differentiation that marks some US citizens with what might be called 'safe forms of Americanness' and other US citizens with 'unsafe forms of Americanness'. If safe US citizens are US citizens who the PSA imagines as easily melting into the PSA's advertised ideal of a diverse yet unified Americanness, then unsafe US citizens are those US citizens who the PSA marks with differences that cannot or will not melt into this ideal of advertised Americanness.

These unsafe US Americans and their unsafe forms of Americanness expose what Barbara Johnson calls 'the critical difference' that keeps an identity like the USA from corresponding to its image of itself, in this case as a patriotically diverse melting pot (1980). More generally, unsafe citizens point to the limits of the liberal promise of inclusion through citizenships and nationalisms that persistently invent distinctions between good citizens and bad citizens labeling them as 'meltable' or 'tolerable diversity patriots' or 'safe' on the one hand and 'unmeltable' or 'unpatriotic, intolerably dangerously different (potential) enemies' or 'unsafe' on the other. The figuring of some citizens as unsafe leads us to question how perceived racial, ethnic, and cultural differences figure political subjectivity. For they highlight how what is assumed to be a unified, coherent sovereign national political subjectivity fragments into various forms of national sovereignties and 'cultural citizenships' in which perceived 'cultural' differences locate unsafe citizens beyond the bounds of what the sovereign nation will tolerate, because it locates unsafe citizens beyond the bounds of patriotism (Brown 2006, Weber 2008). As such, 'cultural citizenship' marks not only the limits of what the sovereign nation-state perceives as patriotic, it also locates intolerably different citizens as justifiably beyond the bounds of their sovereign entitlement to the state's security and safety. This is a problem that is every bit as acute today with the Congressional passage of a bill that would allow for the indefinite detention of US citizens on US soil[1] as it was in the immediate aftermath of September 11, 2001.

The visual and aural focus of the Ad Council's 'I am an American' campaign is on safe US citizens. As a protest project, I created a practice-based project called 'I am an American': Video Portraits of Unsafe US Citizens that takes mainly unsafe US citizens as its visual and aural focus. After introducing and analyzing the Ad Council's 'I am an American' PSA, I introduce my alternative 'I am an American' project and the visual, aural, and editing techniques it employs to contest the Ad Council's project and to examine how unsafe US citizens refigure Americanness. I conclude by critically reflecting upon both projects as illustrations of 'citizenship protests' and what these projects might tell us about citizenships, nationalisms, Americanness, and political subjectivity.

The American Ad Council's 'I am an American' PSA

On 21 September 2001 – 10 days after 9/11 – the American Ad Council launched its 'I am an American' advertising campaign (Ad Council 2004a). The campaign featured 30 and 60 s PSAs broadcast on US television in which a montage of US citizens of various ages, races, religions, and ethnicities look directly into the camera and declare, 'I am an American' while emotive American music in a style reminiscent of Aaron Copeland's work plays in the background. The US motto appears on the screen, first in Latin, then in English – 'E Pluribus Unum', Out of Many, One. The final shot is of a young girl –

possibly Arab, possibly South Asian, possibly Hispanic. She rides her bike in Brooklyn Bridge Park across the river from where the Twin Towers used to be. Smiling broadly, the little girl waves a US flag. According to the Ad Council (which is the leading producer of PSAs in the USA),[2] the 'I am an American' campaign 'helped the country to unite in the wake of the terrorist attacks' by 'celebrat[ing] the nation's extraordinary diversity' (Ad Council 2004a).

The 'I am an American' PSA illustrates how the US national sentimentality (Berlant 1991, 1997, 2008) and the technologies of mechanical reproduction (Benjamin 1969, Anderson 1983) combine to produce what Alsultany calls 'diversity-patriotism, whereby racialized groups are temporarily incorporated into the imagined community of "Americans"' to the point that '[d]ifference is identified as defining the nation' (2007, p. 598). The cinematic strategies the PSA employs to achieve this diversity-patriotism are masterful. It saturates the visual space with a diversity of sharply focused unnamed US Americans and softly focused familiar Americana backdrops, like a Fire Station in lower Manhattan or the Golden Gate Bridge in San Francisco. It saturates the aural space with the repetitive yet performatively varied mantra 'I am an American' uttered with an array of accents, inflections, and intensities. It sets these visual and aural representations to the emotive American music 'Short Trip Home' by Edgar Meyer that has a Coplandesque quality to it. And it literally spells out what its message is – 'E Pluribus Unum', Out of Many, One – a phrase that, according to the makers of the PSA, communicates 'out of many faces, religions, geographical backgrounds, and ethnicities, we are one nation' (Ad Council 2004b).

By employing these cinematic strategies, the 'I am an American' PSA constructs not only the difference but also the ideal of the *tolerance of difference* as the foundation of the modern US nation (Brown 2006, Weber 2007), as if the US identity announced in the original US motto 'E Pluribus Unum' (which in 1776 referred to the uniting of different US Colonies into one Federal System) always referred to the 'melting' of individual racial and ethnic differences of US Americans into the united citizenry of the USA and as if this melting and the acceptance of all those melted into this pot by all US citizens were a long-ago accomplished fact (Berlant 1997, Marciniak 2006, Fortier 2008). Textually, aurally, and visually, the PSA achieves this rheotorical feat by attempting to solve what R.B.J. Walker refers to as the three problems facing the authorization of the sovereign nation-state – the need to resolve the relationships between (1) the universal and the particular, (2) the self and the other, and (3) space and time (Walker 1990).

The PSA resolves the universal/particular problem by attaching to the sign 'America' a plurality of visible, individual bodily differences (skin color, age, sex, accent) of US American citizens while at the same time denying these individual citizens any invisible, private signs of difference (their names, their lived histories, their easy or complicated relationships with the US state). The PSA resolves the self/other problem by appearing to dissolve all differences – visible and invisible – within the sameness of the US melting pot, whereas it nonetheless excludes or leaves ambiguous differences that might disturb the national melting pot ideal. For example, apart from two ambiguous individuals who might be either Arab or Muslim but cannot be definitively identified as such, the PSA includes 'no visible markers of anything Arab, Muslim, or Sikh [which is misread as Muslim by some US Americans]', 'no veil, no mosque, no turban, no beard; no distinctive Arab, Muslim, or Sikh clothing; no Arab accent' (Alsultany 2007, p. 598). In this way, Alsultany concludes, 'the Ad Council affirms the binary between "the citizen" and "the terrorist"' (2007, p. 598) both inside and outside the US nation-state. Finally, the PSA resolves the space/time problem by domesticating a particular identification – the claim to be 'American' – within the USA rather than within the larger continent that goes by this name and by excluding histories past and present that might make this claim contingent. It does this not only by deploying famous US landmarks as backgrounds in some shots. It also does by excluding any unambiguous signs of Indigenous Americans in the PSA, a population that even today is not containable in the national imagery of either a territorial state like the USA or within the modernist history of progress narrated through the melting pot myth (Sollors 1996, Shaw 2009).

Through these aesthetic and political strategies, the advertising strategy of the 'I am an American' advertisement is invisible because the timeless ideal of an American that the PSA sells to US Americans hardly seems like a product to many of its consumers. As I detail later, for many US viewers of the PSA, this emotive mosaic of modern US citizenship is so overwhelming that the PSA's obvious exclusions that would challenge its frame of reference are not strong enough to disrupt the PSA's emotional impact in the moment of its viewing. Indeed, on one level, the PSA seems to be about having an emotional impact on emotionally impacted 9/11 US citizens. More specifically, the PSA seems to be designed to re-channel US American emotions toward a united citizen ideal and away from a troubling grief, mourning, and melancholia (Gilroy 2006, Maira 2010) that got US citizens stuck on difficult questions such as 'Who are we?' and 'Who might we become?', questions implied in that other question that circulated in the US media as *the* question of 9/11 – 'Why do they hate us?' (Sardar and Wyn Davies 2003, Weber 2006).

Instead, the Ad Council's 'I am an American' PSA participates in transforming this 'bad grief' into a state-sponsored and therefore (from the state's point of view) socially responsible form of 'good grief' – a kind of cathartic release *from* the challenges of US identity posed by 9/11.[3] For the PSA seemed to be telling US Americans *not* to think about what it means to be a US citizen after 9/11 outside of the PSA's frame of reference, even though this was arguably the very time US Americans ought to have been asking questions about America and American citizenship.

That the PSA succeeded in moving many US citizens from a state of not knowing what to think or to feel into a cathartic embrace of their presumed tolerance of difference as the foundation of the US nation is evidenced by the many 'heartening emails' the Ad Council received in response to the campaign, including this one: 'When the twin towers came crashing down, I didn't cry. Like everyone else, I was in shock. When I saw your PSA "I am an American", I did cry. Thank you for putting forth the best and the most appropriate PSA ever' (Ad Council 2004b). This response was not unique. The Ad Council received so many messages of thanks and support for this campaign that it 'complied [them] in a booklet and sent [the booklet] out to volunteers who helped with the project' (Ad Council 2004b).

The effect of these many conscious or unconscious aesthetic, political, and affective strategies is a PSA that aesthetically reifies the illusion of a unified US national citizenry, one that has just enough content to give it resonance with individual US citizens but that is empty enough to make it presumably universalizable among all US citizens, but not to non-US Americans. As such, the PSA's repeated declaration 'I am an American' hails US Americans to identify with their nation and with the specific type of US citizen it constructs – one who recognizes that 'what it is that makes the US nation so unique' is its foundational claim to difference (Ad Council 2004b). More than this, though, the PSA hails these US diversity patriots to become the bearers of this illusion in practice, on behalf of their state and their nation.[4] For as Walker reminds us about the sovereignty of nation-states, 'Absolute authority has itself no absolute ground to stand on. What counts is the degree to which people can be persuaded to underwrite the sovereign power' (Walker

1990, p. 8). Considered in this way, the PSA is an instance of what might be called nationcraft as citizencraft (to paraphrase Richard K. Ashley's famous phrase 'statecraft as mancraft'; see Ashley 1989) in that it exemplifies how political nationalism is localized not only through legal and juridical practices (as Lauren Berlant convincingly claims; see Berlant 1991) but also through particular aesthetic practices that make the body and the citizen indivisible.

It is on the basis of this specific yet universalizable construction of a collective US national identity in which body is nation, diversity is identity, and tolerance is patriotic citizenship that the PSA hails every US citizen to actively tolerate those differences that compose this 'America'. But because of the necessary exclusions and ambiguities the PSA employs to assemble this ideal 'America', what the PSA also does is remind US Americans of how distinct they are from those whose differences – foreign and domestic – cannot be melted into this 'America'. It is these differences that the PSA implicitly instructs US Americans not to tolerate, for these are the differences embodied by those who presumably hate 'us'.

In this respect, then, the PSA not only draws a line between the normative white or normatively melted US citizen and the threatening Muslim, Arab, or Sikh terrorist, as Alsultany argues (2007, p. 598). By representing some 'culturalized' differences as acceptable and failing to represent other 'culturalized' differences at all, the PSA encourages a more amorphous, unanchored fear of any difference – not only racial and religious but also indigenous, sexual, and political, for example – that was not clearly represented in the PSA.[5] For by failing to represent these additional differences as melted into the US ideal of itself, the PSA leaves open the possibility that these, too, might be threatening to US citizens and the US nation-state now or in the future. In this way, the PSA even more narrowly draws a line around what Alsultany calls 'the limits of cultural citizenship' (2007, p. 596). And it is only within the limits of this narrowly drawn, acceptable cultural citizenship that US citizens are hailed by the PSA to transform the aesthetic illusion propagated by the PSA of a united (albeit exclusive) US national identity into a practical fact.

Contrary to its intended purpose of preventing 'a possible backlash against Arab Americans and other ethnic groups after the 9/11 attacks' (Ad Council 2004a), the PSA helps to organize a US national imaginary in which some but not all bodies are equated with the US nation, some but not all differences are equated with US identity, and some but not all forms of tolerance are equated with patriotic citizenship. In doing so, the PSA simultaneously anchors itself in a celebration of diversity on the one hand and a fear of difference on the other. For as Anne-Marie Fortier so persuasively argues, even though individuals, societies, nations, and states regularly conflate the two, the celebration of diversity does not necessarily equate to the celebration of difference. Rather, the celebration of diversity often explicitly refuses difference and thereby refutes the politics of difference (Fortier 2008). It is through this simultaneous conflation of diversity with difference and strategic separation of these two terms that the PSA effectively constructs a complex, mobile system of differentiation in which some differences mark citizens as 'safe citizens' and others mark them as 'unsafe citizens'. 'Safe citizens' are those citizens whose differences can, through their citizenship practices, be made to normatively conform to national ideals during the War on Terror historical moment so that they not only pose no threat to their state but, rather, they defend their state from threats by confirming these national ideals. In contrast, 'unsafe citizens' are those citizens who either will not or cannot make their differences normatively conform to the national ideals of this particular historical moment, making them real or potential threats to 'unifying' national ideals and to the US state itself (Weber 2008).

It is these unsafe citizens – US citizens who are beyond the limits of US cultural citizenship – who are cautioned by the PSA to keep their 'culture' (a euphemism for 'disturbing differences') private so that their differences do not endanger the US nation-state (Brown 2006). For if these unsafe citizens do not melt into/mesh with the US image of itself after 9/11, they are likely to find themselves on the wrong side of the us/them divide, whether they are 'American' or not. In this sense, the 'I am an American' PSA is not only a celebration of US diversity-patriotism, it is a warning to 'different' US Americans to align with the national side by keeping what could be their disturbing cultural differences private or to face the consequences. As such, the PSA reinforces the message President George W. Bush made before a Joint Session of the US Congress the day before the 'I am an American' PSA was broadcast – 'Either you are with us or you are with the terrorists' (Bush 2001). For even though President Bush's words were directed to foreign nations that harbor terrorists, his words, like the 'I am an American' PSA, attempt to persuade US citizens to underwrite the sovereign power of the US state in its War on Terror or face the possibility of having US sovereign power unleashed against them.

Filming the fear of difference[6]

The multi-media project *'I am an American': Video Portraits of Unsafe US Citizens* was crafted in response to the Ad Council's 'I am an American' PSA.[7] The project explores the complicated meanings and practices of citizenship, identity, tolerance, nationalism, patriotism, justice, and memory woven into and around the seemingly simple declaration 'I am an American'. It does this by recounting the experiences of some US citizens who after 9/11 would not or could not normatively conform to the ideal of 'safe citizenship' the PSA hailed them to embody and enact.

The films, photographs, and feedback commentaries that compose this project originated in a series of on-camera interviews I began in 2005 with a wide range of US Americans about their experiences as citizens in the post-9/11 USA. Some of the individuals I interviewed were involved in US foreign wars in Iraq and Afghanistan, others were involved in US domestic wars on immigration primarily at the US–Mexico border, and still others were caught up in the security and immigration crossfire of the War on Terror as a sort of collateral damage. These individuals ranged from patriotic soldiers who served in the Iraq War to patriotic Muslims who found themselves detained as alleged enemy combatants, from undocumented immigrants to the US citizens who either track them and turn them over to US Border Patrol or who offer them humanitarian assistance, and from indigenous US Americans living on both sides of the US–Mexico border who are subjected to extraordinary surveillance by US Border Patrol to Hurricane Katrina evacuees whose needs too often fail to register as urgent in the post-9/11 USA to artists and activists who found themselves suspected of practicing terrorism or aiding terrorists.

These individuals, their stories, and how these stories are told through my project can be understood as enactments of citizenship protests generally and often as immigrant protests specifically, as Tyler and Marciniak define it (2013), because they question the capacity of citizenship to capture how political subjectivity functions. These stories are told from the perspectives of a number of very differently situated protesters – some who are immigrants, some who insist they are not immigrants, and some who are struggling to become immigrants. Let me give an example of each of these types of stories, which highlight tensions among continental versus sovereign Americanness, indigenous versus settler Americanness, and consenting versus contesting patriotisms, respectively.

The story of Mexican citizen and immigrant rights activist Elvira Arellano and her US citizen son Saul highlights some of the tensions around immigration and birthright citizenship that Tyler and Marciniak discuss in their introduction to this volume. For this is the story of an undocumented economic migrant to the USA who worked in Chicago's O'Hare airport and who was discovered to have been using a false social security number when the USA tightened up its immigrant checks on airport workers after 9/11. Elvira received a deportation order which she defied, claiming that to deport her would effectively mean to deport Saul, who was born and raised in the USA. Elvira lived with Saul in sanctuary in a Chicago church for 1 year. When she left sanctuary, she was deported. She and Saul now live in Mexico (Figure 1).

Another story is that of indigenous rights activist José Matus. A Yaqui tribal member and director of the indigenous rights group Alianza Indigena Sin Fronteras/Indigenous Alliance Without Borders, José tells of how the US–Mexico border crosses what are traditional Yaqui tribal lands. Over the years, this has lead to the dismemberment of the Yaqui nation, with part of it in the USA and part of it in Mexico. José works with other indigenous rights activists to ensure the free passage of Yaqui tribal members across the US–Mexico border, whatever their US or Mexican citizenship. But because of increased border security measures in this region, José explains that Yaqui nation members coming from Mexico into the USA are often treated with the same suspicion as undocumented economic migrants coming into the USA. José's immigrant protest is against the idea that Indigenous Americans are being treated like immigrants. As he puts it, 'We didn't cross the border. The border crossed us' (Figure 2).

And then there is the story of Phil McDowell, a former Sergeant in the US Army. A college graduate, Phil enlisted in the military after 9/11 because he believed that 'the USA was a beacon of light in the world and that we were a good society'. By the time he deployed, the US was at war with Iraq, a war for which he saw no legal or moral

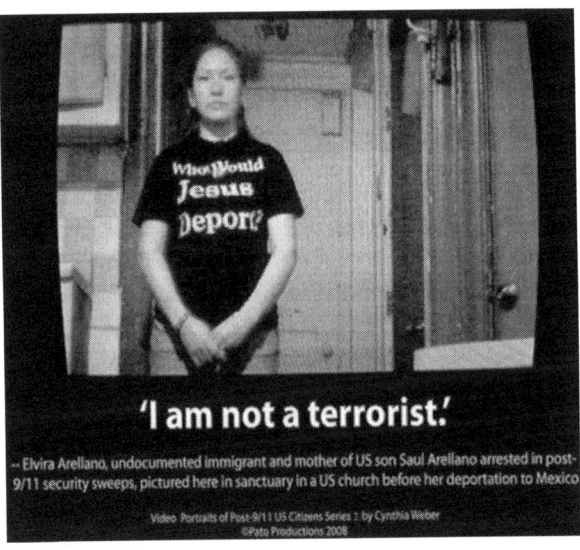

Figure 1.   Elvira saying 'I am not a Terrorist'.
Source: Video Portraits of Post-9/11 Citizens Series I by Cynthia Weber, © Pato Productions 2008.

Figure 2.   José Matus.
Source: Video Portraits of Post-9/11 Citizens Series I by Cynthia Weber, © Pato Productions 2009.

justification. Even though he objected to the US war in Iraq, Phil served out his 4-year term. Deciding not to re-enlist, Phil got his separation papers, cleared base, and took his vacation days. A few days before his vacation was over, Phil was stop-lossed. 'Effectively, I was drafted and told I had to go back to Iraq.' Unable to continue to serve in a war he believed was illegal and immortal, Phil deserted the army and sought asylum in Canada. 'I never thought I'd be a political refugee from the United States', says Phil (Figure 3).

Figure 3.   Phil McDowell.
Source: Video Portraits of Post-9/11 Citizens Series I by Cynthia Weber, © Pato Productions 2008.

I asked each interviewee to narrate their story, reflect upon their experiences of citizenship and patriotism after 9/11, create a pose (with the US flag if they so chose) that epitomized their experiences, and encapsulate their experiences into a sentence that includes the words, 'I am an American'. I edited the resulting 13 major interviews into 13 short documentary films.

Each of my 13 documentary films begins with the emergency call between Fire Fighters on their way to the Twin Towers and their Command Post,

> Firefighter to Command: 'The World Trade Center Tower Number One is on fire. The whole left side of the building…it's just a huge explosion'.

> Command to Firefighter: '10-4. All units stand by at this time'.

As this exchange plays, the name of the film's title character fades up. A few seconds later, the words 'I am an American' fade up below the name. Then the action starts. Over the next three and a half min, the title character narrates their story in their own words as a variety of still and moving images roll across the screen. The typical arc of each story goes like this – normal life before 9/11, how 9/11 changed the character's life for better or usually for worse, how this change was adjusted to or resolved, and how all of this makes the character reflect on US citizenship and what it means to be a US American. After this narration, each film cuts to the title character looking directly into the camera and saying not only 'I am an American' but explaining what kind of US American they are. So, for example, Phil McDowell says 'I am an Iraq War Resister, and I am an American'. Saul Arellano says, 'I am the son of an immigrant without papers, and I am an American'. And another Indigenous American I interviewed Ofelia Rivas says, 'My nation is divided by an international border, and I am an O'odham American'.

As in the Ad Council's original PSA, I end each of my films with a version of the US motto. But instead of displaying the motto in its original form, I turn the motto around so that 'E Pluribus Unum' – Out of Many, One – becomes 'Ex Uno Plures' – Out of One, Many. This reversal is not meant to suggest some revaluing on my part between the One and the Many or a redirecting of the process of transformation between the One and the Many. Rather, it is meant 'to expose the unreliability of the code' (Keenan 1997, also see Barth 1975, Weber 1999) upon which the US national imaginary of the tolerance of difference is founded. Combining this reversed/reversible motto with films that, by R.B.J. Walker's description of them, 'capture the dilemma of a national sovereignty caught between classical sovereignty and biopolitical sovereignty' (Walker 2007), the overall effect is to demonstrate how the US state can at any time – and does during the War on Terror – change direction, rewrite its foundations, and potentially put in jeopardy the Many who are not protected by the always historically contingent promise of the One. This means that those in the safe 'One' may at any time find themselves in the unsafe 'Many'.[8]

Just as in the Ad Council's PSA, my reversed/reversible US motto fades up onto a black screen as a cacophony of US voices repeat all or part of the line 'I am an American'. The final image in each of my films is of the title character looking directly into the camera while (in most cases) holding the US flag. As the film cuts from the US motto to this 'flag shot', the cacophony of voices resolves with an anonymous US voice saying 'I am' and the title character in voice over saying 'American'. Each film then fades to black, and the credit sequence begins.

I used the materials from these short documentaries to produce an alternative 'I am an American' PSA that quite literally speaks back to the original PSA. Like the Ad Council's 1-min PSA, my 1-min PSA features each of my title characters looking directly into the camera and declaring 'I am an American' while the emotive Americana music of Edgar

Meyer plays in the background. Structurally, declaratively, aurally, cinematically, and affectively, my PSA deliberately mimics the Ad Council's PSA. But 20 s into my PSA, my PSA confounds expectations because my characters go on to declare (as they do in their individuals films) just what kind of US American they are – an Iraq War resister, a political refugee *from* America, a wrongly suspected bioterrorist. From this point on, my PSA also includes explicit markers of racial, ethnic, religious, and political differences that are excluded from the Ad Council's PSA. These include shots of a clearly identifiable Muslim character praying in a mosque, of a clearly identifiably Indigenous character posing next to a banner with the emblem of her nation on it (as opposed to the US flag), and of a political protest that features a sign that reads, 'I won't trade my humanity for patriotism'. Finally, as in the individual films, my PSA ends with a twist on the Ad Council's ending, with my characters saying 'I am an American' while the inverted US motto fades in and out.

The final shot of the Ad Council's PSA is of a smiling, brown-skinned little girl waving a US flag. She seems to embody the PSA's post-9/11 affirmation of the tolerance of difference and the promise of carrying this tolerance into our melted American Dream-like future. In contrast, the final shot of my PSA is of a visibly unhappy Saul Arellano waving a US flag, just as he did at his mother Elvira Arellano's press conference in which she announced she was taking sanctuary in a US church to defy her deportation order. As viewers learn from the 4-min film about Saul and Elvira, Elvira was deported when she left sanctuary after a year, and Saul eventually joined her in Mexico. Both because this 8-year-old US citizen had his childhood cut short by political circumstances and because he was in his mother's words 'effectively deported' with her to Mexico, Saul can be read as embodying the post-9/11 American Nightmare experienced by those US Americans whose differences are not tolerated.[9] If read in this way, the future Saul's image predicts is not one that is celebratory of difference and diversity-patriotism but mournful of how some differences are always placed beyond tolerance, especially in times of patriotic fever.

Figure 4. Saul Arellano.
Source: Video Portraits of Post-9/11 Citizens Series I by Cynthia Weber, © Pato Productions 2008.

Saul's image, then, can be read as announcing (to borrow a turn of phrase from Sara Ahmed) that while all US citizens are part of 'America', 'being "in it" does not mean we are all "in it" in the same way' (2000, p. 171, also see Lewis 2004)[10] (Figure 4).

Nor, as this final image of Saul suggests, do we all feel the same way about being in it. In making these different 'feeling states' (Fortier 2008, 2010) explicit, my PSA attempts to make an affective break from the Ad Council's PSA. For my PSA, it meant to play itself out in a different affective register than does the Ad Council's PSA, one which lingers in/on 'bad grief' and the difficult questions it poses to 'America' and 'Americans' after 9/11 rather than affectively attempting to transform this 'bad grief' into a state-sponsored 'good grief' that might release US citizens from the post-9/11 challenges of US identity. As such, my PSA is meant to mark how affect is politically and aesthetically mobilized on behalf of a state-sanctioned national fantasy while suggesting the possibility for new mobilizations of affect, aesthetics, and politics, those that might refigure the complex relationships among citizenship, identity, tolerance, nationalism, patriotism, and memory to make them more just and more politically responsible to populations both within and beyond nation-states.

Viewed as a collection, these 14 films are meant to convey a sense of what Barbara Johnson calls 'the critical difference' that keeps any identity from corresponding to its image of itself (1980). That critical difference is surely expressed in the disjuncture between the lived reality of US citizenship for unsafe US citizens during the War on Terror measured against the ideal of the tolerance of difference as the foundation and lived reality of the US nation-state.[11] But in expressing that critical difference, the films suggest yet another critical difference. This is the radical disjuncture between the citizen and the human – a disjuncture that, according to Kant, need not exist in the modern liberal nation-state because the modern liberal nation-state makes being a good citizen the basis for being a good human (Walker 2007).

It is this equation of the good citizen to the good human that the Ad Council's PSA circulates when it attempts to represent the tolerance of difference as the foundation of diversity-patriotism. But because the Ad Council's PSA organizes the US national imaginary by disavowing many differences in the name of one national ideal of tolerance and censuring many differences in the name of one national idea of justice, the Ad Council's PSA effectively forecloses on a whole range of expressions of humanity that cannot or will not be confined within the limits of diversity-patriotism. The effect of this foreclosure is that the Ad Council's PSA fails in its representation of the good citizen as the good human.

My project is dedicated to communicating this failure so that it can be known, felt, and remembered in ways that not only potentially refigure what it means to be an 'American' but also what it means to be a citizen and a human more generally. For as Judith Butler (paraphrasing Emanuel Levinas) explains, 'For representation to convey the human . . . , representation must not only fail, but it must *show* its failure' (Butler 2004, also see Managhan 2008).[12] By reminding us, as R.B.J. Walker puts it, that 'the modern compromise in political life is that we are citizens first and humans second' (Walker 2007), my 14 films contribute to chronicling the violence and injustice required to make this compromise work on behalf of the modern nation-state. They hopefully suggest that because the US state (like any state) reserves for itself the power to determine who among its citizens is 'safe' or 'unsafe' and to reverse this decision at any time, this modern liberal compromise of humanity for citizenship is a compromise too far. This is not only because citizenship can never guarantee one's safety (meaning there is no such thing as a 'safe citizen' from the citizen's point of view; Weber 2008). More importantly, this is because citizenship not only cannot but willfully does not guarantee one's humanity, much less the humanity of those who are not among the 'One'.[13]

Critical reflections

If the Ad Council's 'I am an American' PSA is a protest *for* citizenship, can my alternative 'I am an American' project be understood as a protest *of* citizenship? Answering this question is not straightforward because of how my project uses and apparently reaffirms the phrase 'I am an American'. As such, one might suggest that my project celebrates both citizenship itself as a regulative ideal of political subjectivity and US citizenship as the most sought-after brand of national citizenship far more than it offers 'a protest against citizenship' (Derrida 1994, p. 46).

These criticisms of my project are not without merit, particularly when one considers the individual films on their own, rather than the films as a collection. Yet if individually the films often express a desire to be included within a unified national ideal of a coherent liberal Americanness – to protest *for* citizenship – collectively these films protest *against* citizenship by challenging notions of coherent liberalism, coherent nationalism, or coherent Americanness. So while both examples of advertised Americanness discussed in this article might be understood as citizenship protests, whether they are for citizenship or against citizenship depends upon how they perform advertised Amercianness.

Aslultany clearly grasps this performative function of advertising in her critique of the Ad Council's PSA in terms of how it attempts to sell 'diversity-patriotism' to the post-9/11 US citizenry. From her perspective, it seems that the Ad Council's PSA 'does not so much represent society *as it is* but society as it *should be*' (Cronin 2004, p. 113), even if, as she points out, how the USA 'should be' for the Ad Council is one in which the limits of cultural citizenship are narrowly drawn. Aslultany's observations sit nicely within Anne Cronin's work on the performative function of advertising more generally. For, as Cronin argues, advertising functions performatively by offers consumers not only products but 'promotional beliefs' and 'invested understandings' that perform divisions in the social order and frame classificatory regimes in relation to their consumption habits, which in this case are about consuming the 'diversity-patriotism' of the US nation (Cronin 2004).

As a protest against citizenship, my 'I am an American' project appears to be in a different register than the Ad Council's original 'I am an American' PSA. For if the Ad Council's PSA takes unified US nationalism as the pre-given basis upon which to sell 'diversity-patriotism' to a unified US citizenry, my 'I am an American' project puts this pre-given category under erasure. It does this by asking, for example, if it means the same thing for an undocumented continental American migrant to the USA like Elvira Arellano to say 'I am an American' as it is for a documented legal immigrant to the USA to say this same thing. It shows a curiosity about why it is that an Indigenous American like Ofelia Rivas refuses to say 'I am an American', opting instead to say 'I am an O'odham American', with O'odham being the name of her tribal nation. More broadly, it ponders how race, class, sexuality, gender, and indigeneity performatively come into existence in relation to the seemingly simple declaration 'I am an American' in ways that not only identify with the USA and with citizenship but also simultaneously dis-identify with citizenship through their creative re-identifications with the phrase 'I am an American'. What this means is that my 'I am an American' project offers what Cronin might call a different 'matrix of transformation' in relation to how the advertised and consumed subjectivities of 'America' and 'American' are performatively constructed, connected, and contested (Cronin 2004), to the point that nationalisms and indeed citizenships might be reimagined.

By inviting the uninvited, unsafe US citizen to make a claim to the USA, then, my 'I am an American' project just might begin to expose how ill-equipped the concept of citizenship is to function as a universal framework for political subjectivity. The effect might well be to shame some specific post-9/11 legal enactments of US citizenship, if not the concept of citizenship itself. Understood in these terms, the performances of citizenship protest in this project may not amount to endorsements of US citizenship in its post-9/11 form or of citizenship more generally. Rather, they might be read as shaming gestures (Souweine 2005, p. 534) that provide some future grounds from which to oppose citizenships, nationalisms, and how they figure Americanness (Parenti 2003) by aiming 'to expose the banal violence of citizenship *as regimes of control*' (Tyler and Marciniak, introduction to 2013).

Acknowledgements

This research was supported by grants from the British Academy and the Leverhulme Trust. My generous network of friends and family helped these funds go further and enabled me to self-fund the final four films in this series by providing accommodation, food, and transportation whenever they could. They include Lucy Suchman, Andrew Clement, Monique Fortier, Roxanne Doty, Spike Peterson, Candy, Heather, and Max Ogle, Cheryl Hill, Nigel Clark, Shelia Rye, Chris Olofson, and as ever Chuck, Nina, Lindsay, and Seth Clovis. Additional grants from the Lancaster University Faculty of Arts and Social Sciences and from the Lancaster University Friends Association helped to fund the production of still images for exhibition. My greatest debt is to those people featured in this project – Lupe Denogean, Phil McDowell, Jamine Aponte, Fernando Suarez del Solar, Cindy Sheehan, James Yee, Greg and Glenda Avery, Chris Simcox, Elvira and Saul Arellano, Shanti Sellz, José Matus, Ofelia Rivas, Julia Shearson, Abe Dabdoub, Will Potter, and Steve Kurtz.

Notes

1. I am referring to the National Defense Authorization Act, which at the time of this writing was passed by both Houses of Congress and threatened with a Presidential veto.
2. For historical background of the Ad Council, see http://www.adcouncil.org/About-Us.
3. My inspiration for thinking about 'good grief' and 'bad grief' in relation to this project was sparked by a presentation by Gaye Chan and Nandita Sharma at the Melancholic States conference at Lancaster University. My use of these terms, however, bears no resemblance to how they used these terms and is not one that they endorse. See Chan and Sharma (2007).
4. On the hail, see Althusser (1971).
5. For example, the US singer Pat Boone recently labeled Gay Rights Activist working to overturn California's ban on gay marriage as 'sexual jihadists'. Writing about these activists in the context of the November 2008 Mumbai terrorist attacks, Boone commented, 'What troubles me so deeply, and should trouble all thinking Americans, is that there is a real, unbroken line between the jihadist savagery in Mumbai and the hedonistic, irresponsible, blindly selfish goals and tactics of our homegrown sexual jihadists. Hate is hate, no matter where it erupts. And by its very nature, if it's not held in check, it will escalate into acts vile, violent and destructive'. See Boone (2007).
6. Thanks to Kate Nash for articulating this form of words to describe my project.
7. Films from my 'I am an American' project can be viewed at http://www. iamanamericanproject.com. For a book-length elaboration of the project, see Weber (2011).
8. In his generous commentary on this project, R.B.J. Walker elaborated this point in grander terms, arguing that my project makes visible 'the reversibility in all modern claims to subjectivity'. And if modern subjectivity is reversible, then the modern promise of progress and meaning the nation presumably guarantees cannot be insured.
9. Saul and Elvira's case is a complicated one. In my collection of films and in my PSA, it is not meant to represent how all foreign mothers of US children were treated by the US government, either before or after 9/11. Rather, because each film is shot as much as possible from the

perspective of the person telling that story, the film about Saul and Elvira represents Elvira's perspective on their situation, a perspective Elvira did much to popularize before, during, and after her sanctuary stay with Saul.

10. Ahmed's quote refers to her description of a globalized economy of difference, not to any particular national economy of difference. But because the US national economy of difference is a colonial and post-colonial economy of difference, Ahmed's point applies to the USA.

11. Another way to think about this is through the notion of what Homi Bhabha calls the split that is inherent in writing the nation. As Bhabha explains, 'In the production of the nation as narration there is a split between the continuist, accumulative temporality of the pedagogical, and the repetitious, recursive strategy of the performative. It is through this process of splitting that the conceptual ambivalence of modern society becomes the site of *writing the nation*' (Bhabha 2004; also see Bhabha 1990, Closs Stephens 2008, 2010).

12. Thanks to Tina Managhan for bringing Butler's formulation of this point to my attention. See Managhan (2008).

13. Barbara Johnson's ideas of critical difference follow on from Jacques Derrida's idea of difference. In this context, both Johnson and Derrida agree that to construct singularity and deny difference is a violent act. It is worth quoting Derrida at length on this point. As he puts it, 'As soon as there is the one, there is murder, wounding, traumatism. The one guards against the other, it protects itself from the other. But in the movement of this jealous violence it compromises in itself its self-otherness or self difference. The difference from within one's self, which makes it one. The one as the other. At one and the same time, but in the same time that is out of joint. The one forgets to remember itself to its self. It keeps and erases the archive of this injustice that it is, of this violence that it does. The one makes itself violence, it violates and does violence to itself. It becomes what it is, the very violence that it does to itself. The determination of the self as one is violence' (Derrida 1995).

References

Ad Council, 2004a. *I am an American (2001–Present)* [online]. Available from: http://www.adcouncil.org/default.aspx?id=141 [Accessed 15 March 2013].

Ad Council, 2004b. *I am an American (2001–Present)* [online]. Available from: http://www.aef.com/exhibitions/social_responsibility/ad_council/2486 [Accessed 20 August 2007].

Ahmed, S., 2000. *Strange encounters: embodied others in postcoloniality*. London: Routledge.

Alsultany, E., 2007. Selling American diversity and Muslim American identity through nonprofit advertising post-9/11. *American Quarterly*, 59 (3), 593–622.

Althusser, L., 1971. Ideology and ideological state apparatuses (notes towards an investigation). *In*: L. Althusser, ed. *Lenin and philosophy and other essays*, trans. B. Bruwster. New York: Monthly Review Press, 127–186.

Anderson, B., 1983. *Imagined communities: reflections on the origin and spread of nationalism*. New York: Verso.

Ashley, R.K., 1989. Living on borderlines: man, poststructuralism, and war. *In*: J. Der Derian and M.J. Shapiro, eds. *International/intertextual politics*. Lexington, KY: Lexington Books, 259–321.

Barth, R., 1975. *S/Z: an essay*, trans. Richard Miller. New York: Hill and Wang.

Benjamin, W., 1969. The work of art in the age of mechanical reproduction. *In*: H. Arendt, ed. *Illuminations*, trans. H. Zohn. New York: Schocken Books, 239–241.

Berlant, L., 1991. *The anatomy of national fantasy*. Chicago, IL: University of Chicago Press.

Berlant, L., 1997. *The queen of America goes to Washington City: essays on sex and citizenship*. Durham, NC: Duke University Press.

Berlant, L., 2008. *The female complaint: the unfinished business of sentimentality in American culture*. Durham, NC: Duke University Press.

Bhabha, H., 1990. *Nation and narration*. New York: Routledge.

Bhabha, H., 2004. *The location of culture*. New York: Routledge.

Boone, P., 2007. *Hate is hate, in India or America, World Net Daily, December 6* [online]. Available from: http://www.worldnetdaily.com/index.php?fa=PAGE.view&pageId=82830 [Accessed 10 January 2008].

Brown, W., 2006. *Regulating aversion: tolerance in the age of identity and empire*. Trenton, NJ: Princeton University Press.

Bush, G.W., 2001. *Address to a joint session of Congress and the American people* [online]. 20 September 2001. Available from: http://www.whitehouse.gov/news/releases/2001/09/20010920-8.html [Accessed 15 March 2013].

Butler, J., 2004. *Precarious life: the powers of mourning and violence.* New York: Verso.

Chan, G. and Sharma, N., 2007. *Good grief! Presentation at the Melancholic States Conference.* Lancaster: Lancaster University, 27–28.

Cronin, A., 2004. *Advertising myths: the strange half-life of images and commodities.* London: Routledge.

Derrida, J., 1994. Nietzsche and the machine: interview with Jacques Derrida by Richard Beardsworth. *Journal of Nietzsche studies,* 7, 7–66.

Derrida, J., 1995. *The gift of death,* trans. David Wills. Chicago: University of Chicago Press.

Fortier, A.-M., 2008. *Multicultural horizons: diversity and the limits of the civil nation.* London: Routledge.

Fortier, A.-M., 2010. Proximity by design? Affective citizenship and the management of unease. *Citizenship Studies,* 14 (1), 17–30.

Gilroy, P., 2006. *Postcolonial melancholia.* New York: Columbia University Press.

Johnson, B., 1980. *The critical difference: essays in the contemporary rhetoric of reading.* Baltimore, MA: Johns Hopkins University Press.

Keenan, T., 1997. *Fables of responsibility: aberrations and predicaments in ethics and politics.* Stanford, CA: Stanford University Press.

Lewis, G., 2004. Racialising culture is ordinary. *In:* E.B. Silva and T. Bennett, eds. *Contemporary culture and everyday life.* Durham, NC: Sociology Press, 111–129.

Maira, S.M., 2010. *Missing: youth, citizenship, and empire after 9/11.* Durham, NC: Duke University Press.

Managhan, T., 2008. Grieving dead soldiers, disavowing loss: Cindy Sheehan and the im/possibility of the American antiwar movement, Paper presented at the Violence, Bodies, Selves Workshop, Manchester, 23 March.

Marciniak, K., 2006. *Alienhood: citizenship, exile, and the logic of difference.* Minneapolis, MN: University of Minnesota Press.

Parenti, C., 2003. *The soft cage: surveillance in America from slavery to the war on terror.* New York: Basic Books.

Sardar, Z.M. and Wyn Davies, M., 2003. *Why do people hate America?* London: Disinformation Press.

Shaw, K., 2009. *Political theory and indigeneity: sovereignty and the limits of the political.* New York: Routledge.

Sollors, W., 1996. *Theories of ethnicity: a classical reader.* New York: New York University Press.

Souweine, I., 2005. Naked protest and the politics of personalism. *In:* M. Narula, S. Sengupta, J. Bagchi, G. Lovink, L. Liang and S. Vohra, eds. *Sarai reader 05: bare acts.* Delhi: The Sarai Programme, 526–536.

Stephens, A.C., 2008. Community, time, security: the persistence of nationalism in Judith Butler's *Precarious Life,* Paper presented at the Globalization, Difference and Human Security Conference, Osaka University, Japan, March 12–14.

Stephens, A.C., 2010. Citizenship without community: time, design, and the city. *Citizenship studies,* 14 (1), 31–46.

Tyler, I. and Marciniak, K., 2013. Immigrant protest: an introduction. *Citizenship studies,* 17 (2), 143–156.

Walker, R.B.J., 1990. International relations/world politics, Unpublished paper.

Walker, R.B.J., 2007. Closing comments at the BISA, Security, Aesthetics, and Visual Culture Workshop, Queens University, Belfast, 10 November.

Weber, C., 1999. *Faking it: US hegemony in a 'post-phallic' era.* Minneapolis, MN: Minnesota University Press.

Weber, C., 2006. *Imagining America at war: politics, morality, film.* London: Routledge.

Weber, C., 2007. 'I am an American': portraits of post-9/11 US citizens. *Open democracy* [online]. 11 September. Available from: http://www.opendemocracy.net/article/democracy_power/america_power_world/citizen_identity

Weber, C., 2008. Designing safe citizens. *Citizenship studies,* 12 (2), 125–142.

Weber, C., 2011. 'I am an American': filming the fear of difference. Bristol: Intellect Books.

Index

Note:
Page numbers in **bold** type refer to figures
Page numbers in *italic* type refer to tables
Page numbers followed by 'n' refer to notes